THE KILLING OF
ROBERT F. KENNEDY

Books by DAN E. MOLDEA

THE HOFFA WARS:
Teamsters, Rebels, Politicians and the Mob
1978

THE HUNTING OF CAIN:
A True Story of Money, Greed and Fratricide
1983

DARK VICTORY:
Ronald Reagan, MCA, and the Mob
1986

INTERFERENCE:
How Organized Crime Influences Professional Football
1989

THE KILLING OF ROBERT F. KENNEDY:
An Investigation of Motive, Means, and Opportunity
1995

The Killing of Robert F. Kennedy

An Investigation of Motive, Means, and Opportunity

by

DAN E. MOLDEA

W · W · NORTON & COMPANY

New York   London

The text of this book is composed in Galliard,
with the display set in Galliard bold.
Composition and manufacturing by the Haddon Craftsmen, Inc.
Book design by Jacques Chazaud

Library of Congress Cataloging-in-Publication Data
Moldea, Dan E. 1950–
The killing of Robert F. Kennedy : an investigation of motive,
means and opportunity / by Dan E. Moldea.
p. cm.
Includes index.
1. Kennedy, Robert F., 1925–1968—Assassination. I. Title.
E840.8.K4M58 1995
364.1'524'092—dc20 95-3533
ISBN 0-393-03791-6
ISBN 0-393-31534-7 pbk.
W. W. Norton & Company, Inc., 500 Fifth Avenue, New York, N.Y. 10110
W. W. Norton & Company Ltd., 10 Coptic Street, London WC1A 1PU

2 3 4 5 6 7 8 9 0

To

Mrs. Nancy Nolte

and in memory of

Walter J. Sheridan

Contents

PART II: The Controversies

PART III: The Crime Scene Revisited

Acknowledgments

This work could not have been completed without the assistance of the following six people: Los Angeles attorney Marilyn Barrett; California state archivist John Burns; Professor Philip Melanson of Southeastern Massachusetts University; citizen-activist Floyd Nelson; former United Auto Workers executive board member Paul Schrade; and, especially, our good friend, the late Greg Stone.

I am also grateful to several others who have played important roles in my research: Dick Billings, Dick Brenneman, Vincent Bugliosi, Beaux Carson, Mae Churchill, David and Christina Convis, John Cosgrove, David Cross, Edward Gelb, Jeff Goldberg, James Grady, Helen Johnston, Robert Joling, Robert Blair Kaiser, Bill Knoedelseder, Larry Leamer, Paul LeMat, Jim Lesar, Scott Malone, Phil Manuel, Dick Mardiros, David Mendelsohn, "Mister In-Between," Don Murdock, Pete Noyes, Tom O'Neill, Bob Pack, Mark Perry, Mike Pilgrim, Francis Pizzulli, Jan Pottker, Barbara Raskin, Kristina Rebelo, Bill Regardie, Dave Robb, Marvin Rudnick, Tom Rumpf, Mike Scott, Carl Shoffler, Kris Sofley, Jenny Stone, Joel Swerdlow, Bill Thomas, Rhys Thomas, Jack Tobin, Jennifer Toy, Shelly Tromberg, Tom von Stein, Garland Weber, Frank Weimann, Tim Wells, Danny Wexler, Peter Whitmore, and Mimi Wolford.

I would also like to thank Adel Sirhan and Lynn Mangan for their efforts and cooperation in helping to arrange my interviews with Sirhan Bishara Sirhan.

And I would like to acknowledge the fine work accomplished by John Burns' fine staff at the California State Archives, who include: Teddi Akers, Melodi Anderson, Anne Applewhite, Julie Calef, Blaine Lamb, Leslie Laurance, Stuart Lauters, Laren Metzer, Fred Myers, Cindy Percival, Joe Samora, Sandy Smith, Dave Snyder, Teena Stern, Genevieve Troka, Elena Williams, and Nancy Zimmelman.

However, I must emphasize that the conclusions made in this book are my own; the above acknowledged people do not necessarily agree with my findings.

Finally, my deepest appreciation is extended to my family and friends, as well as to my literary agent, Alice Martell, of the Martell Agency in New York; my booking agent, Jodi Solomon, of Jodi Solomon Speakers in Boston; my fightin' lawyers Roger Simmons and Ed Law of Gordon & Simmons in Frederick, Maryland, and Steve Trattner of Lewis & Trattner in Washington, D.C.; adviser/ attorneys George Farris of Akron, John Sikorski of Northampton, Massachusetts, and Richard Stavin of Los Angeles; my dedicated writing coach, Mrs. Nancy Nolte, of Boulder, Colorado; Patricia J. Chui and Otto Sonntag at W. W. Norton & Company; and my loyal editor, Starling Lawrence, who believed in me and this project.

QUESTION: Did you kill Senator Robert F. Kennedy?
ANSWER: Yes, sir.

> —Sirhan Bishara Sirhan in response
> to his defense counsel, Grant
> Cooper, at his 1969 trial

Preface

At 12:15 A.M. on June 5, 1968, an assassin shot and mortally wounded Senator Robert F. Kennedy of New York in a narrow kitchen pantry of the Ambassador Hotel in Los Angeles. Just moments earlier, the forty-two-year-old Kennedy had left a ballroom celebration in the wake of winning the California Democratic presidential primary. No fewer than seventy-seven people were crowded in the pantry when twenty-four-year-old Palestinian immigrant Sirhan Bishara Sirhan, using an eight-shot .22-caliber revolver, opened fire on the senator. Kennedy was shot three times and died early the following day. Five other people were each shot once, but all survived.

Many people still remember where they were and what they were doing when they heard that Robert Kennedy had been gunned down. On that terrible day, I was an eighteen-year-old graduating senior at Garfield High School in Akron, Ohio, the president of my class, and a volunteer worker for Kennedy's opponent in the primaries, Senator Eugene McCarthy.

At the early morning rehearsal for our graduation ceremonies to be held later that night in the school gymnasium, an assistant principal told me that Senator Kennedy had been shot. I was given the job of announcing the tragedy to my six hundred classmates. I still vividly remember the shock and horror on nearly everyone's face as I gave them the news.

I had no idea then that years later, in the midst of my career as a crime reporter, I would write a book about the murder—because for many people it was still an open case, even though Sirhan had been convicted of the crime and was serving a life sentence.

At first, indeed, the case appeared to be open and shut. An ostensibly impressive police investigation found no conspiracy and concluded that Sirhan had acted alone. However, responsible critics of the official inquiry later uncovered serious problems with the conduct of the probe. They based their criticisms on eyewitness testimonies and challenges to the existing physical evidence.

By the time I published my first article about this case, in 1987, no one had made a systematic attempt to accumulate evidence from the most objective and experienced people available: the police investigators themselves, especially those involved in the crime scene investigation. That became my project—which also included my extensive interviews with the two people known to have drawn their guns at the crime scene that night: Sirhan Sirhan and security guard Thane Eugene Cesar.

This book is the story of a murder investigation. It is neither a political melodrama nor a paranoid's paradise. I do not attempt to analyze and explain time and space. A *Washington Post* reviewer, Pulitzer Prize winner Jonathan Yardley, wrote of my second book, *The Hunting of Cain: A True Story of Money, Greed and Fratricide,* "It is not an especially reflective book, and Moldea doesn't hammer the reader over the head with the conclusions that can be drawn from it; but this reticence is one of the book's greatest strengths, and it stands in revealing contrast to the breathless tone in which many nonfiction crime stories are told these days."

My approach to this story is quite similar.

Part 1 details the official police investigation, mostly in the words of the investigating officers themselves. Part 2 explains the controversies stemming from the official probe. Part 3 chronicles my own investigation.

In the final chapter, I present my conclusions for the first time, on the basis of my view of the evidence.

As in all of my previous works, everything in this book has been extensively fact-checked. (When necessary, I used the California State Archives as the final arbiter when discrepancies arose over the spellings of proper names.) Nearly all of its major and minor characters and sources—including both Sirhan and Cesar—have been permitted to approve their quoted words, as well as given the opportunity to amend and expand upon them. Also, several experts on this case have read the manuscript to ensure its accuracy and fairness.

Dan E. Moldea
Washington, D.C.
October 3, 1994

Prologue

By June 5, 1968, few Americans felt neutral about Robert Francis Kennedy of Massachusetts, the seventh child of Joseph and Rose Kennedy, the father of ten children, and the husband of Ethel, who was carrying their eleventh child in June 1968. In the view of some, he had risen to power on the coattails of his brother President John F. Kennedy, who made him U.S. attorney general in a blatant act of nepotism. Others insist that Robert Kennedy had become the greatest crime fighter in American history, beginning with his baptism as the chief counsel of the Senate Rackets Committee from 1957 to 1960. There he earned his reputation as a fearless enemy of mobsters and labor racketeers.[1]

---

[1] In 1960, Kennedy published a memoir of his experiences with the committee, *The Enemy Within* (New York: Harper & Brothers).

After the murder of John Kennedy, in November 1963, Robert Kennedy, the man and the public servant, changed dramatically. His quick wit, though still present, became overshadowed by a sense of Irish melancholy. Like a soldier out of combat, he seemed to be searching for himself. Overwhelmed with deep personal guilt, he appeared to blame himself for his brother's death. According to aides, Robert Kennedy privately believed that John Kennedy's murder had been arranged by Teamsters president James R. Hoffa and Hoffa's allies in the underworld—the principal targets of the Kennedy Justice Department. During his final months as attorney general, in 1964, Kennedy successfully prosecuted Hoffa, his arch-nemesis, achieving convictions for jury tampering and defrauding the union's pension fund. Hoffa received a thirteen-year prison sentence, which began on March 7, 1967.

A trusted insider become distant outsider with the presidency of his brother's vice president, Lyndon Johnson, a longtime adversary, Kennedy searched for another power base. He was elected a U.S. senator from New York State in 1964, despite critics' perception of him as a carpetbagger. A restless warrior in a collegial body where compromise is not only a virtue but an absolute necessity, he appeared disenchanted.

Nevertheless, Kennedy continued to search and learn, questioning himself and his long-held beliefs. Although a supporter of civil rights activists while attorney general, he began traveling to the ghettos in Brooklyn, the poor rural black areas in Mississippi, and the poor rural white areas of Appalachia. He wanted a firsthand look at this desperate poverty, as well as the plight of Native Americans and Mexican-American farmworkers in the West, so far removed from his own life of Eastern Establishment wealth and privilege. He went from being a mere supporter of activists to being an activist in his own right.

The escalating war in Indochina, which he and his brother had supported, occasioned his next internal battle. Moved by the relentless U.S. bombing of North Vietnam and the rise of the antiwar movement, Kennedy changed again. He began to oppose the war and considered challenging Lyndon Johnson for the presidency.

Senator Eugene McCarthy of Minnesota, who inspired thousands of young antiwar activists to campaign for him, had already announced his candidacy for the presidency on November 30, 1967. In the New Hampshire Democratic primary election on March 12, 1968, McCarthy polled 42 percent of the vote and nearly defeated Johnson, forcing the president to reexamine his own future. Four days later, sensing a now-or-never urgency, Robert Kennedy announced his candidacy, advocating domestic and international reforms but still appearing to many to be capitalizing on McCarthy's early spadework against the incumbent.

On March 31, 1968, the political drama intensified when Johnson, while announcing a partial hiatus in the bombing of North Vietnam, stunned the world with his televised announcement that he would not seek or accept his party's nomination for president. The following month, on April 27—after the brutal April 4 murder of civil rights leader Dr. Martin Luther King, Jr., in Memphis—Johnson's vice president, Hubert Humphrey, also joined the race but did not enter any of the primaries.

Kennedy scored a major victory on May 7 in the Indiana primary and another one the following week in Nebraska. However, on May 28, McCarthy, openly disdainful of Kennedy, who had refused to debate him, scored a stunning upset by taking the Oregon primary.

This set the stage for the crucial June 4 primary election in California.

I. THE CASE

1. *Intersection*

Tuesday, June 4, 1968. Primary election day in California.

For months, Senator Robert F. Kennedy, brother of slain President John F. Kennedy, had been campaigning hard for the Democratic nomination for the presidency. However, on this day, Kennedy relaxed at the Malibu home of family friend John Frankenheimer, the filmmaker who produced the political thrillers *The Manchurian Candidate* and *Seven Days in May*, among other movies.

Kennedy spent the day swimming, sitting in the sun, talking to friends, playing with his children, and sleeping. He became so relaxed that he considered not attending his own election night party, suggesting that he and his family and friends watch the primary results on television. He wanted to invite the media to join them at Frankenheimer's home. Because the television networks refused to haul their equipment out to Malibu, Kennedy reluctantly decided to go into Los Angeles to await the election returns.

At 7:15 P.M., Senator Kennedy, accompanied by Frankenheimer and other members of the campaign staff, left Malibu and sped downtown in Frankenheimer's Rolls-Royce Silver Cloud III to the Ambassador Hotel for the election night party. Kennedy and several key staffers had reserved suites on the hotel's fifth floor. With the election still in doubt and Kennedy running behind, he went to his suite and remained there, hoping that the tide would turn.

The hotel management had deployed eighteen security guards for crowd control.[2] But no known police officers were assigned to the hotel that night, even though Democratic and Republican candidates for the U.S. Senate were also holding election night celebrations there.

Two principal reasons have been given to explain this. First, presidential contenders in 1968 were not yet provided Secret Service protection. Second, the relationship between the Kennedy campaign and the Los Angeles Police Department (LAPD) was strained at best.

LAPD sergeant Michael Nielsen explains, "When Kennedy came into town, he went into a crowd and a motor sergeant went into the crowd after him. He thought that Kennedy was going to be mobbed and hurt. And the sergeant just got tremendous abuse from campaign followers of Kennedy. 'Get out of here,' they yelled. 'We don't want you guys involved in anything. You give us a bad image.' "[3]

---

[2] George R. Stoner, chief of the Bureau of Investigation for the Los Angeles District Attorney's Office, conducted an interview with Ambassador Hotel security chief William Gardner, which was recorded in a June 19, 1968, memorandum to Los Angeles district attorney Evelle Younger. According to Stoner, "Mr. Gardner stated that he had discussed security with members of the Kennedy organization and, although they did not say they did not want any security, the implication was clear that they did not want anything to interfere with the Senator mingling with the people in the audiences."

[3] An official LAPD report memorialized this May 29 incident, stating, "At one point in the motorcade, at 9th and Santee Streets, the vehicles came to a stop and Senator Kennedy was pulled from his vehicle by a large enthusiastic crowd. A Traffic

LAPD inspector Robert F. Rock says, "The department saw Kennedy as a guy—given the times, given the way things were happening during those days—who was a public figure at risk. We wanted to give him more attention than he wanted to get. They didn't want him to be seen in the same photograph with uniformed police officers."

LAPD Metro officer Robert Bruce Pickard recalls, "The Kennedys did not want any uniformed guys in the hotel, so there were three or four squads, which included eight to ten men each, strategically located within a circle around the hotel."

Thus, on the night of the primary election at the Ambassador Hotel, Kennedy had only a single former FBI man, William Barry, as trained security, and he was unarmed. Two well-known athletes—former New York Giants and Los Angeles Rams defensive tackle Roosevelt Grier and Olympic decathlon gold medalist Rafer Johnson—volunteered as "unofficial bodyguards."

Campaign aides milled around the Kennedy suite, waiting for the election returns. Meantime, Kennedy paced in the bedroom, working on notes for a speech to his eager followers who were jam-packed in the Embassy Room downstairs. Finally, at about 11 P.M., the results started to favor Kennedy.

When his victory became clear, he took the freight elevator down to the kitchen, walked through the pantry and anteroom, and entered the Embassy Room to wild applause. About twenty people, including his pregnant wife, Ethel, were on the platform with him.

Speaking to an ecstatic crowd of eighteen hundred, Kennedy concluded, "I would hope now that the California primary is finished, now that the primary is over, that we can now concentrate on having a dialogue . . . on what direction we want to go in the United States: what we're going to do in the rural areas of this country; what we're going to do for those who still suffer in the United States from

---

Enforcement Division sergeant attempted to assist the Senator back to his vehicle when it appeared to him that Kennedy needed help. Kennedy and his aides berated the sergeant and told them that they had not asked for the assistance of the police."

hunger; what we're going to do around the rest of the globe; and whether we're going to continue the policies which have been so unsuccessful in Vietnam. . . . I think we should move in a different direction. . . . So my thanks to all of you. And now it's on to Chicago and let's win there!"[4]

When he finished to a loud ovation from the huge crowd, he headed for a news conference in the nearby Colonial Room. To get there quickly, an aide told him to go back through the kitchen pantry.

* * *

Twenty-four-year-old Sirhan Bishara Sirhan, an unemployed former "hot walker" at Santa Anita racetrack and apprentice jockey, spent nearly all of Tuesday, June 4, 1968, rapid-firing his .22-caliber Iver Johnson revolver at the San Gabriel Valley Gun Club, in Duarte, California, where he had signed the nonmember roster at 11:00 A.M. He was dark-haired and dark-complected and dressed in a long-sleeve, blue permanent-press shirt, a blue velour pullover sweater, blue denim pants, and gray loafers.

Although alone most of the time at the west end of the pistol range, the friendly and polite young man talked to several other club patrons. Everett Buckner, the range master, complimented Sirhan for being an "expert" shot. Late that afternoon, Sirhan also offered shooting tips to a petite, twenty-five-year-old, green-eyed blond club member whom he had just met. She had been firing a newly purchased, nine-shot .22 revolver. Her husband crouched on the nearby rifle range shooting at a target with his 30-30 caliber Marlin rifle. Sirhan told the woman that her gun appeared to be firing left and offered to let her shoot a few rounds with his Iver Johnson to prove the point; he also fired her gun. However, before she could confirm Sirhan's theory, the range supervisor advised everyone that it was 5:00, closing time.

[4] Kennedy did not capture the Democratic nomination with his victory in California. According to UPI, Kennedy won 172 of California's 174 delegates, as well as 24 additional delegates in the South Dakota primary. Kennedy's total delegate count ran to 393½ convention votes, still far behind Hubert Humphrey's 561½ delegates but ahead of Eugene McCarthy, who had 258. The final battlefield between Kennedy and Humphrey would have been the 1968 Democratic National Convention, in Chicago.

By then, Sirhan, who had fired 300 to 400 rounds of ammunition, had been shooting for nearly six hours and worn out the center of his target.

Five feet two and 115 pounds, the bushy-haired Sirhan climbed into his beat-up, white-and-pink, two-door, 1956 DeSoto, placed his revolver in his car, and returned to Pasadena, where he lived with his Jordanian mother, Mary, and two brothers, Adel and Munir. All in his family were Christians—not Muslims—and members of the Eastern Orthodox faith. They had immigrated to the United States from East Jerusalem in January 1957, when Sirhan was twelve.

Instead of going directly home from the gun range, he stopped at a Bob's Big Boy restaurant on Colorado Boulevard in Pasadena at about 6:10 and met with Gaymoard Mistri, an old college friend. The two men sat at the counter, drinking coffee and discussing horse racing. Sirhan also mentioned a headline he had seen in the *Los Angeles Herald-Examiner* about continuing gun battles in the Middle East. Sirhan told his friend, "This is bad. This is terrible." He then returned to the subject of horse racing.

After Sirhan picked up the check for the coffees, at 6:40, they decided to go to the nearby student union at Pasadena City College, where both had been enrolled in 1963. At the union, they met three other friends—Marof Mohammad Badran, Abdo Jabre Malke, and Anwar John Sayegh. After talking and checking out the coeds, Sirhan and Mistri returned to Bob's Big Boy. By that time, the two men were discussing rabbit hunting. Suddenly, and for no apparent reason, Sirhan pulled a spent bullet from his pocket and showed it to Mistri.

Sirhan wanted to go shoot pool, but Mistri had another appointment. At about 7:15, Sirhan returned to his car, still parked at the restaurant.

Sirhan's own account of this time is as follows: "After I left the student union, I went back to my car at Bob's Big Boy. That's when I picked up the newspaper, mostly to see the next day's horse entries. I noticed that a local Jewish group was going to have a parade near the Miracle Mile to celebrate Israel's one-year anniversary of the Six-Day War. I went downtown, not realizing that the parade was supposed to be the following night. I wasn't going downtown to cause any trouble. I just wanted to see what was happening. . . .

"After I parked my car and realized that there wasn't a parade, I started walking around. I noticed lights in a storefront window, which was the campaign headquarters for Thomas Kuchel, a Republican who was running for reelection to the U.S. Senate.[5] I crashed that party, but there wasn't very much going on. I struck up a conversation with someone there who suggested that a better party was going on for Max Rafferty, another Republican, at the Ambassador Hotel across the street.

"So I left the Kuchel party without even having a drink. I walked across the street to the Ambassador. I saw the Rafferty banner, and the name 'Rafferty' rang a bell. I went to school with his daughter at John Muir High in Pasadena. I thought she might be there. But she wasn't.

"It was a hot night. There was a big party, and I wanted to fit in. I arrived there at about 8:00.[6] I drank four Tom Collins. It was like drinking lemonade. I was guzzling them. My body is small. It was hot in there, and I wasn't used to it. I was feeling it, and I got sleepy. So I wanted to go home. It was late."

During his brief stay at the Rafferty party, Sirhan tried to make conversation with a hostess, but she blew him off, complaining about the manner in which he was dressed.

"I went to my car. I was surprised that I made it to my car. I remember that it was parked uphill, and I was too drowsy to drive. I then made up my mind to go back to the Ambassador to get some coffee."

Before returning to the Ambassador, Sirhan said, he had a brief memory lapse. However, during the alleged blackout, he took his .22 Iver Johnson revolver and placed it in his pocket.

---

[5] Kuchel, a U.S. senator since 1953, was also a partner in the Los Angeles–based law firm Wyman, Bautzer, Rothman, Kuchel & Silbert. Kuchel, a progressive Republican, was defeated by Max Rafferty, a conservative, in the June 4, 1968, GOP primary for the U.S. Senate. Alan Cranston defeated Rafferty in the November general election.

Victory parties for both Cranston and Rafferty were being held at the Ambassador Hotel at the same time as the Kennedy party on June 4.

[6] Because of election day, the bars at the Ambassador Hotel were closed until 8:00 P.M.

He does not remember walking back to the hotel.

Hans Bidstrup, a hotel electrician, remembered that Sirhan, holding some sort of drink, approached him near the hotel's Venetian Room at about 8:45 and asked if he was a Democrat. When the electrician said that he was, Sirhan stuck his hand out and replied, "Shake hands with another Democrat." The electrician believed that Sirhan was "half-drunk."

At about 9:30, auto mechanic Enrique Rabago, standing by the door to the Palm Court Room, saw Sirhan and asked him, "Are we going to win?" Sirhan replied, "I think we're going to win." When Rabago told him that Senator McCarthy held a slight lead in the ballot count, Sirhan, according to Rabago, replied, "Don't worry about [Kennedy] if he doesn't win, that son of a bitch. He's a millionaire, and he doesn't need to win. He just wants to go to the White House. But even if he wins, he's not going to do anything for you or any of the poor people."

Rabago recalled that Sirhan wanted him and a companion, Humphrey Cordero, to return to the party. However, the two other men were concerned about their appearance: dressed for work, not for a party. Sirhan, according to Cordero, simply said, "Why shouldn't we go in there. We are voters. We're putting them in office." Bewildered by this strange man they had just met, Rabago and Cordero walked out of the hotel just after 10:00, leaving Sirhan behind.

At about the same time, Sirhan asked hotel waiter Gonzalo Cetina-Carrillo to hold his drink while he took a folding chair. After Sirhan sat down, the waiter returned his drink and walked away.

Claiming to have had lapses in and out of consciousness, Sirhan next remembers standing in front of a teletype machine cranking away in the Colonial Room. He just stared at it. "I was mesmerized," he says. "I had never seen anything like that before." Mary Grohs, a Western Union Telex operator, spotted Sirhan and described him as "glassy-eyed." Sirhan's own words: "I was shit-faced drunk."

Further disoriented by the bright lights in the hotel, Sirhan walked into the Embassy Room, mingling with the large crowd. "My only goal was to get some coffee," he insists.

Finally, someone in the crowd pointed Sirhan to an anteroom—between the backstage area and the west pantry double swinging doors of the kitchen pantry. Sirhan remembers, "The coffee was in a shiny urn. I remember standing there and saying, 'I like my coffee with cream and lots of sugar.' An attractive brunette was standing next to me, and she said that she liked her coffee the same way. I remember that she was wearing a plain white dress. We had a brief conversation, and I don't remember anything more than that."[7]

Just before midnight, Jesus Perez, a hotel busboy, saw Sirhan nervously holding and twisting some papers, standing in the kitchen pantry, as were several other people. According to Perez, Sirhan asked him, "Is Mr. Kennedy coming this way?" Perez said that he didn't know.

A few minutes later, the throng of Kennedy supporters packed into the kitchen pantry and moved east toward the Colonial Room. Sirhan stood and crouched by a tray stacker to the far side of the ice machine near the east end of the pantry. He then moved west toward Kennedy, picking his way through the crowd until he reached the steam table. The senator had just released a handshake with a kitchen worker.

Karl Uecker, a hotel maître d', thought that Sirhan was just another busboy who wanted to shake hands with Kennedy. Uecker pinned Sirhan against the steam table, stopping his forward motion.

Sirhan then pulled his revolver from his pants and opened fire, drawing the attention of nearly everyone in the pantry.

* * *

Twenty-six-year-old Thane Eugene Cesar, returning from his plumber's job at Lockheed Aircraft, arrived at his Simi Valley home at 4:30 P.M. on Tuesday, June 4, 1968. He and his wife were having problems with their five-year-old marriage, and they barely spoke to

---

[7] Judy Royer, a Kennedy campaign worker, said that she twice asked Sirhan to leave the kitchen pantry between 10:15 and 11:00 P.M. She last saw him leaving the anteroom.

Robert Klase, having been stopped by a security guard from entering the Embassy Room, tried to get in through the kitchen. While standing in the anteroom, he was asked by a television network technician to guard his equipment until he returned. At about 11:00, Sirhan attempted to enter the kitchen, but Klase advised him that only ABC-TV staff were allowed in the area. Sirhan left without an argument.

each other when he walked into the house. Cesar reached into the refrigerator and poured himself a glass of orange juice. Then he went into the living room and turned on the television. In for the night, he expected to fall asleep in his favorite chair before the 11:00 local news aired.

A few minutes later, just as he was getting comfortable, he received a telephone call from Tom Spangler, the manager of Ace Guard Service, where Cesar moonlighted as a part-time security guard. "Gene, I need you to work tonight," Spangler told Cesar. "There are three big parties at the Ambassador Hotel. I need six guards, and I only have four. And I need you for an eight-hour shift, starting at 6:00."

"I can't do it, Tom," Cesar replied. "I just got home from work, and I'm really tired."

"I'm in a jam here, Gene!"

"Tom, I just can't!"

"I'll tell you what. If you report to the Ambassador at 6:00, you can slip out between 11:30 and midnight, and I'll pay you for the entire eight-hour shift."

Needing the extra money, Cesar thought for a minute and then sighed, "Okay, I'll be there."

Cesar chugged his orange juice, walked into the kitchen, and told his wife that he had to go to work for Ace and was expected to be in downtown Los Angeles by 6:00. She shrugged him off, keeping her back to him, saying nothing. He walked up behind her and grabbed her playfully by the shoulders. He kissed her on the back of the neck and pressed his six-foot, 210-pound frame against her. A smile started to break through her anger. He whispered, "Baby, you still got it."

"Get out of here," she finally laughed, stroking his chestnut brown hair and his pudgy face. "Get cleaned up, and I'll make you dinner."

Dressed in his gray uniform and wearing his Sam Brown and attached holster that cradled his .38 Rohm revolver, Cesar kissed his wife and left at 5:00 for the hour drive through rush hour traffic to the eight-story, 512-room Ambassador Hotel, at 3400 Wilshire Avenue.

Cesar arrived in the hotel parking lot at 6:05. He reported to Fred Murphy, the Ace commander and a former LAPD lieutenant, and

William Gardner, the hotel's chief of security, who was dressed in a plain suit and tie. Under Gardner's command were eleven guards who worked full-time for the hotel. They wore brown uniforms and were unarmed.

The hotel was packed. In addition to the political parties, employees from General Electric, Bulova Watch, and Pacific Telephone were at the hotel for their own company conclaves—as well as 144 members of the press, who were there primarily to cover Kennedy.

Murphy instructed Cesar to work crowd control at Kennedy's campaign party. He was assigned to patrol the large Embassy Ballroom on the lobby level of the hotel, where everyone expected Kennedy to deliver either his victory or his concession speech.

At 9:30, because of massive overcrowding in the Embassy Room, Los Angeles fire marshals closed the main entrance to the ballroom and admitted people only on a "one-in, one-out basis." At the same time, Murphy reassigned Cesar to the Embassy Room's kitchen pantry area.

Murphy told Cesar to position himself at the east door, next to the Colonial Room, the designated press room where Kennedy planned to hold a news conference after his speech. Instructed to check the credentials of the people walking in and out of the kitchen, Cesar mostly sat, paced, and occasionally checked the bona fides of those people.

Cesar recalls, "At about 11:15, Murphy came to me and said that Kennedy would be going through the kitchen pantry on his way to the Colonial Room after his speech on the stage in the Embassy Room. Murphy then moved me from the east pantry door to the west double swinging doors, which were next to the backstage area.

"A few minutes later, Bill Gardner told me that he wanted me to accompany Kennedy from the west pantry double doors to the Colonial Room. He just told me, 'Keep the aisle clear. Make sure that everybody's out of the way, so that Kennedy's group can walk freely.' "

While waiting for Kennedy, Cesar talked to several people in the kitchen, including comedian Milton Berle, Roosevelt Grier, and Rafer Johnson. Cesar recalls, "I had the time of my life, because Berle just kept everyone in stitches."

A little before midnight, Kennedy and his entourage, assured of victory in the California primary, stepped off the freight elevator in the kitchen. Kennedy briskly walked past Cesar, through the west pantry double swinging doors, out an anteroom between the pantry and a backstage area, and into the Embassy Room, where his cheering supporters greeted him as he climbed onto the stage.

Thunderous applause and chants of "We want Bobby! We want Bobby!" echoed in the kitchen pantry during and following his speech. "I heard them say he was on his way," Cesar remembers. "Someone said, 'This way, Senator,' as he was walking off the back of the stage. So I moved out of the way of the swinging doors and moved up, letting him come by me."

According to Cesar, Karl Uecker led the way for Kennedy. Standing to the senator's left, the maître d', dressed in a tuxedo, held Kennedy's right wrist, trying to get him through the surging crowd in the kitchen pantry. "I'm on the right side of him," Cesar explains. "And what I'm doing is taking my hand and pushing people back, because Kennedy was having a hard time walking forward.

"About halfway through the pantry, there was an ice machine to the south and some steam tables just a few feet up ahead to the north. Right about then, I went directly behind Kennedy and took his right arm at the elbow with my left hand. The maître d' was now up ahead.

"I let go of Kennedy just as he shook hands with a busboy."

Cesar looked at his watch. The time was exactly 12:15 A.M., June 5. Suddenly, while pressed up against Kennedy's back, Cesar saw flashes coming from the steam table, just in front of him and Kennedy.

Realizing he was under fire, Cesar immediately reached for his gun.

* * *

Forty-three-year-old Paul Schrade, a member of the executive board of the United Auto Workers and also the vice chairman of the Kennedy campaign for labor, was driving home from the Los Angeles airport early that Tuesday evening after returning from a trip to San Francisco. While on the highway, he decided to go instead to the Kennedy campaign party at the Ambassador.

Schrade remembers, "I went up to the Kennedy suite on the fifth floor in the southeast wing of the hotel. We hung around and waited for results. We finally got into a session with [Kennedy aides] Frank Mankiewicz and Fred Dutton. They started talking about what we would do if we won, because the results at about 11:00 were showing that we were moving ahead in the vote."

As the returns began looking good, the men started to make calls to friends and supporters around the country, including UAW president Walter Reuther, Schrade's boss, with whom he had spent most of the day in San Francisco.

Schrade walked into Kennedy's personal suite and found Kennedy putting last-minute touches on his victory speech. After a cordial greeting, Kennedy asked Schrade to jot down the name of Dolores Huerta, a vice president of the United Farm Workers Union and a key Kennedy supporter, so that Kennedy would remember to thank her. As Schrade looked for something to write on, Kennedy, accompanied by several aides, left the senator's fifth-floor suite and took the elevator down to the kitchen.

Schrade recalls, "Because the elevators were so crowded, we just walked downstairs from the fifth floor. And we caught up with Bob and his entourage in the kitchen area, where I gave him an envelope with Dolores's name."

Together, the entire group passed through the pantry, out the double swinging doors, into the Embassy Room, and onto the stage as the overflowing crowd cheered wildly.

"I was on the platform with Kennedy. Bob went through his speech, thanking everybody. The crowd was so excited, really happy. As soon as he finished, I just climbed off and went into the kitchen pantry area to wait. He came by fairly quickly after that. I was several feet inside the pantry, and Bob said to me, 'Paul, I want you and Jesse [Unruh, the speaker of the California State Assembly and a Democratic Party powerbroker] with me.' I turned and looked for Jesse, and he was standing over in the corner of the pantry. And I yelled at him, 'Jesse, Bob wants us with him.'

"At that point, I turned around. Bob had stopped and was shaking hands with some workers in the kitchen about four or five feet in front of me. And I was feeling really good at this point. I remember the thought that was going through my head: 'This is really what we've been fighting for. We're going to have a president!'

"At that point, Bob, who was smiling and walking towards what I know now was a steam table. All of a sudden, I started shaking very violently. There were television cameras all around and cables all over the wet floor, and I thought I was being electrocuted. I just passed out. Other than the heavy trembling, I don't remember hearing anything or feeling anything. I just fell. My next sensation was feeling people trampling on me. I felt pain. Then there was a doctor over me as I came to. He said, 'You're going to be all right. It's not serious.' I felt the blood streaming out of my head. At that point, I realized that I had been shot. The doctor said that Bob Kennedy had also been wounded."

2. *The Scene*

At 12:06 A.M. on June 5, nine minutes before the shooting, Los Angeles Police Department officer George W. Blishak and his partner, Robert J. Velasquez, responded to a report from hotel security at the Ambassador that unauthorized cars were blocking the hotel's back parking lot. "While we were driving up to the hotel," Blishak says, "we could hear the crowd inside the Ambassador cheering and chanting Kennedy's name." Blishak remarked to his partner, "Maybe we ought to go in and see if we can shake his hand." Instead, they started writing tickets for the illegally parked cars.

Inside the hotel, Harold Burba, a photographer for the Los Angeles City Fire Department (LAFD), conducted his own patrol of the

Kennedy campaign party. In 1968, television cameras were large, bulky, and positioned on wheels and had heavy cables trailing behind them. When moved into crowds, they became safety hazards. For the Kennedy celebration at the Ambassador, the LAFD ordered barricades to prevent these cameras from being moved into the crowd. If a camera operator crossed the barricade, the LAFD planned to arrest him and confiscate his equipment.

Burba, who photographed possible fire code violations at the request of the Fire Prevention Bureau, remembers, "It wasn't until about midnight when Kennedy announced his victory. I was sitting in the kitchen area where the kitchen help takes their breaks and drinks their coffee, waiting. Not being a Kennedy fan, I didn't pay any particular attention when he came through [the first time]. He walked right by the area where I was. He came down the service elevator, instead of the regular elevator—which led him into the kitchen area.

"He went in and made the speech. And then on the way back out, a big surge of people came out ahead of him, and he was surrounded by people.

"From where I was sitting, when the shots were fired, I could see the flashes up in the air.

"So I jumped up and grabbed my camera and started taking pictures. There were a couple of them in that struggle there [with Sirhan]. Then I dipped down to take pictures of Kennedy.

"After I took the picture of him lying on the floor, someone bumped me or something, and I almost lost my camera. And then, grabbing it, I inadvertently flipped the lock on so that the shutter wouldn't work. So I was ready to take more pictures, but nothing would happen. By the time I recovered and got the camera working again, some high-ranking politicians decided that there would be no more pictures."

Speaking of the panic in the kitchen pantry, Burba continues, "I never felt so threatened in all my life. I thought the world was going to come to an end. These [Kennedy supporters] were absolutely out of their gourds. I felt very conspicuous in uniform."

Kenneth Held, the captain of the Fire Prevention Bureau, Public Assemblage Unit, had been in the Gold Room, trying to deal with the overcrowding. "We obviously had a leak," Held explains. "We were getting people coming through the side door, leading to the Embassy Room and to the scullery. And we got a guard and had him stationed there. I'm sure that I observed Sirhan as he was over there in the corner [before the shooting]. He, basically, fit right in with the Latin, Mexican help that the hotel had there."

After hearing the shots and the screams from the crowd, Held crossed over into the Embassy Room and then into the kitchen pantry. He was at the crime scene within a minute of the opening shot. "Things fell apart. People went berserk. And we tried to maintain order there, and we did call for assistance. There were no policemen around, because the Kennedys didn't like to have any uniforms around them."

Along with Senator Kennedy, five other people lay on the floor, wounded by gun shots.

At 12:17 A.M., Officer G. W. Hathaway, a Communications Division officer working at Parker Center, LAPD headquarters, in downtown Los Angeles, received a call from L. M. Butler, a switchboard operator at the Ambassador. The conversation was automatically tape recorded.

BUTLER: This is the Ambassador Hotel. They have an emergency.

HATHAWAY: What kind of emergency?

BUTLER: I don't know. Some kind of emergency. You know we have Mr. Kennedy here.

HATHAWAY: Big deal!

BUTLER *(brief pause)*: I think somebody was shot.

HATHAWAY: Oh, great.

BUTLER: You want me to find out more?

HATHAWAY: Yes, ma'am.

BUTLER *(pause lasting several seconds)*: Senator Kennedy has been shot.

HATHAWAY *(realizing the seriousness of the situation)*: He's been shot?

BUTLER: That's right. You'd better send someone here.

HATHAWAY: What's the address there?

Also at 12:17 A.M., Officer Howard L. Schiller, the desk officer at Rampart Station, just a few blocks from the Ambassador, received a telephone call from an anonymous man who asked to speak to the watch commander. Sergeant Raymond M. Rolon, who was just coming on duty, took the call on behalf of Lieutenant Robert K. Sillings, the night watch commander, who was at the end of his shift.

"The male voice, identifying himself as a sheriff's deputy, claimed that Kennedy was shot," Rolon recalls, adding that immediately after the shooting the deputy confirmed that Kennedy had been hit and then called Rampart from a private phone in the hotel. "You could hear a lot of background noise. He was not sure how many suspects, but he felt that they had a perpetrator in custody at the time. He [the deputy] would not identify himself, because he was not supposed to be there."

Why? Rolon replies, "Many times, different law enforcement agencies put people in situations to monitor events. And he was there—but unofficially, in other words. He was not identified as a sheriff's deputy.[8] They [the Kennedy people] didn't wish to have any security by LAPD, but we had a 'need to know.'

"Immediately, I turned around and made arrangements for the night crew to stay on, as well as the entire morning watch, the midnight group. While I was doing all of this, Bob Sillings was standing next to me at Rampart approving it."

At 12:20 A.M., Sergeant Paul Sharaga, who had just picked up a pack of cigarettes at a store at Eighth and Fedora streets, heard the "ambulance shooting call" on his police radio as he returned to his patrol car.

[8] The LAPD's long-standing position has been that *no* known law enforcement personnel were present at the Ambassador in an undercover capacity. Rolon told me that he knew of "three or four plainclothes" sheriff's deputies who were working undercover at the Ambassador that night. However, I could not find anyone at the LAPD or the Los Angeles Sheriff's Office (LASO) who would confirm this.

Sharaga remembers, "I was directly across the street from the rear driveway of the Ambassador Hotel on Fedora. All I had to do was make a U-turn, and I was on station in the back parking lot of the hotel within ten seconds.

"I arrived at the hotel, and there was mass confusion. I got up on the parking lot, and there were people running in all directions.

"Right away, an older Jewish couple ran up to me, and they were hysterical. I asked them, 'What happened?' The woman said that they were coming out of the Ambassador Hotel by the Embassy Room when a young couple in their late teens or early twenties, well dressed, came running past them. They were in a state of glee. They were very happy, shouting, 'We shot him! We shot him!' The older woman asked, 'Who did you shoot?' The girl said, 'Kennedy, we shot him! We killed him!'

"I said, 'Can you describe them?' The lady gave me a description of the gal as 'a female Caucasian, in her late teens or early twenties, blond or light hair, and wearing a polka-dot dress.' And she gave me the description of the man, a male Caucasian in his late teens, early twenties, well dressed, but she couldn't describe him any further. Her attention was with the person she had the conversation with: the girl. Then, she said, they both ran off.

"That put this old Jewish woman into hysterics. She was still in hysterics at the time I talked to her. The one thing I learned during my many years in the police department is that remarks that are made spontaneously are very seldom colored by the people's imagination. These were spontaneous remarks from this couple. As far as I was concerned, that was the most valid description available.

"After she gave me the description, and I determined that Kennedy had, in fact, been shot, I notified the Communications Division. I was given a clear frequency. I radioed in the description of the man and woman a number of times, requesting that it be broadcast every fifteen minutes."[9]

This became the root of later controversy: an eyewitness state-

---

[9] Sergeant Sharaga remembers that he wrote down the names of the older couple. He then gave that page of his officer's field notebook to Rampart Detectives. However, he never saw his notes again, and they are missing from the LAPD's files. As best as he can recall, the couple's name was Bernstein, but he is not sure.

ment indicating that more than one person—one of whom was a woman in a polka-dot dress—might have been involved in the shooting of Senator Kennedy.

Also at 12:20 A.M., Sergeant Rolon reported the shooting to Lieutenant Charles F. Hughes, the chief of Rampart Detectives, who was off-duty and at home. Hughes assigned James R. MacArthur, a twenty-one-year veteran of the department, to take control of the crime scene.

MacArthur explains, "I was at my home in Playa del Rey. The wife and I had been watching television. And we watched the scenes from the Ambassador Hotel when Bobby was up there, accepting and everything. And just as he was getting ready to leave the thing, I turned off the television. The wife and I were going to bed. About three or four minutes after I turned it off, I got a telephone call. It was from my oldest daughter, who lived next door. She said, 'Did you see what happened on television?' And I said, 'Well, no.' She said, 'Well, Bobby Kennedy just got shot.' So I turned on the TV, and I said to my wife, 'I'll betcha it'll be five minutes, and I'll get a phone call to get the hell down there.' The phone rang, and it was the Rampart Detectives, saying, 'Hey, get to the Ambassador Hotel real fast. Bobby's been shot.' I said, 'I know.' So I took off."

Meantime, Inspector John W. Powers, acting commander of all LAPD detectives in the absence of Chief Robert A. Houghton, gave the official authority of the investigation to the Rampart Detectives. A twenty-eight-year veteran of the LAPD at that time, Powers, who said he helped Jack Webb write several "Dragnet" episodes, adds, "The thing we were concerned with was we weren't going to have another Dallas, where the other guy [Lee Harvey Oswald] got knocked off [by Jack Ruby]."

At 12:21 A.M., as Officers Blishak and Velasquez were in the parking lot, ticketing illegally parked cars, they saw two distraught black women running out of the rear of the Ambassador. They told the officers, "Kennedy's been shot!" Blishak recalls, "Velasquez and I ran [to the Embassy Room] to verify that, and we were in the scene of chaos immediately. That was the first and only time in my career I saw

THE KILLING OF ROBERT F. KENNEDY

mass hysteria. And I mean mass. There were people sitting on the floor, crying. I had great difficulty finding out what had happened, because people were not responding."

Velasquez agrees with his partner: "We ran up the [back] stairs and went into the auditorium. You could see that it was just pandemonium there. People were screaming and yelling. Some people were lying down like they were injured. Blishak continued in, and I ran down to the car to put out a help call. While I was running down the back steps, I stumbled and fell. I sprained my ankle. As I got to the car, the call was coming out about the shooting. And it was directed to us: Blishak and myself. So I indicated that we were at the location, and we needed help. I then went back upstairs, attempting to locate doctors to help these people.

"There were hundreds of people there, and everyone was talking at once. It was hard to get the story as to exactly what happened."

At or around 12:22, Officers Sanford S. Hansen and Daniel Jensen were the first from the LAPD to enter the actual crime scene, the kitchen pantry. Hansen remembers, "I was a training officer that night, and Dan Jensen was my probationer. Actually, I never would have taken the call if it wasn't for him. It was right at the beginning of our watch. We were working the Wilshire Division when the call came out for an ambulance shooting in the Rampart area. The kid was all excited, saying, 'Let's go! Let's go!' So I decided to roll up there, and see what was happening.

"When we rolled up, we saw three guys in suits going into the hotel. They looked like FBI agents. So I said, 'Let's follow these guys.' We never said a word to them, and they never said a word to us. We followed them down a corridor, up a stairway, and we came out right in the doorway of the hotel's kitchen. We were running in what seemed to be absolute silence. When that door to the kitchen opened up, it was like someone had turned on amplifiers. There were hundreds of people screaming.

"I ran in, and I stepped right over the legs of someone lying on the floor. It was Senator Kennedy, and I didn't realize it even though the place was well lit. I didn't know that Kennedy was one of the people who had been shot."

42

Among those shot and bleeding on the floor of the kitchen and pantry were the following:

- Paul Schrade of Los Angeles, who was about four to five feet behind the senator. Schrade had fallen backward, bleeding profusely from a head wound. At the moment he was shot, his eyes were fixed on Kennedy, who was smiling and had just shaken hands with a busboy. Schrade never saw the shooter.
- Irwin Stroll, also of Los Angeles, a seventeen-year-old student and Kennedy campaign worker, who was shot in the left leg. After hearing what he believed to be firecrackers going off, he tried to push his way out of the kitchen pantry, running into Ethel Kennedy in the process. He then felt a blow to his leg and noticed that he had been shot. He did not see either Kennedy or the assailant during the shooting spree.
- Ira Goldstein of Encino, a nineteen-year-old Continental News Service reporter, who was shot in the left buttock as he stepped over the wounded Stroll. In the midst of the barrage of gunfire, he felt a pain in his hip and fell against a wall—without ever seeing Kennedy being wounded or the man who shot him.
- William Weisel, thirty, of Washington, D.C., an ABC-TV unit manager, who was shot in the abdomen as he stood in front of the swinging doors and center divider that Kennedy had just stepped through to enter the pantry. When he heard the "numerous cracks," he felt thumping sensations in his side, knowing immediately that he had been shot. In the midst of the shooting, he saw neither Kennedy nor the gunman.
- Elizabeth Evans, forty-two, of Saugus, California, an artist and a close friend of Kennedy aide Pierre Salinger. She had been standing next to Weisel and was shot in the forehead. At the moment of the shooting, she had bent down to find a lost shoe. After the shooting ceased, she heard someone scream that a woman had been shot—not realizing that she was that woman until she felt the blood flowing from her forehead.

Officer Sandy Hansen continues, "I ran toward a commotion a few yards away where everyone was beating on this guy. And I had no idea who he was or what he had done. All I knew was that there had been a shooting, and people were going crazy. I didn't even know that there had been an election that day. I just had never seen this kind of a reaction after a shooting before."

3. *The Arrest of Sirhan*

At 12:22 A.M., in response to Velasquez's call, Officers Travis R. White and Arthur Placencia of Rampart Station arrived at the Ambassador and immediately ran into the crime scene. Placencia recalls, "I had graduated from the police academy on May 17. This happened on June 5. I was a young probationary officer, twenty-one years old. I had hardly seen anything, and Travis was my training officer."

Working the midwatch, White and Placencia had stopped at Seventh and Vermont streets when they received the call of the shooting at 3400 Wilshire Avenue. White shouted, "That's the Ambassador!" He knew the location well. Cops liked to eat at the coffee shop on the lower level of the hotel.

The two officers sped to the Ambassador and parked at its front entrance. "There was a big crowd," Placencia recalls. "Some guy in a black tuxedo was shouting, 'This way, Officer! This way!' We started following him. We went up a ramp that led us into the kitchen pantry."

At the same time, after finishing their meal at the International House of Pancakes near Sixth and Vermont streets and receiving the radio call, LAPD Metro officers Michael G. Livesey, Walter A. Strickel, and Willie Nunley arrived at the hotel and parked directly behind White and Placencia's car. Two busboys directed them to the kitchen pantry.

When Strickel ran into the pantry, the first person he recognized was Kennedy, who was lying spread-eagle on the floor, with the crowd gathering around him. Two doctors were attending to the senator.

Strickel says, "I had lost Mike and Willie in the crowd. I went over to where Kennedy was lying down. Kennedy had a rosary in his hand, resting on his chest. The look on his face made me think that he wasn't going to make it. He had a kind of ashen look.

"Sirhan was down at the other end of the serving table. I started to work my way down there."

Strickel's partner, Mike Livesey, remembers, "We saw about five thousand hysterical people. They were going bananas. All I knew was that there had been a shooting. I didn't realize that it was Kennedy who had been shot down—until I saw him lying on the floor. He was in shock and looked aged. I thought he was dead then. I was more concerned with the crowd and the panic there. Then I was directed over to a table where they had Sirhan laid out on his back."

Placencia continues, "We saw a guy on top of a table. Someone [Ambassador assistant maître d' Karl Uecker] had him in a headlock. Rosey Grier was lying on his body, like dead weight. I remember Rosey was crying. Some other guy [Frank Burns] had him by his legs. Everyone was shouting, 'That's him! That's him!' We figured that this was the guy who did the shooting.[10]

[10] Besides Uecker, several other people battled with Sirhan. According to the LAPD, they included hotel waiter captain Edward Minasian, attorney Frank Burns, Kennedy aide Jack Gallivan and Kennedy bodyguard Bill Barry, businessman Gabor

"We told the guy in a tuxedo [Uecker] who had him in a head-lock to let him go. And then we had to get Rosey Grier off of him.

"Jesse Unruh [the speaker of the California State Assembly] was on top of one of the tables with his knee in Sirhan's back, shouting, 'We don't want another Dallas here!'

"Travis and I were yelling out, 'Who has the gun?' Somebody said, 'Rafer's got it!' Travis yelled at Rafer Johnson, 'Give me the gun!' Rafer says, 'No, I'm not going to give you the gun!' We didn't fight with him, because we had other problems."[11]

Joined by Livesey, Nunley, and Strickle, White and Placencia battled with people in the crowd who were trying to get to Sirhan. Unruh continued shouting, "This one's going to stand trial! He's going to pay! No one's going to kill him!"

Two other Rampart officers, Randolph B. Adair and Patrick G. Metoyer, had been on foot patrol in the area and received the call when they returned to their car. Once in the hotel, Metoyer recalls, "[w]e basically threatened Grier. He didn't want to turn him over to the police. We convinced him that we were going to take the suspect. So he backed off."

Adair remembers, "Placencia and White had physically taken Sir-han away from the crowd. If they had left him alone there for a few more minutes, the crowd would have killed him.

"The guy [Sirhan] was real confused. It was like it didn't exactly

---

Kadar, author George Plimpton, Joseph LaHive, Glen Midby, Kilbert Dun Gif-ford, professional football player Roosevelt Grier, and Olympic decathlon cham-pion Rafer Johnson.

The LAPD said that, officially, Uecker was the first to grab Sirhan.

One of the many myths to have survived the assassination is the general belief that Sirhan was initially grabbed by Grier and Johnson. Both were with Kennedy's wife, Ethel, outside the pantry doors when the shooting began. The six-foot-five, 287-pound Grier ran into the pantry and finally wrenched the gun from Sirhan's hand. He then gave it to Johnson, who placed it in his pocket and later delivered it to police headquarters.

[11] Remarkably, at some point after the shooting had ended and several in the crowd wrestled the gun away from Sirhan, Kennedy's official bodyguard, Bill Barry, said in his statement to the FBI, he "called Roosevelt Grier to hold and protect the assailant and at the same time, directed Rafer Johnson to pick up the gun which was lying on the table. . . . [D]uring the switch, the assailant somehow again recovered the gun. . . ."

However, at that point, Sirhan had run out of ammunition.

hit him what he had done. He had a blank, glassed-over look on his face—like he wasn't in complete control of his mind at the time. He might have been scared, too. He didn't look drunk or intoxicated."[12]

Strickel says, "Willie was having a difficult time getting Sirhan's arm around his back, just because of the number of people pushing in on them. I was able to get his arm around and assist in handcuffing him. Then we had to figure a way to get out of there."[13]

Livesey recalls, "I said, 'We've got to get this guy out of here before the crowd tears him apart.' People were screaming, 'Lynch him!' and 'Kill him!' This was not a good scene. We were in jeopardy just being with him. I had been in riot situations all through the sixties, and this was clearly a dangerous situation. Had we not arrived, he would not have survived too much longer. And I don't think we would have either."

Officer White shoved Unruh out of the way and yelled at the other officers, "Let's get him [Sirhan] out of here!" Unruh then grabbed White by the shoulder and screamed, "You're not taking him anyplace!" White again pushed Unruh out of the way, knocking him into the crowd and to the floor. Back on his feet, Unruh lunged at Sirhan and grabbed him by the neck. Hanging on to Sirhan, Unruh shouted at White and Placencia, "Okay, you can take him, but I'm going with you!"

At this point, Officer Hansen says, "I told the other officers, 'I don't think I can find my way out of here!' This one guy [Frank Burns] knew the building. He said, 'I know how to get out of here!'"[14]

Placencia continues, "Travis was on the suspect's right side; another officer was on his left. I walked ahead of them with my baton out, trying to clear a path through the crowd which was coming on all

[12] LAPD records do not list Adair and Metoyer as being among those officers assisting in Sirhan's arrest. Clearly, they did.

[13] According to the official LAPD log, White handcuffed Sirhan with Willie Nunley's handcuffs and with the assistance of Placencia, Livesey, and Strickel.

[14] The official LAPD log does not credit Hansen with assisting in the arrest of Sirhan. However, the official LAPD report about Hansen's activities that night states, "Hansen assisted in the arrest by pulling people away from the officers who had Sirhan in custody."

around us. I remember that I had to jab a few people with the butt of my baton. My adrenalin was pumping."

Livesey explains, "We went through an empty dining room and figured that we were safe. And then we went through another set of doors trying to find the stairway. Lo and behold, we ended up back in the main ballroom and in the middle of the crowd again. Actually, it led to the main stairs. The people were still hollering and screaming. We went down to the main entrance."

Hansen, then six feet and 230 pounds, the largest officer in the group, remembers, "We hit the doors, running. If people tried to get to him, we would knock them over. We had to fight our way all the way down. We actually knocked people over the railing. Finally, we got ahead of the crowd, which was right behind us."

Two Los Angeles sheriff's deputies, Frank Linley and Robert Hussey, had learned about the shooting on a commercial radio station and rushed to the scene. Linley says, "When I got over there to the Ambassador, several LAPD officers had Sirhan. It was almost like they were trying to figure out what to do with him. A patrol officer could not do anything without a sergeant. And they didn't have one."

With Placencia leading the way, the other LAPD officers and LASO deputies formed a tight circle around Sirhan and continued battling through the crowd toward the exit from the Ambassador.

Placencia recalls, "We finally got Sirhan to the car. I held on to Sirhan, while Travis opened the back door on the driver's side. We finally got Sirhan into the car. I then went around and got into the back seat next to him on the passenger side. Travis climbed in the driver's seat. I had rolled down my window, and people were trying to come in through the window. I had to push several people out. And then this other guy got into the passenger's seat. He was a civilian. It was Jesse Unruh."

Six more LAPD officers, who had just arrived at the scene, also helped push the crowd away from the car.[15] One of them, Sergeant William C. Swihart, explains, "When we arrived, some officers were

---

[15] The six officers were Sergeant William C. Swihart, Sergeant Jerry Feinberg, Donald R. Kreiger, Robert B. Pickard, C. C. Craig, and Alan D. Bollinger.

---

just coming out of the door with Sirhan. There were bottles and everything else being thrown at him, but we were getting hit.

"Then Kennedy was brought down. That was probably one of the things that made the crowd so irate—seeing the victim and suspect there at the same place, at about the same time.

"We had to surge our way through the crowd and get Sirhan into the car. There was so much confusion going on—with people pushing and shoving—we just threw Sirhan in upside down, in between the front and back seat to keep him out of the way."[16]

Hansen continues, "People were rocking the car, trying to turn it over. So Jensen and I jumped on the hood with our batons and beat the car out of there. We hit a lot of people, but we had to get the car out of there."

Hansen adds that he radioed the first notification of the shooting to the Communications Division. "I went to the police car and put out the initial broadcast to Communications. I said, 'I need a Tac-Alert. Kennedy has been shot, and he is en route to Central Receiving Hospital. We need police officers there to protect him. The guy who shot him is in a police car, and he's on his way somewhere.'

"A lieutenant came back to me and asked if the suspect was by himself and whether the gun was in custody. I told him, 'The gun is in the possession of a citizen. As far as I know, one person committed the crime.' "

In hindsight, Hansen adds, "As I look back, it was really stupid for me to say that. But, at the time, I had a gut feeling that he was the only one who was involved in the shooting.

"There could have been other conspirators out in, say, the car, waiting for him to run out. Because he was grabbed and the crowd had taken his gun away, I just figured that he was the one and only person involved."

[16] Swihart explains, "That night, my partner, Sergeant Jerry Feinberg, and I were assigned to the area in the near perimeter to the Ambassador Hotel. When we had a big event like that, we usually put cars in the area for crime suppression. Really, we were there so that if something did occur, we would have somebody close at hand to handle it, a quick response. So there was some anticipation that there might be some problems. And we were briefed to that possibility at roll call."

According to the LAPD, Rampart Division had "deployed four two-man radio cars for assignment around the hotel on election night."

Officer George Blishak radioed in the first description of the shooter: "The suspect is a male Latin, 25 to 26, 5-5, light build, dark bushy hair and dark eyes. Wearing blue Levis, blue jacket, blue tennis shoes."

Placencia remembers, "At that point, I still didn't know that Bobby Kennedy had been shot. I never saw him or anyone else who had been shot.

"We started to leave with red light and siren while the crowd banged on the car. After we left the Ambassador, I asked Unruh, 'By the way, who did he shoot?' Unruh said, 'Bobby Kennedy.' I didn't know what to say, so I just said, 'Oh.'

"Travis then told me, 'Advise him of his rights.' I then took out my field officer's notebook, which had the Miranda rights written out. I turned on my flashlight and read him his rights. Sirhan was cuffed behind his back. He was looking down and not saying anything. He wouldn't answer me. I was looking at him, and I thought maybe he was Mexican or Hispanic. I'm Mexican, and I speak Spanish. I asked him, 'Habla Ingles?' He still wouldn't say anything.

"I then poked him in the ribs with my flashlight and said, 'Hey, I'm talking to you!' He looked over and scowled at me. He said, 'I'll remember number 3909,' which was my badge number.[17] I said, 'Good!' At least I knew that he spoke English. So I then advised him of his rights again. I asked him, 'Do you understand these rights?' He still didn't respond.

"I took my flashlight to check his pupils to see if they dilated or constricted. His eyes were reddish, but I didn't smell any alcohol. But I remember I took some criticism, because I wasn't on the job long enough to know whether he was drunk or not.[18]

Unruh asked the suspect, "Why did you shoot him?" Sirhan

[17] Later, Sirhan wrongly stated that an officer with badge number 3949 had brought him in instead of 3909, which was Officer Art Placencia's badge number.

[18] A supervisor later scolded Placencia for not comparing Sirhan's eyes with those of a person who would have a normal reaction. At Rampart Station, Officer White again checked Sirhan's eyes with his flashlight—this time comparing them with Placencia's normal eyes. White stated that Sirhan's eyes appeared to be normal, as well. He did not seem to be intoxicated or on drugs.

replied, "You think I'm crazy, so you can use it as evidence against me."

Placencia says, "We went to Rampart Station, which took us less than ten minutes. We got him out of the car, and walked him in and up some stairs toward the detective bureau, but it was locked. While Travis went to get the keys, I put the suspect in the Breathalyzer room.[19] Sirhan still refused to say anything.

"I was by myself. So I emptied his pockets, and laid everything on the table. I remember that he had an expended .22-caliber slug in his pocket, a live .22, along with his money and car key. Travis told me to start booking this stuff.[20] So I started to make out a property report. The next thing I knew, Sergeant Bill Jordan and some detectives came in. Jordan said, 'We'll take all of that.' They took all the stuff and took him out the back door with these detectives. I didn't see Sirhan again until I testified against him in court."

[19] Sirhan was not given a Breathalyzer test. Although the time was never recorded, a prison doctor took a blood sample from the suspect. However, according to a December 11, 1968, memorandum written by Deputy District Attorney David N. Fitts, "Blood samples of admitees . . . are not subjected to any test which would reveal presence of alcohol in the blood or the presence of any drug in the system." The sample was later destroyed, which is consistent with police procedure. Similarly, a routine urinalysis administered to Sirhan "does not disclose the presence or absence of alcohol or drugs in the system of the individual."

In short, Sirhan received no test or measurement to determine whether he had been drinking—other than the eye comparison test by Officer White.

[20] Removed from Sirhan's pockets were four one-hundred-dollar bills, one five-dollar bill, four one-dollar bills, $1.66 in change, two .22-caliber cartridges (brass cases, lead projectiles), one .22-caliber copper-coated projectile, a brown comb, a car key, two newspaper clippings, and a piece of paper containing a typed verse.

One of the articles was from the *Pasadena Independent Star News* of June 2 and discussed Kennedy's support for Israel. The second clipping was an advertisement, announcing a rally for Kennedy at the Ambassador Hotel on Sunday, June 2, two days before the primary election.

4. *The Desperate Effort to Save Kennedy*

Before being removed from the kitchen pantry, Senator Kennedy received medical attention from two doctors, who immediately realized that he was critically wounded. Dr. Stanley Abo reached Kennedy first, determining that his heartbeat remained very strong and his pulse rate between fifty and sixty. However, Abo noted that the senator's breathing was shallow. Also, his left eye had closed. Dr. Marvin Esher was the second to come to Kennedy's aid. On the basis of a quick examination, Esher concluded that the senator could suffer a possible cardiac arrest. He observed that Kennedy's left eyelid was closed and that his right eye was open, slightly deviated to the right. The doctor became alarmed when he saw no visible movement in Kennedy's chest, but he was relieved to discover that the senator had a strong, although rapid pulse rate. There was no sign of paralysis.[21]

Thirteen minutes after the shooting—just after Sirhan's arrest—two ambulance attendants, Max Behrman and Robert Hulsman, carried Kennedy on a stretcher to their emergency vehicle. Officer Sandy Hansen says, "When Kennedy came out almost right behind us, the people were trying to touch him, kiss him, and grab his clothing. So we had to fight them off of Kennedy. And then we had to fight everyone away from the ambulance."

Officer Strickel continues, "Livesey and I ended up leading the ambulance to Central Receiving Hospital in our car. Willie Nunley was helping the ambulance attendants place Kennedy in their vehicle. Because of the rush, Willie got left behind at the scene."

Ethel Kennedy accompanied her husband to the hospital in the back of the ambulance with the senator's campaign aide Fred Dutton. Kennedy bodyguard Bill Barry and reporter Warren Rogers rode up front with the driver. During the ride to the hospital, Kennedy started gasping for air, prompting Behrman to place an oxygen mask over his mouth.

Central Receiving, just eighteen blocks from the Ambassador, operated as a small trauma center; it generally didn't admit seriously injured people. Once patients were stabilized, the center would send them to Good Samaritan Hospital, just a few blocks away.

Upon the arrival of the Kennedy ambulance, the hospital staff rushed him into Room 2 and began working to keep him alive. The initial diagnosis of Kennedy's condition, according to an official report, was as follows: "comatose, weak thready pulse, in extremis, blood pressure zero over zero, heartbeat almost imperceptible, bullet wound right mastoid area with swelling, and in shock."

Sergeant William Jordan of Rampart Station had immediately gone to Central Receiving.[22] The first victim he saw was Paul

---

[21] Two other doctors who assisted with Kennedy's care at the scene were Dr. Ross Matthew Miller and Dr. Roland Dean. Both men also attended to other shooting victims.

[22] Sergeant Jordan had been sitting in the division's coffee room, talking to another officer, when a third ran into the room. "Bill, we've got a problem at the

Schrade, who Jordan could immediately tell would survive.

"Then, as I started to relax," Jordan remembers, "in came Bobby. He needed help. They took him right in the room, and we blocked off the scene. Ethel went in with him. I went in and told her, 'This might be awhile. We have a private office where you won't be bothered by the press or anything.' She said, 'No, I'm going to stay right with him.' I said, 'Fine.' She was very, very gracious under the circumstances."

Officers Hansen and Jensen were among the first LAPD personnel to arrive at Central Receiving. Hansen recalls, "I didn't see any police officers there. No perimeter had been set up yet. When I walked into Central Receiving, we saw about fifteen people crowded in front of one of the emergency rooms, screaming and stuff.

"I saw another officer in there, and he didn't know what was going on. So I told him to grab his partner, quick. When he asked why, I told him, 'In about a minute, there's going to be about two thousand people that are going to try to come through that door to get to that room. We have to stop them right here.'

"So the four of us formed a line. Within minutes, the hospital was totally filled with people. When people tried to get past us, we decked them. Jesse Unruh came up. He said, 'I'm Jesse Unruh, and I have to get to that room!' I said, 'You're too late. No one's going to that room until I get a lieutenant here.' Unruh tried to come through, and I decked him.

"Then Lieutenant [Richard] Tackaberry of Metro came up to me. He said, 'What's going on here?' I explained to him that we had to get those people in the hallway away from the room where Kennedy was. He looked at me and said, 'I need you to hold this line for ten minutes. I'll be right back.'

"When Tackaberry came back, he had a unit of Metro officers. Tackaberry yelled out to the crowd, 'You people have thirty seconds

---

Ambassador," he said, adding that he had seen the aftermath of the shooting on television. Their initial information was that Senator Kennedy, his wife, and several others had been shot.

Jordan tried to get a report directly from the hotel, but the chaos was already evident and radio communication was difficult. Jordan and other officers drove to Central Receiving Hospital.

to get out of this hospital! This is an order to disperse!' The crowd still didn't move. So Tackaberry shouted, 'All right, draw batons!' The Metro guys drew their batons. 'Half-step, forward, march!' And they moved forward with their batons, doing a jab motion. They cleared everyone out."

Sergeant Swihart continues, "There was a uniformed officer stationed outside the emergency room. Ethel Kennedy came up to him, and he didn't know who she was. So he wouldn't let her in there. So she slapped him across the face. I witnessed that. Of course, when I got over there, we let her go in. But he was told not to let anybody in; so he didn't. We could understand her being upset."

There has long been a mystery regarding the missing left sleeves of Senator Kennedy's suit coat and shirt and the manner in which his clothing was finally booked as evidence. Helping to explain how they were cut off—as well as the treatment of Senator Kennedy—is a statement to the LAPD by Margaret Lightsey, a nurse at Central Receiving. When Kennedy was taken into the treatment room, she said, "[w]e could see he was not breathing and his eyes had a glazed look. Dr. [V. Faustin] Bazilauskas started heart massage. I assisted Mrs. [Bette A.] Eby in getting the cardiac machine in place under the Senator and we then started the cardiac massage and resuscitation by machine. . . . By this time Dr. [Albert] Holt came into the room and took charge of the situation. He wanted an intravenous of dextrin and albumin started and he wanted adrenalin injected directly in the heart. . . . By the time I got the intravenous ready the two doctors were cutting the Senator's left suit and shirt sleeves off in order to expose the arm for the intravenous. They had to cut his suit off because they didn't want to disturb the cardiac machine.

"Since the Senator's veins had apparently collapsed from shock and loss of blood, Miss [Reba] Nelson and I removed the Senator's trousers and socks. . . . Mrs. Kennedy [who was in the room] ordered that the clothes be thrown away or destroyed, but Mrs. [Alice] Mejia wrapped them as is our usual procedure. . . .

"As Dr. Holt started to do the cut down he said, 'I want someone to call Good Samaritan Hospital and tell them to alert the operating room and the laboratory. Call Dr. [Henry] Cuneo and Robert Meyers and let me talk to them.'"

Soon after Kennedy received absolution and last rites, he was transferred to Good Samaritan; Dr. Cuneo headed the team that attended to him. Kennedy's wrapped clothing was sent along with him to Good Samaritan.[23]

Officer William Wighton of the LAPD's Accident Investigation Division was initially assigned to the hotel. Then, en route, he was reassigned to Good Samaritan. Wighton, who had a camera, recalls, "Somebody said they needed a camera. So I donned a green gown and spent the night in the operating room about two feet away from Bobby Kennedy's head. I took pictures before they opened up his head. I had to take pictures of the entrance wound, because after they opened up his head to operate, there would no longer be an entrance wound. I could clearly see the powder burns.

"Kennedy was wired for sound, and they were hearing things. He was still alive. I was outside in the hallway when they finally brought him out. He looked good coming out of the operating room. I thought he was going to make it."[24]

LAPD officer Anthony Davis remained at the hospital during the frantic attempt to save Kennedy's life. "He was gray," Davis remembers. "When I looked in that room, it was my opinion that they were keeping him alive until his family got out here. In my view, he was already dead."

[23] LAPD sergeant William Swihart explains, "We had an around-the-clock security around the hospital. And we checked everybody going in and out. We saw a guy going down the side entrance. He was carrying a package. It turned out that he was a priest, but he was not in a priest's garb. I'm a Catholic, and I was as polite as I could be, but I said, 'What do you have in the bag?' He said, 'Well, I have the senator's clothing.' And I said, 'Well, we have to take that, because that's evidence.' There were bullet holes in his suit. I had the clothing locked in the trunk of a police car and had some officers take it down to the Property Division."

Swihart identified the priest as the Reverend James Mundell, who had administered absolution to Senator Kennedy.

[24] LAPD Intelligence Division officer Leroy F. Goforth, who was assigned to Good Samaritan Hospital through most of the day, told me, "On the third floor, there were two offices, like nurses' stations. One of them was for LAPD, and the other was for the Kennedys. One time, I was there and the Kennedy phone was ringing, and I answered it. It was Governor Ronald Reagan's office. His secretary was on the line. Reagan wanted to talk to Ethel. But they had just taken Ethel and her sister, Jean Smith, up, and they were in the room next to Bobby on the fifth floor."

5. Controlling the Crime Scene

While the LAPD captured and arrested Sirhan, from 12:22 to 12:28 A.M., other police officers were swarming into and around the hotel, trying to bring order while collecting evidence.[25]

At 12:23 A.M., after calling in the description of the woman in a polka-dot dress and her male accomplice allegedly fleeing the scene

---

[25] The LAPD's Emergency Control Center became operational on June 5 at 12:50 A.M., thirty-five minutes after the shooting. It continued to be so until 2:30 P.M. on June 6. According to an official LAPD report, "The E.C.C. was activated in order to provide personnel and logistics to the field forces, to collect and disseminate information from field command posts, and to coordinate the activities of the Department."

and claiming to have shot Senator Kennedy, LAPD sergeant Paul Sharaga created a command post in the parking lot of the Ambassador Hotel. Sharaga explains, "The LAPD's departmental manual, at the time, stated that the first supervisory patrol officer on the scene of a major occurrence shall establish a command post and shall maintain command of this post until relieved by a senior supervisor from patrol. I maintained the command post until I closed it down twenty-three hours later."

Across the street, in the IBM Building, a contingent of Los Angeles Sheriff's Office deputies were monitoring the collection of primary election ballots from all county precincts. With their job nearly completed, LASO sergeant John C. Barber and his squad of twelve deputies heard the sirens screaming toward and stopping at the Ambassador. He asked Sergeant Robert E. Lindblom to go to the hotel to investigate.

Sharaga remembers, "A sergeant from the sheriff's department came up to me. He said, 'I have a detail of men over here at the IBM Building. We've been counting ballots. They're at your disposal. What would you like me to do with them?' It was a godsend. 'Get identifications and license numbers of everyone entering or leaving the hotel grounds. Record them, so we can give them to the investigating officers when they arrive.' "

While carrying out this task, the LASO deputies also parked a city bus across Wilshire Boulevard to divert traffic from the hotel.

A few minutes later, Sergeant Sharaga instructed all officers en route to the Ambassador to meet him at the command post. "I asked Communications to have some men sent to me," Sharaga remembers, "a minimum of six two-men units, as fast as they could. I announced that my radio frequency would be TAC-1.[26]

"As soon as my men started showing up, I gave them their

---

[26] During the two-minute period 12:26–12:27 A.M., among the officers responding to the "all units" call were Vasilos T. Karalekas, Thomas W. Duehring, Jeffrey J. Fedrizzi, Lawrence L. DeLosh, Gustavo Ruiz, H. G. "Grady" Dublin, J. D. Hayden, Ronald G. Gould, Steven V. Ebbert, Leo L. Estrada, G. E. Foster, and John T. Weinbeck.

Karalekas, Ruiz, Dublin, Gould, and Weinbeck all say that, at the time, their roles were limited to traffic and crowd control.

assignments. At the command post, I had a logistics officer on the telephone, a log officer, and a radio officer. I dispatched the others to the entrances and exits of the hotel to relieve the LASO's deputies who were there.''

At 12:28 A.M., discrepancies appeared in the police broadcasts about the number of suspects in the shooting. According to the official LAPD log, ''Sergeant Sharaga gave Communications the description of a suspect given to him by an unknown person who claimed to be a witness. His broadcast was as follows: '2L30, description of a suspect in the shooting at 3400 Wilshire Boulevard, male Caucasian, 20 to 22, 6' to 6'2", built thin, blond curly hair, wearing brown pants and a light brown shirt, direction taken unknown at this time.' ''

When Sharaga later was asked about this broadcast in view of his report of the older *couple* seeing *two* people fleeing from the scene, Sharaga insisted, ''I called in a description of two suspects, not just one. To the best of my recollection, the description of the male suspect was very lean. I don't recall having that explicit a description of him. I had a better description of the woman. I wrote these descriptions down in my officer's notebook. I tore the page out of my officer's notebook, and I immediately sent it by courier to Sergeant Bill Jordan at Rampart Detectives.''

Sergeant Jordan says he has no recollection of having received this information.

Also at 12:28 A.M., according to the official LAPD log, at the same time as Sharaga's supposed broadcast of a single suspect other than Sirhan, LAPD detectives Jeff Fedrizzi and Lawrence DeLosh, who had just arrived at the hotel, broadcast a report that a man and woman had fled from the Ambassador after the shooting. On the basis of information supplied by three eyewitnesses, DeLosh radioed in: ''No. 1, male Latin, 30 to 35, 5'9½, stocky, wearing a wool hunter's hat with a small brim. No. 2, described as female Caucasian. No further description.''[27]

[27] According to the LAPD log, this information came from Andrea Busch; her brother, James Busch; and his friend, Richard Rittner—who had been at the Kennedy campaign celebration. According to the Busches, while they were stopped in the parking lot of the Ambassador Hotel and after hearing a radio report about

Later asked whether he was involved in the questioning of these three witnesses and the subsequent radio report, Fedrizzi recalls, "I wasn't, but I think Larry was. Larry said that he had made a broadcast, but I didn't ask him what it was all about."

DeLosh simply says, "I don't remember that. It was an absolute zoo there. We just received the description. All of that information was written down and passed on. We had started our systematic interviews of everyone."

The LAPD treated this report as just another false trail.

DeLosh and Fedrizzi were the first detectives at the crime scene. DeLosh remembers, "I was a plainclothes detective assigned to the Juvenile Division at the time. I was with Jeff in downtown Los Angeles, and we were working a juvenile case at the time. We were talking to a drag queen, a female impersonator, down by the bus station, because they were preying on juveniles. We heard the call come out, and we knew that it was the Ambassador Hotel from the address."

Fedrizzi adds, "When we got in the hotel, we went to the main ballroom. There were people hollering and screaming. It was chaotic, even though Sirhan and Kennedy were both gone."

DeLosh continues, "We were trying to get some control, which was almost impossible."

Fedrizzi says, "Some uniformed guys came in right behind us; so they helped us break the crowd up into 'who saw,' 'who heard,' and 'who didn't know anything except what somebody else told them.'

"There was a little guy standing right beside me. His name was Jesus Perez. He was standing there and just looked at me like, 'What's going on?' So I asked him, 'Did you see anything?' He said, 'Yeah.' And I said, 'What did you see?' He said, 'I was talking to the man just before he shot the other man over there.' So I grabbed him, and I said, 'Don't you even leave my side.' "

---

the shooting, they saw the described male and female walking quickly out of the hotel. When James Busch asked them what had happened, the male stated, "They shot him in the head. He's dead." The male added that he was a hotel busboy and had just shaken hands with Kennedy when the shooting began. The male also simulated the shooting "by pulling out an imaginary gun from his left trouser waistband and placing it to his right temple."

One of Sergeant Sharaga's earliest communications had been to notify Lieutenant Robert Sillings, the Rampart night watch commander, of what had happened at the Ambassador. Sillings, accompanied by Sergeant Ray Rolon, immediately left the station for the hotel. Several minutes after his arrival, Sillings belatedly but finally ordered a "security perimeter" to be established around the hotel.[28]

At about the same time that Sillings and Rolon reported to the command post, Sergeant James D. Jones, a field supervisor on the morning watch at the Wilshire Station, also arrived. Jones recalls that he stood around and watched for a few minutes. Soon, he realized that Sillings was in charge. "I saw Sillings standing, just sort of standing. And I went up and said, 'Lieutenant Sillings, I'm Sergeant Jones. If you need any help, I'll be glad to help.' And he turned around at me, with this obviously shell-shocked look on his face. And he said, 'Oh, yeah, Jones! Jones! Kennedy has been shot! Rosey Grier is in there, and he's got a gun! And we have to go inside and do something to take care of it!' "[29]

Sillings ordered Jones and Rolon to take several officers and secure the crime scene.[30]

---

[28] At 12:37 A.M., according to the official LAPD log, Sharaga assigned several officers to guard the hotel's parking lots and street exits: Officers Alan D. Bollinger, Dublin, Ruiz, Karalekas, V. E. Edwards, Edward W. Crosthwaite, Duehring, and Charles A. Wright.

Dublin, Ruiz, Karalekas, Crosthwaite, and Wright all confirmed to me that they had been involved in the perimeter operation.

[29] Actually, Sillings and Jones knew each other. When Jones battled five bandits in a shootout the week before, Sillings of Rampart came into Jones's Wilshire district to assist. A command post was created for the incident, and the two men first met there.

[30] LAPD reports indicate that Officer Robert Velasquez had been part of the team headed by Sergeant's Jones and Rolon that went to secure the crime scene. However, Velasquez says that he never went into the crime scene. As soon as Rolon arrived, Velasquez told him that he had fallen down the back steps of the hotel and sprained his ankle. For the next couple of hours, Velasquez interviewed potential witnesses and helped transport them to Rampart Station. At 3:30 A.M., Velasquez was finally taken to Central Receiving for treatment.

Also, the LAPD reports and its official log for Officers John W. Grogan and C. A. Brewer stated, "Both assisted other officers and sheriff's deputies in [clearing the crime scene]. While in the kitchen clearing out newsmen, etc., an unknown male told Grogan that he observed another unknown male (possibly a busboy) throw a towel over the Kennedy blood spot and wipe it up."

Grogan insists that he never went to the kitchen pantry at any time—and that

Jones recalls, "We started walking for the back door of the hotel, and there was a newspaper reporter we used to see. He was huge, 300, 350 pounds. And as we were walking toward the back door of the hotel, the reporter came up to Sillings and said, 'Lieutenant! Lieutenant! Let me ask you a few questions!' And Sillings stopped and started talking to him. And we're standing around. And I thought, 'What are we doing standing here? It's crazy!' So I said to the other sergeant [Rolon], 'Hey, let's go.' And he said, 'Okay.' And we took the troops and went inside. That was the last I saw of Sillings for hours.

"I remember we went through a back door and wound up back in the kitchen area. The crowd treated us with total indifference. It was pandemonium. We could have been stick furniture. We went in, and people were hysterical and crying. So when we came into the kitchen pantry, I still wasn't too sure whether Kennedy was in there, whether the man who shot him was in there. I wasn't sure whether Roosevelt Grier had shot Kennedy or had taken the gun away from the person who shot him. I just didn't know what the connection was.

"When we got in there, there was a steward, a small fellow, Filipino or something, in a white steward's uniform. And he had towels [on his hands and knees], wiping up blood off the floor. And I remember saying, 'Oh my god! Stop it! Stop it!'

"My next thought was to seal off the entire area and capture everybody until the detectives can get here and at least get their names—so the people don't just drift off and go home. I went up to the microphone in the Embassy Room and said, 'Can I have your attention? I'm Sergeant Jones, LAPD, please would anybody who saw or heard anything stay right here in this room.' "

Sergeant Rolon continues, "We tried to find out if there were any

---

his partner, Officer Brewer, never did either. When I read him his LAPD report, Grogan appeared completely baffled by what had been written about him. "By the time we got there, the crime scene had already been cleared. We never went into the kitchen." Brewer is deceased. The official LAPD log contradicted the LAPD's own individual reports about these officers and cited Brewer as finding the blood-soaked rag.

The erroneous reports written by the LAPD on Velasquez, Grogan, and Brewer are just three of the many that are clearly in error.

additional suspects. [Witnesses said,] 'Yes, somebody else was running; other people were running.' But there was nothing that we could really substantiate."

Jones adds, "First, you gather the witnesses, then you get them on the road. This took some time. It took me probably a half-hour, forty-five minutes to where I was smart enough to say, 'Gee, maybe this is a conspiracy. Maybe they're going to shoot a lot of Democrats.' It took me maybe a hour or longer to get some patrols out there to find out where the other VIPs were and try to put some protection on them. And I ultimately did that."

Rolon explains that the process of interviewing was extremely difficult. He says, "People who were staying at the hotel, no problem. People who were not staying at the hotel were asking, 'How long am I going to have to wait? I want to get home.' Many of them were transported over to Rampart. And then you had to get some teams to interview them. We couldn't do it at the hotel. We had to get them quietly away. And these were elimination interviews. In other words, 'What exactly did you see?' 'Well. I saw everything.' 'Where were you standing?' 'I was standing back here.' 'What did you see?' 'People screaming.' 'Did you see the man who had the gun?' 'No.' "

At approximately 1:05 A.M., the LAPD began a search of the fifth floor, where the suites of Senator Kennedy and his supporters were. Sergeant Rolon explains, "We made a physical search of the Kennedy rooms—to make sure that there was no one hiding in any of the rooms. We did find people in them. We had to identify them, because we were getting an awful lot of people who were out-of-towners who were traveling with the Kennedy people. They were not local people whom we could get to later. We wanted to make sure that we could identify them so that investigators could talk to them. As long as we could place them either upstairs or in the ballroom, we wanted to indicate that. It is a very large physical area to go through. And I felt that if there is anyone they're going to nail to the wall, it's going to be myself. So I physically entered every room.

"Also I had to determine the validity of the rumors that were going around: 'Is this an assassination plot against the family, too? What is going to happen to the rest of the family? How do we secure them?' We had an awful lot of young, political workers who had been down in the room drinking, prior to and especially afterwards, because there was an unlimited amount of liquor available in the rooms that they were staying in. Quite a few of them, when we went into the rooms, were completely passed out from drinking. And we're talking about the young girls, the twenty-year-olds and so forth. It was a very dramatic point in their lives. 'What's going to happen to us? Are we all going to die?' So there was a very emotional group, especially for the first couple of hours."

By 1:00 A.M., four LASO mobile units and thirty-four deputies on foot had reported to the command post. Sharaga had assigned most of the deputies to secure the perimeter around the hotel. But a little after 1:00, he requested a contingent of LASO personnel to go to the Embassy Room and report to Sergeants Jones and Rolon. Jones ordered them to clear the crime scene.[31]

Jones explains, "We had to get the reporters out of the kitchen pantry. I told the deputies, 'We have to clear this area and protect the crime scene.' Realizing that no one was really in charge, a deputy sheriff said, 'I will help, but I do not want to be responsible for this. I will work for somebody else.' The other sergeant I was with said, 'Don't look at me.' And he [the LASO sergeant] said, 'I want a name [for my report].' And I said, 'Give him Jones.' What were they going to do to me? I was a brand-new sergeant. They weren't going to come back and say that I did anything wrong.

"And the deputy sheriff sergeant said, 'We've got to get going.' He wrote my name down. He says, 'While we're here, we work for you.' I said, 'Good. Line 'em up; clear 'em out!' "[32]

---

[31] According to the LAPD official report, the LASO personnel were Sergeants Lindblom and Barber and Deputies J. R. Armstrong, G. Barrett, Thomas A. Beringer, H. J. Foster, Robert G. Hussey, Frank H. Linley, R. Peterson, and R. F. Salo.

Present at the crime scene with the LASO people—but not reported to have been present in LAPD reports—were Deputies Walter Tew and Charles H. Wood. However, Deputies Hussey and Linley, whom the LAPD listed as being among those present, both told me that they never went into the kitchen pantry. They said that their only job was crowd control, mostly on the outside of the hotel.

[32] The official LAPD log states that Sharaga "redesignated his parking lot command post as the staging area [and] assigned Jones to take over as Field Commander" at 8:40 A.M. Prior to this, the LAPD appears to have viewed Lieutenant Robert K. Sillings as the officer in charge. According to the LAPD log, Sillings selected Jones as the "supervisor in charge of internal security" at 2:20 A.M. How-

Sergeant Lindblom, who led the LASO contingent, remembers, "These reporters were milling all around in there. The first thing you know as a policeman is you have to protect the crime scene. I could see that all of this evidence was going to be destroyed. My immediate thought was, 'We've got to get all of these people out of there.' I don't believe in freedom of the press at a crime scene."

Within fifteen minutes, Lindblom and his men formed a wedge and pressed their way through the kitchen, driving everyone out the swinging double doors at the west end of the pantry.

As the LASO finished its work, Jones noticed a piece of evidence: "I remember seeing what I thought might have been a bullet hole in a door jamb."

After the securing of the crime scene was completed, Sergeant James MacArthur of Rampart Station, who was in charge of the crime scene, posted several officers at all of the entrances to the kitchen pantry.

LASO sergeant John Barber adds, "Once they had enough peo-

---

ever, from all available sources, the evidence is clear that Sergeant Jones of the Wilshire Station and Sergeant Rolon of the Rampart Station ran the operation, with Sergeant James MacArthur in charge of the crime scene.

When later asked about the confusion, Rolon explains, "Being that it was so close to change of watch, in theory, Sillings would be in charge up to midnight—until I turned around and say, 'You're relieved; I'm taking over.' But since it was coming on to our shift, I said, 'Do you want to take this?' And he just looked at me and said, 'No, it's yours. You're going to be on it.' But then again, the title of watch commander is the one who assumes the responsibility. And the rank, whether he was a sergeant, lieutenant, or senior lieutenant, doesn't enter into it. Because you're assuming the position."

Jones also continues, "I saw Inspector Bob Rock and Sillings come strolling through the Embassy Room. Rock looked at me—and maybe I was being a little paranoid—but I looked in his eyes, he looked at me and says, 'You're the field commander?' I said, 'Yes, sir.' He said, 'Okay, what have you done, and what are you doing?' And I told them. And he said, 'Okay.' And he went off. And later Sillings came back—who I thought really should have taken over that thing. And he says to me, 'Is there anything I can do to help?' And I was out of supervisors; so I said, 'Yeah, you could. Could you take this group of people and drop them off at these posts?' And I had a map where I had them all laid out. So he took these officers and went out and did a little supervisor's sort of job. And that was the last I think I ever saw of him."

There were no known clashes between Jones and Rolon; each had his own specific responsibilities and performed them with distinction.

ple there to secure the evidence area, we moved out in the main ballroom, where Kennedy had been speaking. And then we moved out into the main lobby. And there was a fountain. And the hotel manager came through and asked us to assist them in getting the crowd out of the hotel. A real phenomena had occurred there. These people were in shock. You had people around that fountain who were actually kneeling and praying. They were dipping their hands in the water in the fountain and using it to cross themselves."

LAPD Rampart officer Kenneth Vogl says, "After everything calmed down, I was just keeping all of the reporters out of the kitchen. We were looking for bullet fragments and stuff in the kitchen where the shooting occurred." Two other Wilshire Division officers, Robert Rozzi and Charles Wright, also were posted at the crime scene and participated in the search for firearms evidence.

LAPD patrolman Edward Crosthwaite, also of Wilshire, recalls that he arrived at the hotel after hearing an "all units" shooting call on his patrol car radio. After being assigned from the front entrance of the Ambassador to patrol duty near the crime scene, he saw what he believed to be bullet holes in the kitchen pantry while "walking into the room to see what was happening." He adds that it was his understanding that the bullets inside the holes were later recovered.

At 2:00 A.M., Sergeant William J. Lee and Officer DeWayne Wolfer of the Scientific Investigation Division (SID) of the LAPD arrived at the crime scene, along with photographer Charles Collier and police surveyor Albert LaVallee. Even though Lee outranked Wolfer, he refers to Wolfer as "my senior partner." Lee explains that he and Wolfer had been partners since their days in the LAPD's police academy.

Charged with taking photographs of the crime scene, Collier explains, "I'll give you Standard Operating Procedure. The first policeman, often a patrolman, who gets on the scene is supposed to guard it, see? Guard the scene and not let anybody do anything—pick up anything, clean up anything. Save it for the photographer. They want pictures—before anything is moved or disturbed."

After Collier's photography, Wolfer and the SID commenced the official crime scene search for evidence—a search that would become the most controversial portion of the Kennedy investigation.

6. *Interviewing Witnesses*

Two plainclothes detectives, Albert L. Lamoreaux and Cecil W. Zachary, reported to the command post and were ordered "to mingle with people inside the hotel and act as an intelligence unit." Lamoreaux says, "I remember the pandemonium. People were throwing chairs in the air, and they were coming down in the fountain. They were screaming and hollering about Bobby Kennedy being shot.

"So we had tried to locate who had been close to it, who had seen it. We got a room in the hotel. We grabbed as many people as we could and herded them into the room so that we could get some of the witnesses together. We were trying to make a sweep and keep not only guests—people who were present at it—but also hotel personnel. Because at that point, we didn't know who was an employee and who wasn't. Just because they had a white jacket on, it didn't mean that they were a busboy. We just passed them off to the higher-ups when they showed up on the scene."

Lamoreaux adds that he entered the crime scene. "I do recall seeing one or two holes in the door around wherever he had shot him. . . . It was just obvious. Just being a dumb cop, you look and see where the bullets went."

Upon the arrival of the Rampart detectives at the Ambassador, Juvenile Division detectives DeLosh and Fedrizzi, who had already been interviewing witnesses, turned them over to Sergeant James MacArthur and his team.[33] Fedrizzi told them, "This is what we did. We put these people in this room who actually saw something or thought they saw something. These people here in another area heard something. And these are the people who didn't see or hear anything but were told this is what happened."

Sergeant MacArthur arrived at the Gold Room where most of the witnesses were being sequestered. The room was overflowing. MacArthur received permission from Lieutenant Hughes at Rampart to move all of the witnesses to that station to be formally interviewed. Up to that time, only about twenty-five witnesses had been interviewed at the hotel, including busboys Jesus Perez and Juan Romero and waiter Vincent DiPierro; the rest were taken on a bus to Rampart.[34]

MacArthur says, "When I arrived, it was utter chaos. So one of

[33] All LAPD personnel carried their field officer's notebooks, which were their own property. One officer told me, "It is for their own reference—and they take them in court to help their recollections. The notebook fits in your pocket. You scribble things down. You try to keep a chronology."

Interviewing officers also filled out standard 3 × 5 "F.I." cards—field interview cards—that included the witness's name, address, phone number, Social Security number, physical description, and driver's license number. "On the back of the card," the officer explained, "you would put their location [at the moment of the shooting] and other details."

[34] According to the official LAPD log, "A total of one hundred and twenty-six recorded interviews were conducted by various investigators during the period of June 5, 1968, through June 11, 1968." Twenty-three of the witnesses would be called to testify before the grand jury on June 7.

the uniformed officers updated me a little. The first thing I tried to do was to close off the crime scene [once again].

"I was the senior detective, but some of the big brass arrived, too—deputy chiefs and what have you. But they didn't get involved, because it was the Rampart Detectives' investigation. And the news media was driving us nuts. They wanted an interview every two seconds or an update. 'Is there a suspect?' All I knew was that there had been a suspect picked up and taken to Rampart.

"The first thing that was decided was that we didn't want what happened in Dallas to happen. We wanted to find out if there was a conspiracy.

"Also, we wanted to keep the witnesses separate from one another—so that they didn't talk [among themselves] and discuss the shooting. You want what they saw and observed—which was quite a problem.

"There was this one gal who claimed that she was up on the fire escape. And she was sitting there, and she heard a couple of people running. It was a gal running in a polka-dot dress and the two came running by, [saying,] 'We got him! We got him!' So, basically, we thought, 'Well, we've got other people involved.' So the news media got wind of the polka-dot dress."

The woman who saw the girl in the polka-dot dress is Sandra Serrano, who at that time was the co-chairwoman of Youth for Kennedy in the Pasadena-Altadena area.

Serrano had approached John J. Ambrose, a deputy district attorney for Los Angeles County, fifteen minutes after the shooting and told him what she had seen. Ambrose directed her to the police. Several detectives then questioned her. Soon thereafter, she was interviewed by NBC reporter Sander Vanocur.

Serrano told Vanocur the same story she had given to Ambrose:

"Everybody was in the main room, you know, listening to him [Kennedy] speak. And it was too hot, so I went outside. And I was out on the terrace. And I was out there for about five, ten minutes, you know. I started to get cold. And then, you know, everybody was cheering and everything. And then I was standing there just thinking, you know, thinking about how many people there were and how wonderful it was. Then this girl came running down the stairs and said, 'We've shot him! We've shot him!' 'Who did you shoot?' And she said, 'We've shot Senator Kennedy.' And aft—she had—I can remember what she had on and everything. And after that a boy came down with her. He was about twenty-three years old, and he was Mexican-American. I can remember that, because I am Mexican-American. . . . She was a Caucasian. She had on a white dress with polka dots. She was light skinned, dark hair. She had black shoes on and she had a funny nose."

Vanocur appeared baffled by Serrano's bizarre story. But, at the end of his report to the LAPD, deputy district attorney Ambrose concluded, "Sandra Serrano impressed me as a very sincere girl who had been a dedicated Kennedy fan, not interested in publicity in any way."

The LAPD stated that Serrano also claimed in her initial statement to the police to have heard "six quick backfires," which were interpreted as shots, before seeing the mysterious polka-dot dress girl and her male companion.

Thus, the speculation over a possible conspiracy intensified, particularly after Serrano's remarks on national television.[35]

Sharaga, still a one-man command post in the rear lot of the hotel, had not yet been officially informed that the alleged assassin was in custody, nor had he received any communication about his previous reports of a white man and a woman in a polka-dot dress who were seen fleeing from the scene, gleefully telling the elderly couple that they had murdered Senator Kennedy.

According to the official LAPD log, Sharaga rebroadcast his previous report, saying, "2L30, until I establish, or at least have been informed at the C.P. that the suspect is in custody, request you repeat the broadcast of the *suspect*'s description I gave earlier this evening. Repeat at least every ten minutes on all frequencies."

Again, according to the official LAPD log, Parker Center radioed back to Sharaga "that the only description they had was the one

---

[35] According to Chief Robert Houghton in his 1970 book, *Special Unit Senator*, "The All Points Bulletin went out about 3 A.M. requesting information from all agencies on a 'female Caucasian, 23–27, 5'6", wearing white voile dress with small black polka dots, three-quarter sleeves, and wearing heels.' Her companion was also sought: 'Male, Mexican-American, 23, wearing a gold sweater.' "

broadcast at 12:36 by Blishak. This description was that of a male Latin."

However, Sharaga continues to maintain that during the course of that night, he *always* broadcast the descriptions of two suspects.[36]

Inspector Robert F. Rock arrived at the command post and assumed responsibility as the LAPD's press relations officer. Upon hearing of Sharaga's report, Rock did ask Parker Center to "confirm the validity of there being only one suspect involved in the shooting." He was assured that only one person was involved and that he was in custody.

According to a LAPD property report, detectives located Rafer Johnson at Central Receiving Hospital. He had refused to surrender the

[36] Sergeant Sharaga, who had earlier reported his conversation with the older couple who had a story remarkably similar to Sandy Serrano's, told me, "This gal in the polka-dot dress—I never heard anything more about it. I didn't know Sandy Serrano. I never met Sandy Serrano, nor had I ever talked to her, nor had I ever heard about her and the woman in the polka-dot dress until some years after I retired."

At 1:44 A.M., according to the official LAPD log, "Inspector J. W. Powers contacted Sgt. Sharaga on the radio, at the Command Post, and requested to know the origin of the 'second' suspect's description. Sharaga had obtained this information from a person who allegedly had been pushed over by the 'suspect.' This suspect, according to the witness, ran from the crime scene into an adjacent room where this witness had been standing. The witness had only surmised that this person was a suspect because of his hurried actions. Powers ordered Sharaga to disregard the broadcast on the second suspect. He informed Sharaga that other witnesses who had been near the Senator at the time of the shooting described Sirhan as being the only suspect involved."

When I read this notation in the log to Sharaga, he replied angrily, "Bullshit!"

When I read the same notation to Inspector Johnny Powers, he replied angrily, "I'm sure I did that. We had the guy in custody. There are a lot of people in the big city who have guns. Don't jump to conclusions. If you want mental exercise, dig up the facts. We could go off on a half-dozen other tangents about this thing."

At 1:45 A.M., according to the official LAPD log, Sharaga yielded to Powers, radioed Parker Center, and canceled his report on the "second suspect."

However, Sharaga vehemently denied this, telling me, "Negative. It didn't happen that way. I talked to Captain Kirby of Communications, and he said, 'Why aren't you broadcasting a description of these two suspects?' I said, 'I broadcasted it. I don't know whether Communications is putting it on or not, because I'm not listening to anything but TAC-1.' Kirby said, 'Well, they're not putting it out. I'll call and find out why.' He called and came back and said, 'Inspector Powers made a direct order to them not to rebroadcast the description.' "

gun to anyone other than a police officer at "police headquarters." The detectives were ordered to bring Johnson to Rampart, where he surrendered the gun.

Detective Jeff Fedrizzi recalls, "After we accompanied Kennedy up the elevator to surgery at Good Samaritan, Inspector Johnny Powers told us to find Rosey Grier and Rafer Johnson and take them to Rampart Station. We found out later that Rafer had Sirhan's gun in his pocket. Author George Plimpton and his wife were also in the car. There was a team of detectives waiting for us at Rampart. Rafer gave up the gun there [to Sergeant R. L. Calkins]."

According to the LAPD log, "Calkins, while examining the weapon, removed one shell from the chamber to determine the caliber. The remaining seven shells were left in the cylinder for possible prints. Calkins later booked the gun as evidence at the Crime Lab."

The gun was identified as an Iver Johnson Cadet model .22-caliber eight-shot revolver with a two-and-a-half-inch barrel. It had a blue steel finish and dark brown plastic grips. Its serial number was H53725. The revolver contained eight brass shells, all of which had been expended.

7. The Interrogation and Identification of "John Doe"

Sergeant William Jordan, who had tried to comfort Ethel Kennedy at Central Receiving, left the hospital at 12:35 A.M. and started out for the Ambassador Hotel. But after receiving a report that a suspect was in custody at Rampart, Jordan returned to the station. Upon his arrival, he called Lieutenant Charles Hughes, the chief of Rampart Detectives, who told Jordan "to call everybody in."

After making his calls, Jordan went to the interrogation room. He saw the then unidentified shooter, who appeared disheveled and extremely nervous. Jordan had already been told that the crowd at the hotel had badly roughed up the suspect.[37]

Jordan then placed several of his own men outside the interroga-

[37] Jordan later wrote up the commendations for Officers Placencia and White for getting Sirhan out of the Ambassador Hotel in one piece.

tion room for security, telling them, "I don't give a damn if the chief of police comes here, nobody gets in that room!"

When Sirhan refused to identify himself, Jordan told him firmly, "Through fingerprints, you will be identified."

The suspect asked Jordan his name, and the detective told him. When he asked him to repeat his name, Jordan repeated it and then spelled it. "That's a nice name," the suspect replied. Jordan says that the shooter appeared to be quite intelligent and spoke with a slight British accent. "But he didn't seem to be remorseful for anything."

Jordan adds, "The suspect had obviously taken some whacks. There is a little, tiny interrogation room at Rampart. And the guy is sitting there, already beat up. And then I walked in—and I'm not real happy about this—I think he thought he was going to get bounced off the walls. I could just see it in his face. So I got him settled down and introduced myself. I don't think he weighed 130 pounds. So I went through the Miranda business, innumerable times. This was no Mickey Mouse case. That's why I made sure I taped myself. I put a good man on it and told him to knock on the door when he needed time to reload. I wanted everything taped.

"The suspect had no ID. Normally, I started thinking in terms of, maybe, a hit. That's typical. No ID, a little cash in case he got caught. And he was very quiet at first. When I asked him if he understood his rights, he said yes, that they had given them to him in the police car, which was good. He said, 'I wish to abide by that.' I said, 'Okay. I'm going to ask you questions, but they have nothing to do with the case. I have a right and a duty to identify you.'

"We kibitzed back and forth. It was just a game. As soon as he realized that he was not going to be physically hurt, he relaxed. I got him some coffee." However, the suspect refused to eat or drink anything unless Jordan tasted it first.

Sergeant Jordan, who was officially placed in charge of Sirhan, says, "Sirhan was at Rampart for only about thirty minutes to and hour, maximum, but a crowd had started to gather. Sure, we had Dallas on our minds. This guy [Kennedy] would have been the next president. I don't have a doubt in my mind. I tell you, as I was sitting there looking at this little, tiny nothing guy, I thought, 'Man, it just goes to show that we're all vulnerable.'

"I knew that if you make mistakes, you blow your cases, especially the big ones. You just have to kick your personal feelings out the door. If this was the guy who did it, I wanted to find out and convict him. I didn't want anyone to do anything that would detract from that conviction. There are so many things that can happen.

"I called downtown about moving him for security reasons. So we hustled him down in the basement and into a car. I was in the back seat. Sirhan was next to me. We buzzed down First Street as hard as we could go. Somebody thought we had a car following us, but it turned off."

Jordan continues, "Once we arrived downtown, I called the jail doctor [Dr. Elwin C. Lanz] to come up and look at him. I searched Sirhan again in the interrogation room. I took his shoes and socks off. His one ankle was still sore. I tried to be as gentle as I could, which he thanked me for later. I told him, 'I'll get you looked at as soon as I can.' And we took him to the third-floor detective bureau. As best as he could determine without X rays, the doctor decided that Sirhan didn't seem to have any life-threatening injury.[38]

"Sirhan seemed to be in pain, and the doctor wanted to medicate him. I told him, 'Not right now,' because I didn't want him medicated until more people had seen him and talked to him. He wasn't in a lot of pain. Obviously, if he was screaming, we would have let him sedate him and take him to the hospital. It wasn't that way."

Kept under maximum security, Sirhan still wasn't talking and still refused to identify himself. The police booked him simply as "John Doe" at 2:15 A.M. on June 5, charging the mystery man with assault with intent to commit murder. He made his one telephone call to John Howard, a deputy district attorney whom he had met briefly upon arriving at Parker Center.[39]

---

[38] According to the LAPD's official medical treatment record, Sirhan suffered from a swelling of his left ankle, which was determined to be a possible sprain but no fracture; a hematoma on his forehead; a minor abrasion on his face; and a contusion of the left index finger.

However, a subsequent medical report indicated that his left index finger had been fractured. This might have occurred after Sirhan lost and then regained his gun—probably with his left hand—during the battle in the kitchen pantry.

[39] LAPD chief of police Thomas Reddin held a press conference at Parker Center at 3:00 A.M. to discuss what was known about the shooting, like the Kennedy campaign's refusal to accept police protection, and not known, like the identity of the suspect.

The police conducted a strip search of Sirhan and provided him with a pair of loose-fitting prison fatigues. After again reading Sirhan his rights at 3:15 A.M., Jordan, Howard, and Sirhan engaged in rambling small talk—touching on anything *but* the shooting—for about an hour. They were trying to figure out how the alleged shooter got in the pantry and why hotel security never challenged him. But they could never come up with a very good answer. Sirhan refused to discuss the matter or anything else about the shooting.

Jordan remembers, "Sirhan had it all together. When I talked to the DA upstairs, he said, 'What do you think?' I said, 'Well, the only way you can go is dead-bang—unless he pleads insanity or diminished capacity. There's no other way for him to cop out.' He said again, 'What do you think?' I said, 'I won't violate his Miranda, but I'm going to ask him everything in the world that has to do with this case to try to demonstrate that he's sharp, he has a good mind, and that he's control of his faculties.' Which is what I did.

"He wasn't really stalling. I told him a couple of times, 'Through fingerprints, you will be identified.' He said, 'Oh, fine. Let me know when you have me identified.' He wasn't being bitchy about it. At this point, I think Sirhan realized that he wasn't going to be physically hurt, so he was enjoying himself. He talked about Jack Kirschke, an ex–deputy DA. He killed his wife and her lover. I talked to him a lot about that. He was obviously more comfortable with me than the others. It was a combination of my name and the fact that I was so scrupulous about not having him hurt. I told him flat-out, 'I can't afford to have anything happen to you. If I have to protect you with my life—I may not like it but—you're the man right now, and I'm going to take good care of you.' So apparently he believed that.

"The brass asked me after one of the first sessions, 'What's with this guy? He doesn't seem to be remorseful. He doesn't seem to be anything.' I said, 'The only thing I can figure out is that one of the things I found in his pocket was an article about where Bobby had come out very pro-Israeli.' In his mind, my theory always has been and to this day I think it's right, is what it would be like if I was able to parachute into Germany in the middle of the war and shoot Hitler. To the German people, I would be the worst scumbag of all time. In my own mind, I'd say, 'Hey, I'm a hero. I did the right thing for the world.' And that's the way he struck me. He really believed that he had done the right thing."

Sergeant Jordan concluded his final interview with Sirhan at about 5:30 A.M. Later, he summarized his thoughts in his official report: "Sirhan was in good spirits and quite stimulated. He acted like he was playing a game and enjoying it. He appeared anxious to match wits with [us]. He wanted to talk and was happy to talk about anything other than the Kennedy case. We talked about gardening, types of employment, books, literature, family, children, golf, barbers, and the Kirschke case. . . . I was impressed by Sirhan's composure and relaxation. He appeared less upset to me than individuals arrested for a traffic violation. I thought that his mind was keen and that he fancied himself somewhat of an intellectual."

Earlier in the morning, Lieutenant Hughes of Rampart had ordered Officers Travis White and Art Placencia, the two men who officially made the arrest of Sirhan, to take a key found in Sirhan's pocket and find his car, which they expected was parked somewhere near the Ambassador. Placencia explains, "The car key said Chrysler on it. So Travis and I went around the Ambassador after we finished at Rampart and started looking for Chrysler cars."

At about 4:00 A.M., Placencia and White reported to Jordan that the suspect's key had fit the lock of a blue-and-white 1958 Chrysler, parked on Alexandria Avenue between Sixth Street and Wilshire Boulevard, about one-half block north of the hotel. When Placencia tried to start the car with the suspect's key in the ignition, it worked.

However, the Chrysler was registered to a Robert Gindroz, a cook at the Ambassador.

Jordan recalls, "The officers came up with a Chrysler. And they ran it and got a name: Robert Gindroz. So I got it, and I said, 'Now, I think we're getting someplace.' And I laid the name on Sirhan. He didn't even quarrel about it. He said, "Robert Gindroz. What a wonderful name—yeah, a good name. I like that.' I thought, 'Well, we struck out on this one.' "

Of course, that wasn't the alleged shooter's name.[40]

[40] A radio reporter did create a stir about Gindroz when he broadcast a report, based on "reliable sources," that "the Secret Service [has] a file on this kitchen

As dawn broke in Los Angeles and news about the shooting spread throughout the United States and around the world, Jordan and other LAPD officials decided that the suspect had to be moved again—this time to be arraigned. Jordan made the arrangements with a superior-court judge, Joan Dempsey Klein.

Jordan remembers, "It was about seven or seven-thirty in the morning. I was still worried about somebody trying to do something to Sirhan. An assistant chief said, 'Well, what do you want? Do you want a police car?' And I said, 'No.' So we called around, and we found a guy on duty in the jail who had a camper. We borrowed it and put the suspect on the floor. About six of us just kind of packed ourselves around him. So Johnny Powers and somebody else followed us in the police car. And we drove him to the Hall of Justice. We backed right in to the morgue, because there's an overhang. And then we took him to the courtroom in the elevator."

Inspector Johnny Powers recalls, "If anyone wanted to execute this man, they would figure we'd be there at 10:00. We were guarding someone like this who a lot of people would like to kill and wouldn't care if they got killed either.

"Three cars of us went over, and we got the suspect up in the courtroom. And there wasn't anybody there except the judge and the DA. I don't think there were even any newspeople there."

At the arraignment before Judge Klein, Sirhan, still identifying himself as "John Doe" and represented by attorney Richard Buckley of the Los Angeles County Public Defender's Office, was formally charged by Deputy District Attorney John Howard with six counts of

---

worker, and had it been the President who was in the hotel, the Secret Service would have detained the man before the President ever came to town. . . . [The Secret Service] did apparently consider this kitchen worker in question at least a threat to presidents."

The LAPD investigated this charge with Secret Service special agent Tony Sherman, who stated that "Criminal Identification and Investigation had no record on Gindroz," according to a LAPD report.

"On December 16, 1974, Robert Powis, Special Agent in Charge of the Los Angeles Secret Service Office, authorized a new search. Neither the Los Angeles files nor the Protection Intelligence files in Washington, D.C., contain information on Robert Gindroz. He has never been in the files."

The FBI stated that, at the moment of the Kennedy shooting, Gindroz was working in the kitchen and not in the pantry area.

---

assault with intent to commit murder. The judge ordered his bond set at $250,000.

In the continuing attempt to discover Sirhan's identity, the LAPD ran a check on Sirhan's gun, discovering that it was registered to Albert Leslie Hertz of Alhambra, California, who had reportedly purchased it on August 10, 1965, at the Pasadena Gun Shop. At 3:15 A.M. on June 5, police officers awoke Hertz and his wife at their home. However, the couple no longer owned the gun. They had given it to their daughter, Dana Westlake, who lived in Marin County, California. County sheriff's deputies contacted Mrs. Westlake, who told them that in December 1967 she had given the .22 Iver Johnson revolver to a former neighbor in Pasadena, George Erhard. Immediately upon receiving the information about Erhard, investigators went to his home and questioned him. Erhard told police officers that he had sold the gun for $25 on February 15, 1968, to a man he only knew as "Joe," who worked at Nash's department store in Pasadena.

After arriving at Nash's, at 8:00 A.M., the police identified "Joe" as Munir Sirhan, who had been to the store earlier, borrowed a car, and then left. The employee who gave Munir his car told police officers that Munir told him he believed that his brother had been arrested for the shooting of Senator Robert Kennedy. When he returned with the car to the store, Munir was taken to the Pasadena Police Department for questioning.

By the time the police arrived with Munir, Adel Sirhan, an older brother of Sirhan and Munir, had gone to the Pasadena police station at 9:35 A.M. to identify the mysterious "John Doe" as his brother Sirhan Bishara Sirhan. Adel had seen his brother's picture in the morning edition of the *Los Angeles Herald-Examiner*, which he brought to the police station. Pasadena police officials asked Adel to wait until the arrival of LAPD detectives so that he could be questioned. Adel agreed to cooperate fully.

Two LAPD detectives arrived to interview Adel at 10:15 A.M.; they read him his rights before questioning him. Adel again pledged to work with the police and refused the right to call an attorney. When Adel told the detectives that Sirhan lived with his mother and Munir at 696 East Howard Street in Pasadena, the officers asked him if he would permit a search of the house. "As far as I'm concerned," Adel replied, "you may search the house." Adel also agreed to aid in the search of his home.

At 11:15 A.M., the search of the Sirhan family's home began, starting with Sirhan Sirhan's bedroom. Three green spiral notebooks were found: one near the bed, another on top of a dresser, the third in a dresser drawer. Also in a dresser drawer, officers found an envelope; the words "RFK must be disposed of like his brother . . . . . reactionary" were handwritten across the front.

Also found was gun-cleaning equipment, a strip of three pictures of Sirhan, and a certificate from the California Cadet Corps of John Muir High School that had been presented to Sirhan on June 13, 1963. These and other miscellaneous items were brought to Rampart Station and booked as evidence at 2:00 P.M. Adel Sirhan accompanied the detectives to the police station.

While protecting the Sirhan home from people who might seek revenge on the family, the Pasadena police found additional evidence in a trash box in back of the house, including two more notebook papers written in Arabic, a label torn from Sirhan's gun box, and another envelope with a handwritten message: "R.F.K. must be disposed of D D D Disposed of Sidposed Disposed of properly Robert Fitzgerald [*sic*] Kennedy must soon die die die die die die die die die die."

After the incredible coincidence of the car key in Sirhan Sirhan's pocket opening and starting a 1958 Chrysler owned by an Ambassador cook was sorted out, law enforcement officials continued to search the streets around the Ambassador Hotel for Sirhan's car. Finally, at 4:00 P.M. on June 5, FBI special agent Joseph A. Hanlon found Sirhan's 1956 pink-and-white DeSoto two blocks from the hotel on South New Hampshire Avenue, between Wilshire and Seventh Street.[41] A parking ticket had been placed on the windshield at 8:35 A.M.

---

[41] According to the official LAPD report of the murder, "At 4 P.M. on June 5th, an FBI agent located a 1956 DeSoto bearing a license number JWS 093. . . . Lieutenant A. S. Hegge ordered the vehicle secured until another search warrant [different from the one received for the 1958 Chrysler] could be obtained from

With Sirhan's ownership of the car confirmed, Lieutenant Albin S. Hegge—who had set up the control system for all logged information coming into Rampart Station—obtained a search warrant. Hegge, who was accompanied on the search by Rampart detective Clifford White and two FBI agents, remembers, "We found some expended bullets in the car. They were mashed pretty good. I think the crime lab was able to identify one of the bullets. They found two of them."

Hegge and White found Sirhan's driver's license in his black leather wallet. They also found two books—one in Arabic and the other in English, *Healing: The Divine Art*, by Manly Palmer Hall. Other items booked as evidence included copies of six newspapers and a June 1 receipt for .22-caliber ammunition from the Lock, Stock 'N Barrel Gun Shop, in San Gabriel.

While Senator Kennedy barely clung to life in Good Samaritan Hospital, the man who allegedly shot him had finally been identified.

After discovering the assassin's name, Sergeant Jordan says, "I stopped by the hotel briefly, but they wanted me at the hospital. Bobby was still alive, and I had set up security for him through Rampart. I just sort of bounced between the hospital and downtown, trying to fill them in on what I had done, getting my reports together. And then a lieutenant called me—because one of the nurses said that—somebody in the entourage had ordered a private ambulance and plane standing by at the airport to fly Kennedy back to Hyannis Port. I said, 'Wait a minute! The doctor tells me that as soon as they unplug the respirator, he's dead. We have to have an autopsy!'

"Then I got nervous—rightly or wrongly. The Kennedys had a reputation for doing what they wanted to do. I told the lieutenant, 'I don't want to be stuck here with the homicide of a presidential candidate and no body and no autopsy. Because without an autopsy, Sirhan will walk.' "

Judge Klein. At 5:30 P.M., Lieutenant Hegge returned to the vehicle and directed a search. . . ."

8. The Autopsy and the Bullet Audit

R obert Kennedy died in Good Samaritan Hospital at 1:44 A.M. on June 6, twenty-five and a half hours after he was shot.[42] At 9:15 A.M., after six hours of precise work, Los

[42] Upon the death of Senator Kennedy, the LAPD rebooked Sirhan Sirhan, who had been held for assault with intent to commit murder, and charged him with murder.

According to author Robert Blair Kaiser, attorney A. L. Wirin of the American Civil Liberties Union informed Sirhan of Kennedy's death. "Suddenly Sirhan's manner changed," Kaiser wrote in his book, *"R.F.K. Must Die!"* "He dropped his head, then looked up at Wirin with moist eyes. 'Mr. Wirin,' he said, 'I'm a failure. I believe in love and instead of showing love . . .' He didn't finish his sentence."

Also, Wirin claimed that Sirhan had confessed the murder to him. During my interviews with Sirhan, he denied having made any such confession to Wirin.

Angeles county coroner Dr. Thomas T. Noguchi, a native of Japan who had moved to Los Angeles in 1952, removed one intact bullet, as well as fragments of another bullet, from Kennedy's body.[43] After removing the intact bullet, he initialed it with a sharp, pointed instrument for future identification. Among others, three forensic pathologists from the Armed Forces Institute of Pathology in Washington and two of Noguchi's assistants witnessed Noguchi's careful work.

Years later, when asked what went through his mind while he conducted the autopsy on Senator Kennedy, Noguchi recalls, "I respected him greatly. In an autopsy, there is no pain. Nothing in our surgical procedures is not respectable. Not too long before, I had seen Senator Kennedy [on television], giving the victory sign and giving his victory speech. All of us felt emotionally involved. During the autopsy, I did ask to cover his face. I felt that my assignment was very serious, and I wanted to make sure that I concentrated on the details and performed a very thorough examination. I think all of us had learned from five years prior to that, with the death of President Kennedy, that the work on him had been done too fast under the circumstances. As I understand it, it was not as thorough an autopsy as it should have been, which had since caused considerable speculation. I said to myself, 'Not again. Remember Dallas.'

"I called the senator's support leadership and Joe Kennedy II [Senator Kennedy's oldest son], emphasizing the importance of the autopsy. I was shocked when one of Senator Kennedy's supporters, I don't remember who, suggested that an autopsy wasn't necessary. But I understood where he was coming from. Everyone was in considerable pain. It appeared to be an open-and-shut case. Someone was in custody."

[43] Sergeant Bill Jordan was present for the autopsy. He explained the removal and custody of the bullets taken from Kennedy. "There must have been fifteen people there," Jordan remembers. "I had to be there. They took X rays first of the body. The bullet in his brain had disintegrated; the one by his neck area, in the spine, had not. And I told Noguchi, 'Be as careful as you can, because that's it. We need that slug for [firearms identification].'

"That's normal. There's always a detective in attendance at the autopsy, because you have to take any evidence that they find and book it. He got the slug. I signed for it and gave him a release. I put the bullet in a little evidence envelope, and I took it up to Rampart. And it was booked. Then I made my reports, and I went home."

Noguchi determined in his sixty-two-page autopsy report that the fatal shot had entered through the mastoid bone, an inch behind the right ear and had traveled upward to sever the branches of the superior cerebral artery. The bullet had exploded and fragmented on impact, and the largest deposit of lead had lodged to the right of the brain stem. Chips of lead and bone were scattered throughout the senator's brain. Noguchi's detailed tracings of the track of the bullet determined that it had entered at an upward angle of 15 degrees and a leftward angle of 30 degrees.

Another shot had penetrated Kennedy's right rear armpit, traveled sharply upward at a 59-degree angle, and exited through the topmost portion of the chest. Noguchi stated that for the bullet to have taken this path, Kennedy's arm must have been raised when the shot was fired.

A third shot also entered the right rear armpit, one and a half inches below the wound caused by the second shot. The bullet arched upward at an angle of 67 degrees and burrowed in the neck near the sixth cervical vertebra. This was the only bullet taken out of Kennedy's body intact.

A fourth bullet pierced the right rear of Kennedy's suit coat. It traveled upward through the fabric without penetrating the lining. It exited three-quarters of an inch to the rear of the shoulder pad seam and never touched Kennedy's body.

The other five people—Paul Schrade, Irwin Stroll, Ira Goldstein, William Weisel, and Elizabeth Evans—wounded in the shooting spree all survived. The bullets that struck them were recovered during their surgeries and subsequently retrieved and booked by police officers. The last two slugs—taken out of Schrade and Weisel—weren't booked as evidence until 6:00 P.M. on Thursday, June 6.[44]

Eight known wounds, therefore, had been caused during the attack: three in Senator Kennedy and one each in the five other victims. The number of bullets and their flight paths would be crucial

[44] According to the LAPD, the Stroll and Goldstein bullets were booked on June 5 at 5:00 A.M. and 5:20 A.M. respectively; the Evans bullet was removed later that day at 5:10 P.M.

All of the bullets were .22-caliber, copper-coated, hollow-point, long-rifle ammunition.

evidence for the reconstruction of the crime and for the determination of whether more shooters were involved.

DeWayne A. Wolfer, the chief criminalist of the LAPD's Scientific Investigation Division (SID), personally participated in and supervised the crime scene search. Starting soon after 2:00 A.M. on June 5, he became acutely aware of the significance of bullets, bullet holes, and bullet flight paths. Wolfer filed a bullet accounting report on July 8, 1968. In a subsequent, undated, schematic police drawing that depicted the victims' locations at the crime scene and the suspected bullet flight paths that struck them, Wolfer attempted to reconstruct the shooting. Data collected by Wolfer supported his conclusion that the paths Sirhan's eight bullets traveled were as follows: Bullet number 1 "entered Senator Kennedy's head behind the right ear." Bullet number 2 "passed through the right shoulder pad of Senator Kennedy's suit coat (never entered his body) and traveled upward, striking victim [Paul] Schrade in the center of his forehead." Bullet number 3 "entered Senator Kennedy's right rear shoulder approximately seven inches below the top of the shoulder." Bullet number 4 "entered Senator Kennedy's right rear back approximately one inch to the right of bullet #3. This bullet traveled upward and forward and exited the victim's body in the right front chest. The bullet passed through the ceiling tile, striking the second plastered ceiling and was lost somewhere in the ceiling interspace." Bullet number 5 "struck victim [Ira] Goldstein in the left rear buttock." Bullet number 6 "passed through victim Goldstein's left pants leg (never entering his body) and struck the cement floor and entered victim [Irwin] Stroll's left leg." Bullet number 7 "struck victim [William] Weisel in the left abdomen." And bullet number 8 "struck the plaster ceiling," ricocheted, and then "struck victim [Elizabeth] Evans in the head."[45]

[45] The flight paths of the bullets are difficult to match with medical records, particularly in the cases of Evans and Schrade. According to Wolfer's reconstruction, the Evans bullet penetrated a thick acoustic ceiling tile, ricocheted off the ceiling, exited through a second tile, and then struck Evans, who was fifteen feet away, with enough force to lodge in her forehead. This description contradicts the official medical report of her wound, which says, "The bullet entered the scalp of the forehead just below the hairline, off center to the right and traveled *upward* to approximately one inch above the hair line" (emphasis added).

This bullet audit succeeded in reconciling the large number of bullet holes and wounds acknowledged by officials with the firing of only eight shots. If, however, *any* other bullets were evident at the crime scene, Sirhan's gun alone would not account for them.

Challenging DeWayne Wolfer's conclusions, Dr. Noguchi emphasized that there was no way to determine the exact sequence of the bullets that hit the senator and the other victims. It was, however, clear that neither of the armpit shots would have killed Kennedy. It was the shot behind the right ear that had lodged in the brain that was ultimately fatal.

The kill shot had left a severe nitrate burn, irregular in outline, causing a powder "tattoo" that measured about one inch across. Noguchi concluded that the fatal bullet had been fired at extremely

---

Wolfer described the bullet as traveling down, not up. What makes that seem unlikely is Evans's testimony at Sirhan's trial that at the time she was hit, she was bending down to retrieve a lost shoe. Also puzzling is the fact that after traveling all that distance and striking the ceiling and two of its tiles, the hollow-point bullet—which should have mushroomed and fragmented on initial impact—retained three-quarters of its original mass and weight when recovered and examined.

Schrade has long been skeptical about the official account of the shot that hit him. According to the police reconstruction, the bullet that passed through the shoulder pad of Kennedy's suit coat had to travel nearly straight up, at about an 80-degree angle, to hit Schrade. He found that hard to believe, in light of the fact that he was standing four or five feet away from Kennedy when he was shot. "The only way I could've been hit by that bullet," he says, "was if I was nine feet tall or had my head on Kennedy's shoulder."

The more obvious question with the Schrade bullet is its direction. Schrade was walking behind Kennedy. How could a bullet that passed through the *back* of Kennedy's jacket have hit him? Kennedy would have had to be turned almost completely around to fit Wolfer's diagram of the shooting victims and the bullets' flight paths—a diagram that also contradicts the angles of the shots as shown in official police photographs of the crime scene reconstruction, as well as the statements of the twelve people identified by the LAPD as actual eyewitnesses to the shooting.

In March 1986, at a public meeting of the Los Angeles Police Commission, Schrade presented LAPD chief Daryl Gates with a copy of Wolfer's diagram and conflicting photographs from the reconstruction. He asked for an explanation of the shot that had struck him in the head. Neither Gates nor any of the other police officials were willing to respond. Months later, Schrade requested the return of his photographs, but the police denied all knowledge of this incident, which was memorialized in the official transcript of the hearing and occurred in a packed auditorium with numerous television cameras.

close range—contact or near-contact. When asked at Sirhan's trial where the gun would have had to have been to produce such a burn, he said "between one inch and one and a half inches from the edge" of Kennedy's right ear.

Based on his observations, he also concluded that the other shots were fired at "very close range." When asked what the "outside limit" of "very close range" was, Noguchi replied, "When I say 'very close,' we are talking about the term of either contact or a half inch or one inch in distance."

Even without the telltale powder burns, Kennedy's wounds posed a problem. The angles at which the bullets hit him showed that they came from shots fired from his right rear side—not from the muzzle of a gunman's weapon that was one to three feet in front of him, as many of the eyewitnesses had already told the police. Assuming that he had been partially turned to shake hands with one of the busboys on his left, it seemed unlikely that the bullets could have been fired by someone in Sirhan's position.

Noguchi and a team from the LAPD, including the SID's Wolfer and his staff, tested Noguchi's judgment of the muzzle distance at a police academy firing range on June 11, six days after the shooting. They test-fired a gun of the same make and model as Sirhan's into a piece of cloth similar to that of Kennedy's suit coat and into an area adjacent to a pig's ear.[46]

"We used the inside of the pig's ear," Wolfer's assistant, Officer David Butler of the SID, explains, because it is less subject to damage. "Pigskin is the closest thing to human skin, biologically. And what we do is take and tack the pigskin, flay it so we can get more surface area. Then we can simulate the shot behind the ear from behind the mastoid bone. During the autopsy, photographs were taken of that ear [and] that gunshot wound. Then we can approximate the range of the barrel."

The shots were fired into the pigskin at the same angles described

[46] The serial number of the Iver Johnson test gun was H18602, which would later become the source of a major controversy. Also, a Walker H-acid test conducted on Senator Kennedy's suit coat by the LAPD/SID corroborated Noguchi's findings that the muzzle distance between Sirhan's gun and Kennedy's jacket was no more than six inches.

in Noguchi's autopsy. The police tests confirmed Noguchi's conclusions regarding the close range and the steep angles of the shots that struck Kennedy.

Wolfer's official LAPD report on these activities, dated June 11, 1968, stated, "Tests indicate that the powder residue pattern of the right ear of Senator Kennedy was caused at a muzzle distance of approximately one inch."

When pressed about what he believed had really happened that night, Noguchi explains, "In my career as a forensic pathologist and coroner, I consider that the most important thing is that my work is professional and believable. Credibility is very important. I am very reluctant to get involved in the speculative areas. If I had been responsible for the investigation, I may have done it differently. But the crime scene belonged to the local police department. There are lessons to be learned from this case: Do not take for granted that the one who is in custody is the one who committed the crime. And in a well-known case, there should be a thorough inquiry, making sure that the evidence is handled carefully and that the chain of custody must be provable. Just one incredible event will destroy credibility."

However, in his 1983 autobiography, *Coroner,* Noguchi noted the contradictions between the eyewitness reports of Sirhan's location and the scientific muzzle distance data concerning Kennedy's wounds. "[U]ntil more is positively known of what happened that night," Noguchi concluded, "the existence of a second gunman remains a possibility. Thus I have never said that Sirhan Sirhan killed Robert Kennedy."[47]

[47] Thomas T. Noguchi, with Joseph DiMona, *Coroner* (New York: Simon and Schuster, 1983), p. 108.

9. The Grand Jury

On June 7, the Los Angeles County Grand Jury, presided over by Judge Arthur Alarcon, convened at 9:00 A.M., receiving physical evidence from the SID and hearing testimony from twenty-three witnesses, including Thomas Noguchi and DeWayne Wolfer.[48] Seven and a half hours later, the twenty-two-

---

[48] Others called to testify included shooting victims Ira Goldstein and Irwin Stroll; LAPD arresting officers Art Placencia and Travis White; fire inspector Harold Burba; Lieutenant Albin Hegge and Lieutenant Charles Hughes of Rampart Division; Sergeant Albert J. LaVallee of LAPD/SID; ambulance drivers Max Behrman and Robert Hulsman; two of the physicians who worked to save Kennedy, Dr. V. Faustin Bazilauskas and Dr. Henry Cuneo; eyewitnesses Vincent DiPierro, Edward Minasian, Jesus Perez, Karl Uecker; Henry Carreon, a person who saw Sirhan firing his gun at the San Gabriel gun range; and Los Angeles attorney Paul Ziffren, who officially identified Kennedy as the murder victim.

member grand jury indicted Sirhan for the murder of Senator Kennedy and five additional counts of assault with intent to commit murder. Revoking Sirhan's $250,000 bail, the judge ordered him held without bond. Sirhan remained in custody.[49]

Contrary to popular belief, no known television cameras or recording devices in the pantry were operating at the moment the shooting began.[50] Without this aid, the grand jury had to base its decision on eyewitness and forensic evidence.

As the murder was not memorialized on tape or film, it is worth examining the testimony of the key eyewitnesses in detail. The discrepancies between their accounts of events and that of coroner Noguchi, who based his version on the autopsy, and LAPD investigators, who corroborated Noguchi's findings, would become a key to future controversies.

Speaking of the muzzle distance, Noguchi recalls, "They did ask

[49] Not requiring Sirhan to enter a plea until a later date, Judge Alarcon authorized the selection of two psychiatrists to assist the defense in its examination of Sirhan.

[50] The only photographs snapped *during* the actual shooting may have been those taken by Jamie Scott Enyart, then a fifteen-year-old high school student, who was standing ten to fifteen feet behind Kennedy, holding his camera above his head and aiming it at the senator. But the young photographer has no idea what ten of his pictures had memorialized. Later that night, law enforcement officials impounded his film when the student was taken in for questioning. Two weeks later, after repeated requests, he was given some but not all of his pictures. In 1988, John Burns, the California state archivist, informed Enyart that his pictures were not in the LAPD files and might have been among 2,400 photographs that had been destroyed by the LAPD.

ABC News was the only television network broadcasting when the shooting began. Its equipment was recording from the back of the Embassy Room. Both Andrew West of Mutual Broadcasting and Jeff Brent of Continental Broadcasting switched on their microphones after the shooting began.

In November and December 1982, these three audio sound recordings were subjected to scientific, but controversial, acoustic analysis, in an attempt to determine if a distinctive gunshot "audio signature" can be identified and the number of gunshots counted. According to Dr. Michael H. L. Hecker—an electrical engineer with the Stanford Research Institute, in Menlo Park, California—who conducted the tests, "On the basis of auditory, oscillographic and spectrographic analyses of these three recordings, it is my opinion, to a reasonable degree of scientific certainty, that no fewer than 10 (ten) gunshots are ascertainable following the conclusion of the Senator's victory speech until after the time Sirhan Bishara Sirhan was disarmed."

Experts disagree as to the reliability of such tests.

me about it at the grand jury. I indicated that it was one inch away from the edge of the right ear. It didn't have any impact at that time, because every member of the grand jury had no question. They assumed they had a watertight case against Sirhan. No one paid any attention to this detail. But, afterward, one of the deputy district attorneys came up to me and said, 'Inches or feet? If it's feet, then you might want to change your testimony.' This was after my grand jury testimony. I just told him, 'My goodness, it's an inch, not feet, because of the black powder behind the ear.' He didn't pressure me or call me back. During the trial, Grant Cooper [Sirhan's attorney] was focusing on insanity or a different legal tactic. So he wanted me to leave the stand. The distance again was offered, because I was asked by the district attorney. But there was no challenge from Cooper. He said something like, 'Spare us the gory details.' "

Describing the final seconds before the shooting began, Karl Uecker, the assistant maître d' for the Ambassador Hotel, has proven to be among the most credible witnesses. He testified before the grand jury that after delivering his brief victory speech, Kennedy stepped off the platform and passed through some curtains in back of the temporary stage onto a permanent stage, to the wild applause of his supporters. Kennedy's next stop was the hotel's Colonial Room, where a press conference had been scheduled.

As Kennedy approached the rear stage door, an executive at the Ambassador Hotel who had escorted Kennedy down the elevator a few minutes earlier, innocently called out, "This way, Senator," indicating their route through the kitchen pantry.

Uecker took Kennedy by the right arm and led him out of the stage area. The entourage turned to the right, down a corridor leading back to the kitchen pantry. Walking west to east, the senator passed through two swinging doors that were separated by a wooden center divider where Gene Cesar, the armed security guard, was standing. As they proceeded through the pantry, the senator occasionally broke loose from Uecker and Cesar to shake hands with well-wishers.

Uecker continued to lead Kennedy forward through the crowd, holding the senator's right wrist. Kennedy was immediately followed by Cesar, who was simultaneously holding the upper portion of Kennedy's right arm.

Uecker told the grand jury, "[Kennedy] got loose of my hand again and shook hands with one of the dishwashers. . . . I was trying to get as fast through the kitchen area there, through the pantry, as I could." Uecker again grabbed Kennedy's right wrist and tried to lead him through the crowd.

Suddenly, several feet ahead, Sirhan emerged from behind a tray stacker at the end of an ice machine on Uecker's right and crossed, east to west, over to the side of a steam table about four to six feet in front of Kennedy, who was walking toward him. The five-foot-ten-and-a-half-inch, 190-pound Uecker saw Sirhan and assumed that he was just another kitchen employee who wanted to shake hands with Kennedy.

Because Uecker was anxious to get Kennedy through the pantry, he aggressively moved to block Sirhan and pinned him against the steam table, which was bolted to the floor and, thus, immovable.

Sirhan then reached out around the left side of Uecker's face and pointed his gun in Kennedy's direction.[51] According to the maître d', the barrel of Sirhan's gun never got closer than one and a half to two feet from the senator.

In fact, not a single witness who testified before the grand jury investigating the murder, or at Sirhan's subsequent trial, said or would say that Sirhan's gun ever got closer to Kennedy than this. Noguchi and the LAPD had concluded that Sirhan had shot Kennedy from contact or near-contact range.

According to Uecker, when the shooting began, at exactly 12:15 A.M. on Wednesday, June 5, Sirhan immediately became the focus of attention in the pantry. Many people, realizing that he was shooting into the crowd, reacted by diving to the floor, instinctively and under-standably trying to save their own lives. Thus, general pandemonium erupted.

"I heard the first shot and the second shot right after that," Uecker told the grand jury, "and Mr. Kennedy fell out of my hand. I lost his hand."

---

[51] There is testimony that Sirhan shouted, "You son of a bitch!" before opening fire.

Seeing the gun in Sirhan's out stretched arm reaching in front of him, Uecker grabbed "the arm [Sirhan] was holding the gun in, pushed [it] down towards the steam [table]. And my right arm, I [wrapped] around his neck as tight as I could and [began] pressing him against the steam [table]."

While Uecker battled for control of Sirhan's gun and others rushed to help him, Sirhan began to shoot wildly into the crowd. "In the meantime," Uecker continued, "somebody else came behind me and pushed me against the steam [table]. The guy in front of me [Sirhan] couldn't get loose.

"While I was holding the hand he had the gun in, I was trying to get the point of the gun as far away from the part where Mr. Kennedy was lying. . . . I was trying to push the gun away to the right side where I didn't see too many people, while he was still shooting. . . . I was standing there and he was shooting, and I could feel when he was turning his hand towards the crowd."

Uecker claimed during his grand jury testimony that he had grabbed Sirhan's arm after the second shot was fired. Uecker added that he thought Sirhan blindly got off another six shots while they were wrestling for the gun.

Edward Minasian, another assistant maître d' at the Ambassador, was walking to the right of Uecker when the shooting started. "Out of my peripheral vision," Minasian testified before the grand jury, "I noticed someone dart out from this area . . . and lean against the steam table. And I saw a hand extended with a revolver. . . . I heard two shots. They were very, very deliberate shots. There was just a slight pause."

Then he saw and heard "some more wild-type firing which was more rapid-fire than the first two, as they were struggling for the gun. . . . I know the first two were deliberate and the others came in quick spurts." Minasian said that the barrel of Sirhan's gun was approximately three feet away from Kennedy.

When asked whether these wild shots were fired in Kennedy's direction, Minasian replied, "I doubt it. . . . We had him and his arm somewhere on the steam table here. And I doubt if it was the same direction as the first two shots."

Eyewitnesses Uecker and Minasian testified before the grand jury and, later, at Sirhan's trial. Both were reliable witnesses who stuck to their original accounts of the shooting.[52] The third was busboy Jesus Perez, who barely spoke English and was not asked very penetrating questions about the shooting. The fourth was a student and part-time waiter at the Ambassador, Vincent DiPierro, who has changed his version of the incident over the years. DiPierro is the son of Angelo DiPierro, at the time the Ambassador's maitre d'.

At the trial, Vincent DiPierro would claim under oath that Sirhan was standing four to six feet away from Kennedy when he began shooting. DiPierro said he heard the first shot and then a pause between it and the next three, which were rapid-fired. DiPierro was distracted, however, when his face was splattered with the blood of Paul Schrade, who was shot in the forehead and then fell against him. DiPierro himself was knocked down when a second shooting victim toppled on him.

The questions of how many clear shots Sirhan had fired at Kennedy and from how far away become critical when the evidence of the murder is reexamined.

The discrepancy between Noguchi's autopsy conclusions and eyewitness accounts of the shooting did not arise at Sirhan's trial—because, as Noguchi has said, the prosecution and the defense both assumed from the outset that Sirhan had been the lone assassin. Sirhan's defense team would not contest the crime scene and physical evidence data that would be entered as evidence at the trial, for fear that drawing attention to the "gory details" of the shooting would inflame the jury. For this reason—and because of the imprecision and sparseness of the prosecution's presentation—few of the specifics involving the locations, distances, and direction of the shooting would receive much attention in court.

Why the discrepancy between the conclusions of both Noguchi

---

[52] The first wrinkle in Uecker's credibility came in March 1992 when he told an interviewer for the television program "A Current Affair" that he heard a "shot fired right over [the back of] my head," meaning originating from a gun other than Sirhan's. During the interview, he also stretched the muzzle distance of Sirhan's gun from one and a half feet to "two and a half to three feet." Uecker had never mentioned any of this to anyone before, despite the obvious significance, which he clearly understood. Uecker's most credible statements remain his sworn testimonies during the grand jury hearing and at Sirhan's trial.

and the LAPD with eyewitness accounts of the shooting would not be discussed at Sirhan's trial is an important question. Los Angeles district attorney Evelle Younger, who supervised the prosecution's case, was later asked about that, but he dismissed the problem, saying, "If somebody says one inch and somebody else says two inches, that's a discrepancy. But the jury didn't think it was a significant discrepancy, and neither did I. What worries me more than a discrepancy in a criminal trial is where you've got all of the witnesses saying exactly the same thing. That's when you have to worry, not when there's a reasonable discrepancy."

Of course, the problem was not a matter of "one or two inches," and Younger conveniently ignored the fact that the jury was not asked to deal with muzzle distance at Sirhan's trial—and that the witnesses were all saying the same thing about that. Once again, *no one* who testified either before the grand jury or later at Sirhan's trial placed Sirhan or his gun to the rear and within six inches of Kennedy. Indeed, law enforcement officials have never dealt with the contradictions between the scientific evidence and statements by eyewitnesses. The LAPD simply tried to ignore the eyewitnesses or to insist that their statements were ambiguous and unclear.

In the official police summary report on the Kennedy murder case, five witnesses were identified as being "closest to the Senator at the time of the shooting." Those five were Karl Uecker, the Ambassador's assistant maître d'; kitchen workers Juan Romero and Jesus Perez; waiter Martin Patrusky; and attorney and Kennedy campaign official Frank Burns.

Busboy Juan Romero, who was pictured kneeling next to the senator after the shooting, said, according to a June 7, 1968, FBI report, that Sirhan's gun "was approximately one yard from Senator Kennedy's head."

Perez, who, again, didn't speak English very well, was never asked about the muzzle distance in official transcripts, and no known statement by him on this matter exists.

Ambassador waiter Martin Patrusky stated in a December 12, 1975, sworn affidavit that "Kennedy's back was not facing Sirhan. Sirhan was slightly to the right front of Kennedy. I would estimate that the closest the muzzle of Sirhan's gun got to Kennedy was approximately three feet. After Sirhan fired the first shot, Uecker grabbed Sirhan around the neck with one hand, and with the other hand he grabbed Sirhan's right wrist. But Sirhan continued to fire."

Burns, who also served as the Kennedy campaign's liaison to the LAPD investigation, told Dan Rather during a January 5, 1976, CBS broadcast that after Uecker grabbed Sirhan's arm and held him against the steam table, he dove for Sirhan's legs. He added that Sirhan's gun was "never closer than a foot and a half to two feet" from Kennedy. When asked whether the muzzle distance of Sirhan's gun might have been closer, Burns replied, "Well, it wasn't that gun. . . . No way."

Other eyewitnesses who have made statements on the muzzle distance controversy include newspaper columnist Pete Hamill, who told LAPD investigators on October 9, 1968, that the gun was at least two feet away.

Television producer Richard Lubic, who had been walking a step behind and to the right of Uecker, issued a similar statement in February 1975 for the American Academy of Forensic Sciences: "The muzzle of Sirhan's gun was two to three feet away from Senator Kennedy's head. It is nonsense to say that he fired bullets into Senator Kennedy from a distance of one to two inches, since his gun was never anywhere that near to Senator Kennedy."

Security guard Gene Cesar told the LAPD, "Senator Kennedy was approximately two feet from the gun."

Valerie Schulte, a Kennedy volunteer, would testify at Sirhan's trial that the gun was "approximately three yards from the senator."

Two witnesses, according to the LAPD, said that Sirhan fired from "point-blank range," which is generally considered to be a foot or less between the muzzle of a gun and a victim's body. One was Boris Yaro, a photographer for the *Los Angeles Times*. However, Yaro was in the midst of focusing on the scene through a camera lens when the shooting started. Yaro told the FBI on June 7, 1968, "The senator and the assailant were little more than silhouettes." Yaro, the only witness to claim the Sirhan's gun was within a foot of Kennedy's head, was never called to testify either before the grand jury or, later, at Sirhan's trial.

The second supposedly to claim that Sirhan fired "point-blank" was eyewitness Lisa Lynn Urso, who was standing just behind Sirhan. According to the June 27, 1968, LAPD report of the interview with Urso, "She indicated she was not sure of the distance, but from what she observed she thought the shot was fired from 'point-blank' range." However, when later questioned by police detectives on tape, Urso, who apparently didn't know what "point-blank" range really meant, told the LAPD that the muzzle distance from Sirhan's gun to Senator Kennedy's head was between "three and five feet."[53]

However, as coroner Noguchi and the LAPD agreed, *all* of the bullets that struck Kennedy entered from the right rear—and at point-blank range.

Meanwhile, the LAPD, in cooperation with other law enforcement agencies, continued the investigation with the establishment of a special investigating task force: Special Unit Senator (SUS).

[53] As late as 1977, the Los Angeles district attorney's "special counsel," Tom Kranz, continued to characterize the eyewitness testimony issues as "a supposed contradiction" and "a false trail." However, when asked at a subsequent Los Angeles Board of Supervisors meeting to name any eyewitness who described a point-blank shot at Kennedy by Sirhan, Kranz admitted, "[N]one of the witnesses ever put Sirhan point-blank next to Mr. Kennedy. . . ."

10. SUS and Its Probe of Sirhan

Although the LAPD clearly controlled the Kennedy murder case, numerous law enforcement agencies involved in investigation agreed to participate in a meeting to sort out anticipated jurisdictional problems and to coordinate efforts. It took place on Sunday, June 9, at Parker Center—the same day President Lyndon Johnson declared as a national day of mourning for Senator Kennedy's death. Attending this interagency meeting were the following:

Assistant Attorney General William Lynch of Washington
U.S. Attorney Matt Byrne of Los Angeles and Assistant U.S. Attorney Robert Brosio

Four representatives from the Los Angeles DA's office: Buck
   Compton, John Howard, John Miner, and George Stoner
LASO Captain Clifford Montgomery
FBI special agent William Nolan
Secret Service agent Stewart Knight
LAPD chief of detectives Robert Houghton
LAPD inspectors Johnny Powers and Kenneth McCauley
Rampart Detectives's Charles Hughes, Verne Sorensen, and
   Danny Lodolo
LAPD Scientific Investigative Division's John Bigham, DeWayne
   Wolfer, and Riley W. Maxwell

Chief of Detectives Houghton ran the meeting. He recalls, "I
could see that this was going to be a tough investigation. It had
historical potential. I had fifteen or twenty people there. Because the
murder had been committed in the city of Los Angeles, we [LAPD]
took jurisdiction. However, I wanted all of the assistance and advice I
could get.

"Powers, McCauley, and I believed that Rampart Detectives or
the Homicide Division couldn't handle the entire investigation alone.
That's when we decided to create our special task force: Special Unit
Senator, SUS."[54]

The following day, Monday, June 10, Hugh Brown, the LAPD's
commander of the homicide division, became Houghton's handpicked SUS commander, overseeing the day-to-day operations of the
unit. On June 11, Room 803, heavily secured and well equipped, on
the eighth floor of Parker Center, became the official headquarters of
SUS.

Under Houghton and Brown, Lieutenant Manny Pena wound
up as the day watch commander; Lieutenant Charles Higbie headed
the night watch. Houghton told the SUS team, "We're not going to
have another Dallas here. I want you to act as if there was a conspiracy
until we can prove that there wasn't one."

The key man in the investigation became Pena. He had served in
the Pacific during World War II, had been a counterintelligence offi-

---

[54] A second interagency meeting was held on July 22, 1968.

cer in Latin America and France,[55] and had held command of an LAPD detective bureau. Pena says, "We picked just about the forty sharpest guys on the department in every category: intelligence, auto theft, any specialized area that we could. I was assigned to supervise the case preparation for trial, the conspiracy allegations investigations, and the background of the Sirhan family. I separated all of the paperwork in those three categories. And so we went to work."

With the link between Sirhan and his Iver Johnson .22 revolver, SUS had proof that Sirhan had the means to kill Senator Kennedy. With other physical evidence and the eyewitness testimony, SUS had proof that Sirhan had the opportunity. Thus, the SUS investigation of the motive for Robert Kennedy's murder began with Sirhan and his background.

Here's what SUS found:

Sirhan Bishara Sirhan was born on March 19, 1944, in Jerusalem, Palestine. He was the fifth son of Bishara Salameh Ghattas Sirhan, a mechanic with the local sanitation department, and Mary Bishara Salameh (Muzher). Both were seventeen years old when they married in 1930. Neither was of the Islamic faith; both were Jordanian Christians and members of the Eastern Orthodox church. They were also the parents of a daughter, Aida, and other sons: Saidallah, Sharif, and Adel. Their oldest son, Munir, was hit by a car in Jerusalem in 1946 and killed. The Sirhan family contributed the financial settlement received in the wake of Munir's death to their church. The following

---

[55] For years, some critics of the Kennedy murder case have tried to portray Pena as a tool of the intelligence community. Pena has been extremely upset with the way he has been depicted, telling Los Angeles attorney Marilyn Barrett, "I didn't come back [to the LAPD] as a sneak to be planted. The way they have written it, it sounds like I was brought back and put into the [Kennedy] case as a plant by the CIA, so that I could steer something around to a point where no one would discover a conspiracy. That's not so."

For the record, all direct quotations from Pena in Chapters 10 and 11 are based on Marilyn Barrett's September 12, 1992, exclusive, tape-recorded interview with him. Barrett was the first interviewer to hit Pena with the home run questions about the Kennedy case.

I have chosen to allow Pena's fascinating interview by Barrett, a trusted friend and colleague of mine, to stand. I did not attempt to interview Pena; I only made a courtesy call to him to fact-check the quotations, allowing him to amend or expand upon them.

year, their sixth son, also named Munir, was born.

In the war-torn aftermath of the 1947 creation of Israel, the Sirhan family, by then poor refugees who had survived repeated shelling, moved to East Jerusalem.

Sergeant Mike Nielsen, an SUS member, explains, "There was probably a tremendous amount of trauma when Sirhan was small. There were villages that were being wiped out. I could easily see why and how Sirhan would be affected by his early childhood upbringing and how this hatred between the Arabs and the Jews affected him."

In 1956, the Sirhan family applied and qualified for U.S. visas as Palestinian refugees. Sponsored by a minister in the Church of the Nazarene who was active in the Church World Service, the Sirhans arrived in New York City by boat in 1957 and soon moved to Pasadena, California. Two sons, Sharif and Saidallah, remained in Jerusalem until 1960, when they joined their family at the Sirhan home in Pasadena. They eventually rented their own apartments.

Settled in Pasadena, Bishara Sirhan—a strict disciplinarian, who beat young Sirhan—could not hold a job and failed to adapt to American life. Consequently, he abandoned his family and flew to Jordan in 1957, leaving Mary Sirhan, a kind and hardworking woman, to take care of their children. Two years later, he returned to New York and obtained a job with a construction company. In 1966, reportedly without ever contacting his family in Pasadena, he went back to the Middle East for good.[56] Mary Sirhan remained in Pasadena, raising her family and working as a teacher's aide at the Westminster Nursery School in Pasadena while her children attended public school. The family, which had bought a Pasadena home in 1962 for $11,500, became members of the local First Baptist Church.

According to the LAPD, Sirhan Sirhan, who had a dark, swarthy appearance, was "unique" at his all-white high school. One of his teachers described him as having "a language handicap" but added that he "tried hard and was showing improvement in all areas. He was also cooperative [and] well-mannered," but quiet and reclusive. An-

---

[56] Sirhan's father died in late 1987 in the village of Taibe, in the occupied West Bank of the Jordan River.

other instructor told the FBI that "Sirhan got along well with the other students, was somewhat reserved but was always cooperative and friendly. The instructor said that Sirhan was a good student, did his homework faithfully, and his entire impression of him was very favorable." While at John Muir High School in Pasadena, Sirhan studied German for three years and Russian for two years. Also, he was a member of the California Cadet Corps, a type of high school ROTC. The LAPD stated that Sirhan "did not receive any training in the use of firearms, with the exception of possibly a trip once or twice a year to the National Guard Armory where all of the cadets were permitted to fire a few rounds with the .22 caliber rifle. None of the cadets received any training in the use of handguns."

After his graduation, Sirhan enrolled in Pasadena City College in the fall of 1963. He had a poor attendance record and didn't seem to be interested in his classes. He was not known to have dated any women on campus but was occasionally seen with friends at a local Denny's restaurant, a student hangout, or at a Pasadena pool hall. Despite his lack of success in romance, he fancied himself a ladies' man who usually didn't hesitate to ask women out when he felt attracted to them.

Known as a nondrinker who occasionally bought drinks for the house, Sirhan had a good sense of humor—although he usually became very intense while discussing the Arab-Israeli conflict.

In 1964, Sirhan began returning home from school immediately after his classes to care for his sister, Aida, who had leukemia. She died in March 1965 at age twenty-nine. Her death devastated the Sirhan family.

Three months later, Sirhan dropped out of college.

Sirhan's employment record was long. He had delivered newspapers and worked as a gardener, waiter, short-order cook, and service station attendant.

During the fall of 1965, Sirhan went to work at Santa Anita racetrack as an exercise boy and "hot walker." After races, he cooled down horses by walking them. His racetrack friends nicknamed Sirhan "Sol." On December 16, 1965, he applied to the California Horse Racing Board for a hot walker's license. As part of the application process, he was fingerprinted and photographed. He received his license in January 1966.

While working at the racetrack, Sirhan also trained to become a jockey. The LAPD quoted the foreman at a horse ranch as saying that "Sirhan was a poor horse rider and was constantly being thrown or falling from horses that he was working." He quit his job at Santa Anita on March 31, 1966.

In June 1966, Sirhan went to work for Bert Altfillisch, the owner of Granja Vista del Rio Thoroughbred Horse Farm, near Corona, California, as an exercise boy and groom.[57] He was known to come to the stables early and work late into the evening. At the time, he was living at a motel close to Del Mar racetrack, near San Diego, and making $375 a month.[58]

The man who hired Sirhan was horse trainer Henry Ronald Ramistella, aka Frank Donnarumma, a short and slender sixth-grade dropout who was born in the Bronx in 1933 and had a record of petty crimes and a 1956 guilty plea to possession of marijuana.

According to an LAPD report, Ramistella, a former jockey, had changed his name after having his stable license revoked in New Jersey. Racing authorities accused him of "making an unsatisfactory

[57] Altfillisch told me, "Sirhan—we knew him as 'Sol'—just showed up, looking for a job exercising horses. He had done it someplace else. He wasn't completely green getting on a horse. Green enough—but not totally green. He was exercising and grooming and doing some sales preparation. He really wanted to become a jockey. And that's what he would do here: exercise horses and ride. But these were horses that had already been broken, and he didn't ride in a race. . . .

"He got along fine at the farm, but I really didn't think he was going to make it as a jock. He used to get a little excited when the fellows would goad him a little bit with politics. He loved politics, but he got carried away with it. He was always defending the Arabs and what not."

According to a July 3, 1968, FBI report, actor-producer Desi Arnaz was the owner of Corona Breeding Farm in Corona, California. Sirhan jotted down the names of the farm and Arnaz in his notebooks seized by the LAPD. Altfillisch remembered, "We broke his yearlings here. Arnaz paid by the day; his yearlings were in our care and custody."

[58] Upon being contacted by the FBI, Edward Van Antwerp, another employee at the farm, insisted that he didn't know Sirhan—when, in fact, he had lived with him for five months while they were working at the Corona farm. Finally, during a second interview, he conceded that he did know Sirhan, whom he knew as "Sol," but added little to the body of information about the accused assassin.

ride" and then providing "false testimony before the track Stewards." Under his alias in 1966, he applied for and received a license at Santa Anita, where Sirhan had worked as a hot walker. However, the licensing commission in California later found out Ramistella's real name and again pulled his license.

Interviewed by the FBI on April 5, 1969, Ramistella described Sirhan "as being a 'loner' who had few friends and who used to go without meals in order to save his pay check. Sirhan was very meek and had no 'nerve.' Sirhan was generally afraid of horses and lacked the nerve to become a jockey."

Ramistella was present in late September 1966 when Sirhan fell from a chestnut mare, named Hy-Vera, while she was in full gallop. After the fall, Sirhan was taken to a local hospital for X rays. He was not badly injured and returned to full-time work just six days after the accident. He later received a $1,705 settlement from an insurance company for his injuries. A week after his return to work, Sirhan fell off another horse and was taken to the hospital. Once again, his injuries were minor, and he returned to work the following day. But Sirhan didn't last. On November 13, 1966, he quit his job at Corona.

After a brief job at Del Mar and another fall off a horse, he returned to Corona in early December 1966. But he quit that job again just a few days later.

According to an LAPD document, Sirhan "bet most of his salary on the horses. During this same period of time . . . a school acquaintance frequently met Sirhan at Santa Anita racetrack. He described Sirhan as a heavy bettor, betting as much as sixty to eighty dollars on one race."

SUS discovered that before the murder, Sirhan had been going to the track nearly every day—and losing.

At the time, he was making only $75 a week, according to the FBI, which claimed that he made bets with a Pasadena bookmaker who operated at a local bar. The FBI also said that Sirhan and his mother often argued about his gambling habit and the debts he accumulated.

In September 1967, Sirhan went to work as a salesman and delivery man at Organic Pasadena, a local health food store, for two dollars an hour. In March 1968, Sirhan was fired from his job at the store after an argument with his boss. The Pasadena Police Department had to be called to remove Sirhan from the store's premises. Upon the arrival of police officers, Sirhan was asked to leave, and he complied without incident. Soon afterward, he appeared at a hearing of the California State Division of Labor Law Enforcement to complain that his boss had refused to pay him all the money he was owed. Sirhan lost the case.

Sirhan had no prior criminal or arrest record. He received two traffic violations in 1966 and was questioned twice by police officers for minor matters.

The largest-known sum of money Sirhan ever had at one time was the $1,705 he received from the Argonaut Insurance Company for his September 1966 fall from a horse. The check arrived in early April 1968, and he gave it to his mother to hold for him. The $410.66 Sirhan had in his pocket at the time of his arrest for shooting Senator Kennedy came from the insurance settlement.

He had no credit cards and no credit rating. The only property he owned was his 1956 DeSoto.

As an alien, Sirhan did not have the right to vote in American elections. Although he felt strongly about the Middle East situation and expressed the belief that he was "disenfranchised from the American establishment," Sirhan did not belong to a political party. But, during several conversations with friends, Sirhan appeared to support the Baath Party, which operated in the Middle East.

A seemingly spiritual young man, baptized in the Eastern Orthodox faith, Sirhan infrequently attended a Baptist church in Pasadena, flirted with atheism, and then accepted some brief training in the Seventh Day Adventist church.

He also had an interest in the occult and mysticism. Sirhan applied for membership in the Ancient Mystical Order of the Rosy Cross (AMORC), also known as the Rosicrucian Order, which is "nonsectarian and nonreligious although the ethics of the Order adhere to the principles of Christianity," according to its literature. In his June 1966 application, he wrote, "By reading your book *Mastery of Life*, I have discovered how much I do not know about myself despite all the philosophical works that I have been reading. I sincerely want to better myself, and on that basis I submit my application." Once dropped from the organization's roster in April 1967 because of his failure to pay his four-dollar monthly dues, Sirhan was a member in good standing at the time of the Kennedy shooting. On May 28, just eight days before the murder, he made a rare appearance at a meeting and left immediately after it adjourned.

Houghton explains, "You would be surprised to know how much time we spent and manpower we spent trying to make a connection between Sirhan and anybody who might have been a hypnotist. We even went into a Rosicrucian meeting."

Sirhan also expressed an interest in the Theosophical Society, founded in 1875 by Madame Helena P. Blavatsky. Her book *The Secret Doctrine* articulated the chief theosophical concept, which is based on the brotherhood of man. In fact, after his arrest for shooting Senator Kennedy, Sirhan requested Blavatsky's book, as well as the first volume of *Talks on the Paths of Occultism,* written by Annie Besant, one of Blavatsky's protégés, and Charles W. Leadbeater in 1926. However, Sirhan attended only one meeting of the society, in March 1968, and had not applied for membership prior to the shooting.

SUS clearly understood that its best evidence of motive revolved around the notebooks found in his bedroom at his family's Pasadena home. "Robert F. Kennedy must be assassinated before 5 June 68," he wrote in one entry. In another, he stated, "My determination to eliminate R.F.K. is becoming more [and] more of an unshakable obsession. . . . R.F.K. must be assassinated. . . . We believe that Robert F. Kennedy must be sacrificed for the cause of the poor exploited people."[59]

Some entries contained incoherent scrawling in English, Arabic, and Russian. They also gave evidence of an obvious obsession Sirhan

---

[59] The only witness found by SUS to substantiate a verbal threat to kill Senator Kennedy was Alvin Clark, a Pasadena trash man, who made regular pickups at the Sirhan family's house. According to the LAPD, on April 10, 1968, "Sirhan asked Clark whom he was going to vote for and Clark told him, 'Kennedy.' Sirhan replied, 'Well, I don't agree. I am planning on shooting the son of a bitch.' Clark did not take him seriously and thought it was only an exaggeration."

had with a woman he met but never dated while working at the Corona farm—she is mentioned nearly sixty times—and obsessions with Ford Mustangs and the phrase "please pay to the order of," an obvious reference to money, which appeared over a dozen times.[60] On one particular page of his notes, Sirhan wrote the name of Frank Donnarumma—which he spelled "Donaruma"—in context as the person who was supposed to pay.[61]

Regardless of Sirhan's apparently mindless chitchat in his notes,[62]

[60] Lawrence W. Sloan, an expert handwriting analyst, examined Sirhan's alleged writings and concluded in a September 20, 1968, memorandum, "It is my specific and unqualified opinion that Sirhan Sirhan is the person responsible for the writing of his name on the 'sign-in' sheet at the San Gabriel Rifle Range. It is also my specific and unqualified opinion that he is the person responsible for more than 90 percent of the writings found in the two spiral notebooks." Regarding the other 10 percent, Sloan stated that the handwriting "indicates a writer who apparently 'experiments' with his writing construction from time to time."

[61] Donnarumma—or Henry Ramistella, the man who had hired Sirhan at the Corona farm—disappeared after the shooting of Senator Kennedy. At the time, Ramistella, who had left the Corona farm in early 1968, had an outstanding bench warrant pending against him in the wake of his "failure to report for weekends" after a drunk driving arrest. His dismissal from the farm resulted from his heavy drinking, according to the LAPD.

The FBI did not interview him until April 1969.

[62] In the midst of his threats to kill Senator Kennedy, Sirhan wrote, "I believe that I can effect the death of Bert C. Altfillisch," who had been his boss at the horse farm near Corona. When I asked Altfillisch about this, he replied that the FBI had brought a copy of the notebook for him to see. "When I saw that he had threatened me, I thought to myself, 'That son of a bitch. I never had any run-in with him.' But, really, I was just the closest authority he could strike out against. I think that's all that meant. Heck, you can't apologize for something you never did."

The FBI also asked if Altfillisch could identify some of the other names in the notebooks. "The FBI saw some names of women, which really turned out to be names of horses," Altfillisch said.

However, there were two women Sirhan did write about: Gwen Gum, a college acquaintance who had rejected Sirhan, and Peggy Osterkamp, an "exercise girl" at Altfillisch's farm whom he admired pure and chaste from afar. Osterkamp appeared to be the woman of his dreams. He wrote her name fifty-eight times, saying in one section, "I love you, Peggy." He also referred to her as "Peggy Sirhan."

Altfillisch said of Osterkamp, "She was a very pretty girl, and she rode. She did show horses and jumpers. She knew her horses. But she had never done thoroughbreds, so I hired her as an exercise girl. She had the same work status as Sirhan at the farm. Her father lived about a half a mile from me. He owned a pretty good size dairy. And he was a very fine man.

"Sirhan had a thing for her at the time, and I don't think he was the only one

SUS interviewed witnesses who positively identified the young man as having attended two rallies for Kennedy. Joseph and Margaret Sheehan saw Sirhan in a crowded assembly for Kennedy at the Los Angeles Sports Arena on May 24. Joseph Sheehan, who worked as a clinical psychologist, pointed Sirhan out to his wife, noting that he was "completely out of character with the crowd [and] very intense and sinister."

William Blume, who worked near the health food store where Sirhan sold and delivered products, saw him at a June 2 rally for Kennedy at the Ambassador—the day after Sirhan spent over two hours on the pistol range at the Corona Police Department Gun Range, where he had signed the register.[63]

Having collected all this information about Sirhan's background and movements, SUS now had evidence that Sirhan had apparently stalked Kennedy for nearly two weeks before allegedly shooting him.

Lieutenant Manny Pena insists, "Sirhan was a self-appointed assassin. He decided that Bobby Kennedy was no good, because he was helping the Jews. And he was going to kill him."

Sergeant Nielsen of SUS continues, "Sirhan didn't have much going on in his life. He didn't have any personal goals, like a profession or schooling. In retrospect, I can see why he could be swept into this and ultimately acted on it."

---

who did. I never saw anybody do anything out of the way toward her. If they did, they would have been gone."

Later, at the trial, Sirhan refused to allow his attorney to call either Gum or Osterkamp as witnesses.

[63] Curiously, no one saw Sirhan on the firing line at Corona that day. And the range master who identified a photograph of Sirhan also described him as being tall and heavy, as well as "accompanied" by a smaller man, who spoke with an "unknown foreign accent." SUS claims that the range master mistook Sirhan for another shooter, who was later identified.

SUS investigated and discredited a similar sighting of Sirhan—allegedly accompanied by two other men—by employees at the Lock, Stock 'N Barrel Gun Shop, where Sirhan had stopped to buy more ammunition on June 1 on his way back from Corona. Both employees reportedly failed their polygraph tests.

Also, the range master at the San Gabriel Valley Gun Club, where Sirhan had been rapid-firing his revolver on June 4, claimed another Sirhan sighting with nefarious overtones, which SUS also dismissed after the range master failed his polygraph test.

11. *Investigation of Conspiracy and the Trial of Sirhan*

Did Sirhan Sirhan plot and execute the murder of Senator Robert Kennedy alone? Or was he part of a conspiracy?

SUS member Thomas J. Miller says, "SUS tried to look at the failings that were pointed out with the John Kennedy case. We didn't want anybody pointing at the Los Angeles Police Department and saying, 'Well, they messed up' or 'They didn't look into this.' So there were various aspects of conspiracy angles we looked into: the polka-dot-dress girl, some minister who picked up a hitchhiker [supposedly Sirhan] and gave a long scenario about being involved in the Kennedy homicide.[64] There were all kinds of leads like that.

[64] Oliver Brindley Owen, aka Jerry Owen, an ex-prizefighter described by the LAPD as a "self-styled minister," claimed that he had picked up Sirhan and another

"Then other people would call up and say, 'I was in a bar the other night, and I heard these guys talking.' We had to see if there was anything more than the gossip."

Working thousands of man-hours, SUS discredited numerous rumors revolving around an Iranian national who worked as a

---

man hitchhiking on June 3. Owen dropped off Sirhan's alleged companion at Wilshire Boulevard and Western Avenue. Owen noticed that he was greeted by four young people. Remaining in Owen's truck, Sirhan asked Owen to take him to the Ambassador Hotel and wait while he talked to a friend who worked in the hotel's kitchen. When Sirhan returned, Owen continued, he asked Owen to take him to a location in Hollywood.

During their conversation, according to Owen, Sirhan offered to buy a palomino horse Owen was selling for $250.

Owen said that he and Sirhan met again that night. Sirhan was now accompanied by a man and a woman whom Owen had earlier seen at Wilshire and Western. Sirhan asked Owen to give him until the following day to raise the purchase price for the horse. Owen agreed and checked into a Los Angeles hotel.

On June 4, the day of the California primary election, Owen claims, he came to the scheduled location for his meeting with Sirhan. Instead, the man and his blond female companion, whom he had met the previous day, showed up to meet with Owen, telling him that Sirhan could not make the meeting. The mystery couple asked Owen to meet Sirhan at the Ambassador Hotel that night. Sirhan would have the money then.

Owen told them that he had another appointment and could not make the meeting. He supposedly gave the couple his card and told them to have Sirhan call him when he had the money for the horse.

The following day, Owen saw Sirhan's picture in the paper as the accused shooter in the Kennedy assassination attempt. Owen then went to the LAPD with his story.

SUS member Gordon McDevitt explains, "When Owen said, 'I picked Sirhan up,' we couldn't ignore a statement like that. We had to run it down. Time and time again, we picked away at every detail of everything Owen said, and anyone who saw him or said they saw him. The investigation of his story finally petered out. We just concluded that this guy was full of bullshit. He was a terrible waste of time that we couldn't ignore, because he was saying sensational things. We couldn't just say, 'This guy's a nut,' and then ignore him."

Owen also failed a polygraph test, administered at the San Francisco Police Department.

The Owen story is the centerpiece of William W. Turner and Jonn G. Christian's 1978 book, *The Assassination of Robert F. Kennedy: A Searching Look at the Conspiracy and Cover-up, 1968–1978* (New York: Random House). The authors believe that Owens was involved in a conspiracy to murder Senator Kennedy and had invented his repeatedly contradicted story in order to create an innocent reason for his association with Sirhan.

Kennedy volunteer at campaign headquarters, as well as separate conspiracy theories involving several Arab groups and radical political organizations. Many witnesses claimed to have heard Sirhan, while in the company of unknown associates, threaten to kill Senator Kennedy. However, such reports could not be corroborated. SUS concluded that most of these discounted observations came from "opportunists, political adventurers and publicity seekers. . . . The majority of the persons making the allegations were found to be lying for one reason or another."

By far the most troublesome conspiracy theory investigated by SUS focused on Kennedy campaign worker Sandra Serrano's alleged sighting of a woman in a polka-dot dress and her two male companions, including one who looked like Sirhan, prior to the shooting. After the shooting, the woman and one of the men gleefully fled from the crime scene boasting, "We shot Senator Kennedy." According to SUS, Serrano was the only person to have witnessed this.[65]

Manny Pena, the day watch commander, says, "I found no credence that there was a gal in a polka-dot dress who said, 'We shot Kennedy.' What Sandy Serrano, I still believe today, heard was, 'They shot Kennedy.' And she thought they said, 'We shot him.' If we didn't dispel that, we would still be looking for the gal in the polka-dot dress. The stories [by Serrano] about hearing shots and what have you, it's impossible."

Sergeant James MacArthur, a key member of SUS, remembers, "The gal in the balcony [Serrano] said that she had heard the shots fired. And we got to thinking, 'Well, that was quite a ways from where the shooting took place.' So we decided, 'Let's see just how truthful she is.' "

Pena adds, "I requested the reconstruction of the shots. The ballrooms had thick velour drapes all drawn. They had three orchestras going on three floors. Balloons popping everywhere. And I had a decibel graph placed in strategic locations to see if we could pick up

---

[65] Actually, numerous alleged witnesses soon thereafter stepped forward, telling both the LAPD and the FBI that they, too, had seen a woman in a polka-dot dress flee from the scene with a male companion. When pressed, most of them proved unreliable or simply admitted that they had fabricated their stories.

any sound [at the location where Serrano placed herself], and you couldn't hear a damn thing."[66]

Actually, Serrano had said in her original statement to the LAPD that she had heard "six quick backfires," which were naturally interpreted by police officers as her description of gunshots. However, during a taped and transcribed interview with Serrano on June 20—after the sound tests at the Ambassador were conducted—Serrano insisted, "I never said I heard shots. I heard backfires of a car, and I know they were backfires from a car. I know they weren't gunshots."

Pena says, "We got to a point where we had to establish something on an investigative basis that she was mistaken. So I suggested to [polygraph expert and SUS member Enrique] Hernandez that he take her out to dinner, and see if she would take a polygraph."

When asked what constituted a believable polygraph, Pena stated, "It's as good as the objectivity of the operator."

Sergeant Enrique Hernandez conducted the polygraph examination of Serrano. During the preexamination interview, Hernandez attempted to break down her story. The following exchanges are excerpted from the official transcript:

HERNANDEZ: I think you owe it to Senator Kennedy, the late Senator Kennedy, to come forth, be a woman about this. If he, and you don't know and I don't know whether he's a witness right now in this room watching what we're doing in here. Don't shame his death by keeping this thing up. I have compassion for you. I want to know why. I want to know why you did what you did. This is a very serious thing.
SERRANO: I seen those people!
HERNANDEZ: No, no, no, no, Sandy. Remember what I told you about that: you can't say you saw something when you didn't see it. . . .

[66] According to the official LAPD Analyzed Evidence Report, SUS, in cooperation with the LAPD/SID, conducted the sound test at the Ambassador Hotel on June 20, 1968. The same .22 revolver used for the muzzle distance test, Iver Johnson H18602, was used for the sound test, which concluded that Serrano could not have heard gunfire from where she was sitting.

SERRANO: Well, I don't feel I'm doing anything wrong. . . . I remember seeing the girl!

HERNANDEZ: No, I'm talking about what you have told here about seeing a person tell you, 'We have shot Kennedy.' And that's wrong.

SERRANO: That's what she said.

HERNANDEZ: No, it isn't, Sandy . . .

SERRANO: No! That's what she said.

HERNANDEZ: Look it! Look it! I love this man!

SERRANO: So do I.

HERNANDEZ: And you're shaming [him] . . . !

SERRANO: Don't shout at me.

HERNANDEZ: Well, I'm trying not to shout, but this is a very emotional thing for me, too. . . . If you love the man, the least you owe him is the courtesy of letting him rest in peace.

The interrogation of Sandy Serrano went on like that for over an hour. When Hernandez finally gave her the polygraph test, he determined that the badly shaken Serrano had lied about the entire matter.

Some time later, an interviewer questioned Manny Pena about the horrendous tactics used by Hernandez, pointing out that neutrality by the polygraph operator is considered to be essential. "That's just interrogating," Pena explained. "I don't see anything wrong with those words to draw out compassion. It's an interrogative technique."

Pena essentially ceased the polka-dot-dress inquiry after the Serrano polygraph examination. He explains, "She was a young kid, and she was projected into a national limelight. She was on every television set in the country overnight. There were interviews, and she was a real celebrity. She was the hottest thing on TV, nationwide. And for a young kid like that who was a political supporter, a Kennedy girl, to be projected into this kind of limelight, it might be difficult to give it up. It was very difficult for her to say, 'Well, I'm mistaken.' She would be losing a lot of celebrity status. I still think I was correct in the decision I made."

Ambassador waiter Vincent DiPierro reported to the police on the night of the shooting that he had seen Sirhan in the kitchen "talking with a woman in a polka dot dress just prior to the shooting." However, DiPierro later "admitted that he had embellished his statement at the suggestion of Sandra Serrano with whom he conversed at Rampart Station following her television interview," according to SUS.

SUS did *not* interview Sergeant Paul Sharaga, who headed the command post at the Ambassador Hotel for several hours after the shooting, and who had passed on the report by the elderly couple of a woman in a polka-dot dress and a young male.[67]

In the end, SUS probed the backgrounds of six women who were suspected of being the mysterious girl in the polka-dot dress; all of them were cleared.[68] SUS believed that those who claimed to have

---

[67] Sharaga's version is well documented. According to Sharaga's own report, dictated to Officer J. M. Steele, at the end of his twenty-three-hour watch on June 5, "An unidentified female ran by me shouting, 'He's been shot. Kennedy's been shot.' Another female person accompanied by her husband, (name and addresses given to Rampart Dets.) stated that she and her husband were just outside the Embassy Room, on the balcony when a couple in their early twenties ran by them coming from the Embassy Room shouting 'We shot him, we shot him.' The woman asked the young couple who?, and the young woman replied 'Kennedy, we shot him, we shot him.' I immediately broadcast to communications that Senator Kennedy had been shot, a description of the suspects as given to me by the witnesses. . . ."

However, the official LAPD report of Sharaga's activities at the command post added, "[Sharaga] believes that due to the noise and confusion at the time what was said was misinterpreted, and what was probably said was 'they shot him.' He notified communication that the probable victim of the shooting was Senator Kennedy, and gave a description of the suspect as given to him by additional witnesses to the shooting."

Sharaga denied all of this when I interviewed him and insisted that he gave LAPD communications the descriptions of the *two* suspects throughout the evening.

Also, Sharaga executed on July 14, 1988, a sworn statement, saying, "The L.A.P.D. report . . . is not based on any interview of me by any officials in the L.A.P.D. at any time. Further, it also contains false and deliberately misleading statements. It is obviously derived from a much longer report personally prepared by me."

[68] One of the women investigated, twenty-three-year-old Katheryne Renee Fulmer, a dark-haired and attractive model and go-go dancer, checked into a Los Angeles motel on April 7, 1969, and was found dead the following day. The coroner ruled her death a suicide, resulting from an overdose of drugs. She had left a brief suicide message on the mirror of her room, which had nothing to do with the Kennedy murder.

seen a girl in a polka-dot dress near Sirhan probably saw Valerie Schulte, a student campaign worker who was also an eyewitness to the Kennedy shooting. She told SUS investigators that she was wearing a green dress with gold polka dots. Schulte added that she was standing near the tray stacker where Sirhan crouched before his attack on Senator Kennedy.

Sergeant MacArthur remembers, "I got a call one day, and it was a gal, Valerie Schulte. So we went up to Santa Barbara, where this Valerie was a student. We knocked on the door. A nice-looking blond gal came to the door. And she was in a cast, a foot cast. She says, 'I think I'm the gal in the polka-dot dress.' And I said, 'Well, could we see the dress?' So she went and got the dress. It was a very distinctive polka-dot dress.

"So I said to her, 'What happened to your leg?' 'Oh,' she said, 'I've had that for some time.' I said, 'Did you have that [at the time of the shooting]?' She said, 'Yeah, I had that. In fact, when the shooting went down, I got knocked down to the floor . . . and I got up. And I kind of staggered out. And I didn't stay around.' And we checked her out. She didn't have anything to do with it."

On or about June 19, 1968, Russell E. Parsons of Los Angeles became Sirhan's attorney. Parsons was well known for serving as counsel to southern California mobster Mickey Cohen and members of his gang.

Surprisingly, the possible involvement of organized crime in the Robert Kennedy murder case received almost no attention. Manny Pena says, "The FBI may have done some interviewing or some work in which the mob or the Mafia was mentioned. I never supervised any phase of a conspiracy allegation involving the mob. That kind of information, if it came in, might have gone to [U.S. Attorney Matt Byrne] first. They could have done it over there and not said a word to us."

Although the Mafia never became a target during the investigation, former Teamsters president James R. Hoffa did receive a brief

---

Also, Sandy Serrano had told the LAPD that Fulmer was *not* the woman who passed her on the stairway after the shooting.

flurry of attention from the FBI for alleged death threats he had made against Senator Kennedy.

The FBI quickly learned that this was not the first time that an allegation of a Hoffa plan to kill Robert Kennedy had surfaced.[69]

On June 13, 1968—eight days after Robert Kennedy's murder— the FBI received information from a confidential informant that James R. Hoffa, the imprisoned former Teamsters president, had said, "If Hoffa isn't out, Kennedy will never get in."

The following day, the FBI received another report that Hoffa had allegedly stated at breakfast in the prison mess hall on May 30,

---

[69] In September 1962, Edward Partin, a Teamsters official in Baton Rouge, Louisiana, reported to Walter Sheridan, the head of the "Get-Hoffa Squad" at the U.S. Justice Department, that Hoffa was "fixin' " to kill then attorney general Kennedy. Partin explained to me in 1977 that Hoffa's first plan was to firebomb Kennedy's home in Virginia with plastic explosives. Hoffa was careful to note that even if Kennedy somehow survived the explosion, he "and all of his damn kids" would be incinerated, since "the place will burn after it blows up," Partin said.

Hoffa's backup plan revolved around a sniper shooting Kennedy. Partin said, "Hoffa had a .270 rifle leaning in the corner of his office, and Hoffa said, 'I've got something right here which will shoot flat and long. . . .'"

The "ideal setup," Hoffa went on, would be "to catch [Robert] Kennedy somewhere in the South," where extremist "segregation people" might throw investigators off the track by being blamed for the crime. The "ideal time" to hit Kennedy would be while he was driving his "convertible." Partin thought that the Kennedy brothers' crusade against Hoffa had driven the union leader to desperation. "Somebody needs to bump that son of a bitch off," Partin remembered Hoffa saying. "Bobby Kennedy [has] got to go."

Soon after giving his story to Sheridan and the Justice Department, Partin took and passed a polygraph test. Then FBI agents taped a telephone call between Partin and Hoffa—in which Hoffa and Partin had a brief conversation about plastic explosives.

For unknown reasons, Hoffa relented in his plan to kill the attorney general, who, at the time, was prosecuting Hoffa for extortion in Nashville. The trial ended in a hung jury. Partin became the key government witness against Hoffa in his 1964 trial for jury tampering in Chattanooga, which stemmed from the hung jury during the Nashville trial.

Later, on March 1, 1967—six days before Hoffa reported to Lewisburg to begin his prison sentence for jury tampering and a subsequent conviction for pension fraud—Frank Chavez, the head of the Teamsters in Puerto Rico, left San Juan and headed for Washington, allegedly to kill Robert Kennedy on his own. But Hoffa reportedly talked Chavez out of committing the crime. Chavez gave Hoffa his gun and returned to Puerto Rico. A few months later, Chavez was murdered by one of his own associates.

1967, "I have a contract out on Kennedy. And if he ever gets in the primaries or ever gets elected, the contract will be fulfilled within six months." The informant said that Hoffa remarked in a later conversation, "Right now [May 1967], Kennedy's in no danger. But if he gets into a primary or gets elected, I won't say how or when, but he'll get knocked off."

Of course, Hoffa, upon being interviewed by the FBI, denied any role in a plot to kill Robert Kennedy. Without corroborating witnesses, the information went nowhere and was simply dismissed as gossip.

SUS member William Jordan explains, "When you're a cop, you have to take the guy into court and prove beyond a reasonable doubt. So a lot of these things—believe me, they were all investigated diligently. Hell, if there was a conspiracy, we wanted to prove it more than anybody else. Nobody likes to be made a fool of. You don't want to pass something off as a simple homicide and then find out a couple of years later that there were more people involved. It makes you look like an amateur in the profession.

"People ask, 'Was Sirhan acting alone?' To the best of our knowledge, he was acting alone. We could find no evidence that he wasn't acting alone. If you're asking me to swear that there wasn't anybody else, I can't do it. If there was somebody who could successfully brainwash him or something, how do I know? That's beyond my scope. But, sure, I've thought about it. We used to sit and rack our brains. These guys were the cream of the investigative crop at LAPD, the sheriffs, the bureau. These weren't a bunch of foot soldiers. Everybody put their top people on it."

Sergeant MacArthur insists, "We wanted to get everybody who was involved in it. Well, we had a suspect. It was an open-and-shut case against him. But, if there were other individuals involved, we wanted it. And I actually believe—my own personal feelings—that Sirhan acted alone."

Sergeant Gordon McDevitt adds, "If you read the concluding sentence on at least two of our reports: 'We found no evidence of a conspiracy.' We didn't say there wasn't a conspiracy—you can never say that. But we found no evidence of a conspiracy."

On August 2, 1968, Sirhan officially pleaded not guilty to the murder of Senator Kennedy and the attempted murders of the other five victims. Parsons's defense of Sirhan immediately revolved around his state of mind at the time of the shooting—the diminished-capacity defense. Parsons also insisted that the LAPD had erred with an illegal search of Sirhan's home on the morning of the shooting, at which time Sirhan's incriminating notebooks had been recovered and booked as evidence.[70] However, Judge Herbert V. Walker, the designated trial magistrate, ruled that the search had been legal, since Adel Sirhan—whose name appeared on the deed to the house, along with his mother's—had voluntarily permitted the police to enter the Sirhan home and even unlocked the door for them.

On December 3, Sirhan's lead attorney, Grant Cooper of Los Angeles, finally joined the defense team; Parsons became co-counsel.[71] Later that month, Cooper brought in a third attorney, Emile Zola Berman of New York.[72]

The prosecutors were Chief Deputy District Attorney Lynn Compton and Deputy District Attorneys John Howard and David Fitts.

Sirhan's trial began on January 7, 1969, under tight security, with the selection of the jury and the hearing of several pretrial motions.

[70] Soon after the notebooks were recovered by the LAPD, Mayor Sam Yorty of Los Angeles called a press conference and read from them, concluding, "We know, of course, he killed Kennedy." Many complained that the mayor's indiscretion might jeopardize the defense's ability to provide Sirhan with a fair trial.

Soon thereafter, Superior Court Judge Arthur Alarcon issued a court order prohibiting anyone associated with the case from issuing "extra judiciary statements" or releasing any evidence. Even though the Los Angeles District Attorney's Office opposed this, the American Civil Liberties Union endorsed this precaution, because it further safeguarded Sirhan's rights as a defendant.

[71] At the time, Cooper was in the midst of his defense of Maurice H. Friedman, the principal defendant in the infamous Friar's Club card-cheating scandal, which involved Chicago Mafia figure Johnny Rosselli.

[72] The Cooper-Parsons-Berman defense team had hired three investigators: Ronald Allen, Michael McCowan, and Robert Blair Kaiser. McCowan worked for Allen in his private investigations agency. Kaiser, a respected journalist and a former correspondent for *Time,* came into the case as an investigator—so that he could write about Sirhan's defense "from the inside."

Actually, the prosecution and defense tried to strike a deal that would have mooted the need for a trial. On February 10, attorneys from both sides met in Judge Walker's chambers to discuss a possible plea bargain: Sirhan would plead guilty but would be spared execution in return for a life prison sentence. The prosecution was willing to go along with the deal. District Attorney Younger explained, "Our psychiatrist, in effect, says that the defendant is psychotic and his report would support the position of the defense because of diminished capacity and the death penalty then wouldn't be imposed."

After hearing the attorneys' arguments, Judge Walker decided, "I think you have got a very much interested public. I don't let the public influence me, but, at the same time, there are a lot of ramifications. And they continually point to the Oswald matter, and they just wonder what is going on, because the fellow wasn't tried. . . . [T]hey would say that it was all fixed; it was greased. So we will just go through the trial. . . . I am not going to argue it any further, gentlemen. My mind is made up."

On February 13, the defense did file a motion for a mistrial after publication of a February 11 article in the *Los Angeles Times,* reporting that defense attorneys had offered the prosecution a guilty plea on the first-degree murder charge in an effort to spare Sirhan's life. But each juror told Judge Walker that he or she had not been prejudiced by the article and could judge the case by the evidence presented in the courtroom. The motion for mistrial was denied.

Taking no further chances, Judge Walker ordered the jury sequestered and placed in the Biltmore Hotel.

On February 14, the prosecution called its first witness and rested twelve days later, after calling fifty-six witnesses to testify and introducing 132 exhibits.[73]

---

[73] Among those called to testify by the prosecution on direct testimony were the five other shooting victims (Schrade, Weisel, Evans, Goldstein, and Stroll), six forensics experts, fifteen witnesses at the crime scene who saw either the shooting or the arrest of Sirhan, the two officers who arrested Sirhan (Placencia and White), the detective who interviewed Sirhan after the shooting (Jordan), five people who witnessed the search of Sirhan's car and residence, five people who could trace the history of Sirhan's gun, thirteen witnesses who testified about Sirhan's purchase of ammunition, target practice, presence at the crime scene, and a statement (from Sirhan's trash man Alvin Clark) indicating intent to kill Senator Kennedy.

On February 25, during a discussion about his notebooks, Sirhan shouted out, "It's not admitted into evidence yet!" He had to be restrained by his attorneys then and again that afternoon after he attempted to address Judge Walker, who had just ruled that the search of Sirhan's home was legal. A recess followed during which Sirhan told Judge Walker that he was being railroaded, insisting that he wanted to plead guilty and be put to death.

Sirhan's defense began on February 28. Fifty-three items were placed in evidence. Over nineteen days, twenty-eight witnesses testified for the defense; many of them recounted Sirhan's horrific childhood. According to the official LAPD account, "It was testified that on several occasions after witnessing such events he [Sirhan] lapsed into a trance, his body stiffened, his fists clenched, and his mouth became contorted. . . . The defense contended that these experiences created a twisted mind which diminished Sirhan's capacity to premeditate murder."

Defense witnesses also testified that Sirhan suffered a major personality change after he was thrown from his horse at the Corona farm in September 1966. After the accident, they said, Sirhan became withdrawn and irritable, paranoid and unstable.

After another outburst on the opening day of his defense—which forced the judge to send the jury out of the courtroom—Sirhan repeated, "I, at this time, sir, withdraw my original plea of not guilty and submit the plea of guilty as charged on all counts." He added, "I also request that my counsel disassociate themselves from this case completely," and said that he wanted to be executed.

On April 1, Sirhan again disrupted the court, during the testimony of Dr. Seymour Pollack—who, as a prosecution witness, stated that Sirhan was sane and not clinically psychotic at the time of the shooting. Sirhan had to be removed from the courtroom.

Explaining why Sirhan kept trying to plead guilty during his trial, defense investigator Robert Blair Kaiser, who was in the midst of

---

On rebuttal, the prosecution called three officers who witnessed Sirhan's "sobriety" after his initial arrest; a psychiatrist who testified that Sirhan was not insane; a clinical psychiatrist who corroborated the results of the psychological tests administered to Sirhan; and a handwriting analyst who compared Sirhan's normal handwriting to that while he was hypnotized by the defense.

writing a book about the Kennedy case, said, "He did it, because we were getting closer to the revelation in the courtroom that he was a paranoid schizophrenic. And Sirhan didn't want to be viewed as 'crazy.' To him, that would have been a disgrace.

"Dr. Bernard Diamond [a member of the psychological team for the defense] viewed schizophrenia as a mind that has been cracked like a mirror—but it hasn't fallen apart yet. It's still in the frame, but it has all of these cracks in it. So the schizophrenic does everything he can to keep that frame intact. If he takes off one part of that frame, then the whole thing will crumble and fall to the floor.

"If you believe this metaphor, then it was crucial for Sirhan to remain in control. When he realized during the trial that he was not in control—he couldn't tell the attorneys or the experts what to say about him—that's when he wanted to stop everything, just plead guilty, and be done with it."

Sirhan did testify in his own defense. However, he claimed that he had no memory of getting his gun from his car or shooting Senator Kennedy in the kitchen pantry of the Ambassador Hotel. Although he said that he was angered by Senator Kennedy's support for Israel,[74] he continued to insist that he was drunk prior to the shooting.

All in all, many of Sirhan's defense witnesses, and his own testimony, wound up aiding the prosecution's case. Although Sirhan claimed that he was drunk at the time of the shooting, several wit-

---

[74] On May 26, 1968, Senator Kennedy delivered a speech at Temple Neveh Shalom in Portland, Oregon, advocating the sale of fifty Phantom jets to Israel. According to law enforcement officials, this announcement brought Sirhan to the brink in his decision to kill Kennedy.

Also, a television documentary, "The Story of Robert Kennedy," which implied but did not detail Kennedy's support for Israel, had aired for the first time in Los Angeles, on KCBS-TV on May 20.

The problem here is that Sirhan—who claimed to be angry at Kennedy over his advocacy of sending the jets to Israel—had written about his "determination to eliminate R.F.K." on May 18—two days before the television broadcast and eight days before the speech at Temple Neveh Shalom.

On p. 421 of his book "R.F.K. Must Die!" Bob Kaiser writes, "It is doubtful that Sirhan heard anything about Kennedy's 'promise' to send fifty jet bombers to Israel until John Lawrence [the head of an Arab antidefamation group] told him about it *after* the assassination." Lawrence also gave him an earlier *New York Times* story about this.

nesses, including Enrique Rabago and Humphrey Cordero, testified that he was *not* intoxicated when they saw him at the Ambassador Hotel. A former employer testified that Sirhan had been a good worker, but under cross-examination he conceded that Sirhan had a quick temper.

Clinical psychologist Dr. Martin Schorr testified on behalf of the defense that he had run a battery of tests on Sirhan and concluded that he was a paranoid schizophrenic psychotic. The state's psychologists concluded that although Sirhan had a paranoid personality and might suffer some neurosis, he could still distinguish right from wrong. Schorr concluded that Sirhan's rage resulted from the beatings and mistreatment he had received from his father. Supposedly, Kennedy had become "a symbolic replica" of his father.

After the defense rested, the prosecution called additional rebuttal witnesses to counter claims by the defense.

The defense virtually ignored all of the eyewitness testimony regarding muzzle distance, as well as the prosecution's firearms evidence, attempting to prevent the jury from being prejudiced against Sirhan by the accompanying autopsy photographs of Senator Kennedy. These omissions would later spark critical debate.

In all, eighty-nine witnesses testified during the fifteen-week trial. Other than Sirhan's outbursts, nothing unusual or unexpected occurred during the trial. After final arguments, which began on April 9, the case went to the jury, composed of seven men and five women, on April 14. On April 17, after three days of deliberation, the jury convicted Sirhan of first-degree murder and five counts of assault with a deadly weapon with the intent to commit murder.

On April 23, the jury voted that Sirhan should be put to death in California's gas chamber.

A month later, on May 21, Judge Walker sentenced Sirhan to death.[75]

[75] After the jury's verdict and before Judge Walker passed sentence, Senator Edward Kennedy sent District Attorney Evelle Younger a moving, five-page, handwritten letter, saying, in part, "My brother was a man of love and sentiment and compassion. He would not have wanted his death to be a cause for the taking of another life."

What did Sirhan's own trial attorney think of the case? In a confidential declaration, executed on November 3, 1972, Grant Cooper stated, "Because of my belief that Sirhan performed the assassination independently, solely, and unassisted, my defense was never directed toward the defense that Sirhan did not fire the shots. . . . Had I any inkling or belief that Sirhan had not acted alone or not fired the fatal shot, it is obvious that our entire investigation would have been wholly reoriented. Indeed, I offered, prior to trial, to the prosecution to stipulate to the ballistics' testimony and other prosecution testimony such as the handwriting in the 'diaries' seized from the bedroom of Sirhan was Sirhan's handwriting but [I] was advised that the prosecution preferred to establish these facts and opinions in open Court.

"Additionally, because of my sincere belief that Sirhan alone fired the shots, my associates and I offered to plead Sirhan guilty to the crime of First Degree Murder provided the Court would impose a term of life imprisonment instead of death. Sirhan personally joined in this offer on the record, as did the prosecution. The Honorable Herbert Walker, Judge Presiding, denied this proffer for the reasons stated by him on the record. . . .

"I had innumerable consultations during trial preparation with all the defense psychiatrists and particularly with Dr. Bernard Diamond, M.D., a psychiatrist of the University of Southern California. . . . Dr. Diamond hypnotized Sirhan alone and in my presence and interrogated him attempting to lead him through the events of the past up through the actual minutes of the assassination. . . .

"On many occasions, I conferred with Sirhan preparing him for his direct examination at trial. Sirhan at all times stated he could not remember the killing nor remember firing the shots. Because of my firm and conscientious belief that Sirhan alone fired the shots, engendered among other reasons by his re-enactment of the shooting under hypnosis by Dr. Diamond in my presence,[76] I advised Sirhan to

[76] On p. 355 of *"R.F.K. Must Die!"* Robert Blair Kaiser describes this very dramatic moment of reenacting the shooting, quoting Dr. Diamond as saying, "Sirhan, open your eyes and look at Kennedy. Sirhan, open your eyes. He's coming. Reach for your gun, Sirhan. It's your last chance, Sirhan. Reach for your gun. Where is your gun?" Kaiser notes that Diamond stated out loud that Sirhan "was

testify in substance that notwithstanding his lack of memory, that if everyone said he did fire the shots he must have done so. Sirhan followed my advice and so testified."

Facing the gas chamber, all Sirhan could say to his beloved mother, Mary Sirhan, was, "Mom, I'm sorry. I don't remember anything." Forever faithful and loyal to her son, Mrs. Sirhan publicly protested, "My son did not have a fair trial."

On July 25, 1969, SUS officially disbanded. Its legacy became its confidential ten-volume report, "An Investigation Summary of the Senator Robert F. Kennedy Assassination, June 5, 1968."

---

reaching into the waistband of his pants and also into 'his lap.' "

Diamond continued, "All right, what happened, Sirhan? Take the gun out of your pants. You've got the gun in your hand now. Let me see you shoot the gun, Sirhan. Shoot the gun. Shoot the gun. Shoot the gun. Sirhan, take the gun and shoot it."

Kaiser concludes, "Then Sirhan's right hand pounded climactically on his right thigh—five times. His right forefinger squeezed and twisted three more times in a weakening spasm. Then he was still."

The victory speech *(California State Archives)*

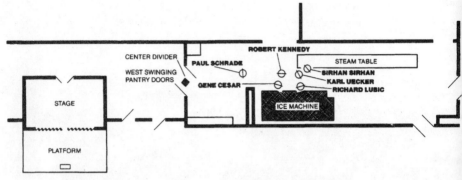

Diagram of the crime scene *(LAPD/Regardie's)*

LAPD orientation photograph of the crime scene, looking
east to west; steam tables on right, tray stacker and ice
machine on left, double swinging doors straight ahead
(California State Archives)

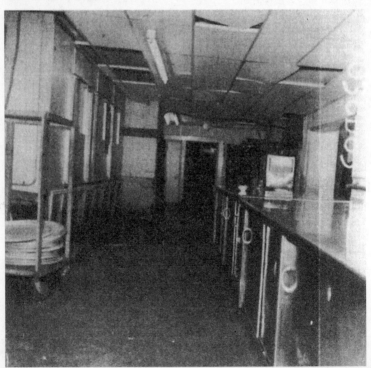

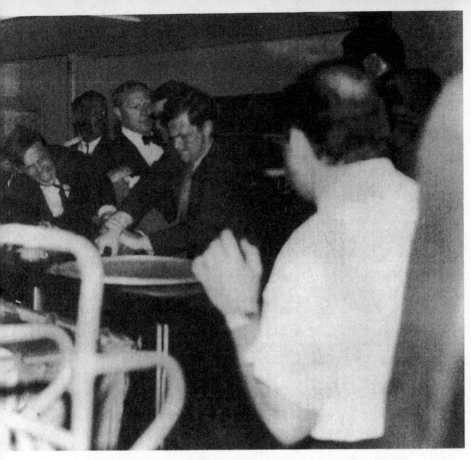

The battle with Sirhan Sirhan: *left to right,* Uno Timanson,
George Plimpton, Richard Aubry, Karl Uecker, Frank Burns,
Jack Gallivan, Gonzalo Cetina, and Roosevelt Grier; Sirhan is
face-down on the steam table *(Harold Burba/California State
Archives)*

The first person to grab
Sirhan:Ambassador maître
d' KarlUecker *(California
State Archives)*

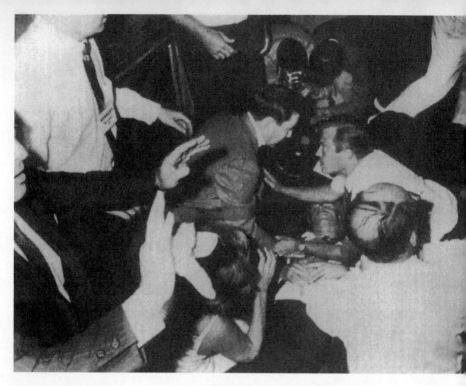

The desperate effort to save Senator Kennedy *(California State Archives)*

The arrest of Sirhan *(California State Archives)*

Arresting officer Art
Placencia *(Art Placencia)*

Other arresting officers: *left
to right,* Willie Nunley,
Walter Strickel, Michael
Livesey, and Travis White,
who is in civilian clothing
(California State Archives)

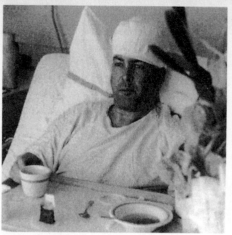

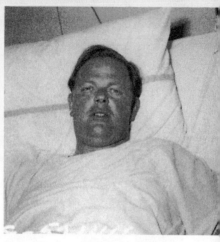

Shooting victim Paul Schrade *(Paul Schrade)*

Shooting victim William Weisel *(California State Archives)*

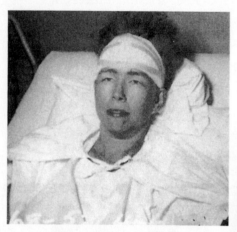

Above: **Shooting victim Elizabeth Evans** *(California State Archives)*
Above right: **Shooting victim Ira Goldstein** *(California State Archives)*
Right: **Shooting victim Irwin Stroll** *(California State Archives)*

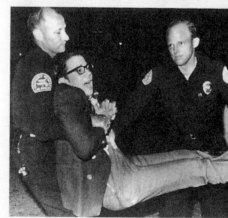

Bloodied and beaten: Sirhan in custody *(California State Archives)*

Sirhan's interrogator: Sergeant William Jordan *(William Jordan)*

The murder weapon, eight shell casings, and three intact bullets *(California State Archives)*

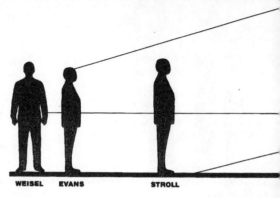

WEISEL   EVANS   STROLL

Sergeant Paul
Sharaga headed the
command post *(Paul
Sharaga)*

At the staging area in the Ambassador Hotel: Sergeant James
Jones, holding radio *(California State Archives)*

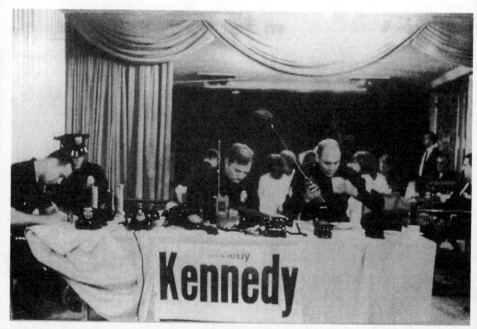

Kennedy

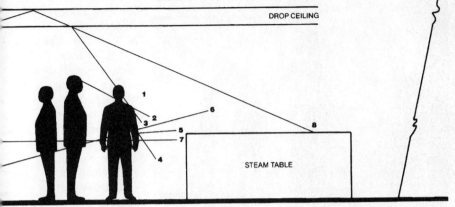

GOLDSTEIN SCHRADE KENNEDY

Reproduction of criminalist DeWayne Wolfer's diagram of shooting victims' locations and the flight paths of bullets striking them; Sirhan's location is not depicted *(LAPD/*Regardie's*)*

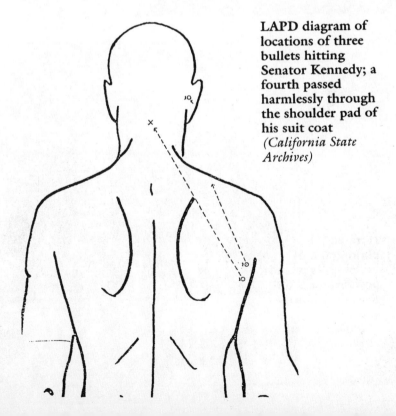

LAPD diagram of locations of three bullets hitting Senator Kennedy; a fourth passed harmlessly through the shoulder pad of his suit coat *(California State Archives)*

Coroner Thomas Noguchi and DeWayne Wolfer, who is wearing Senator Kennedy's suit coat, using copper rods to reconstruct the flight paths of bullets hitting Senator Kennedy or his clothing *(California State Archives)*

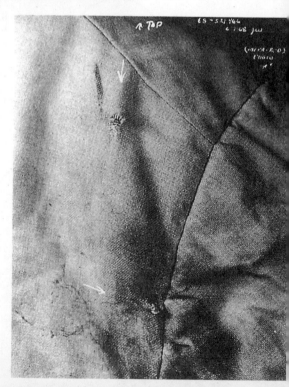

Infrared photograph of bullet holes in and powder burns on Senator Kennedy's suit coat *(California State Archives)*

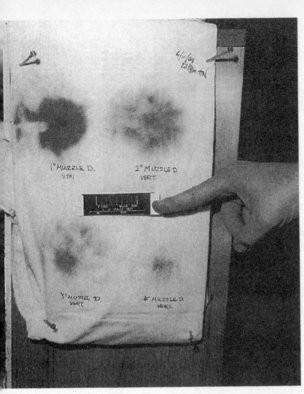

Muzzle distance test into cloth, showing that the shots hitting Kennedy's clothing were fired from point-blank range *(California State Archives)*

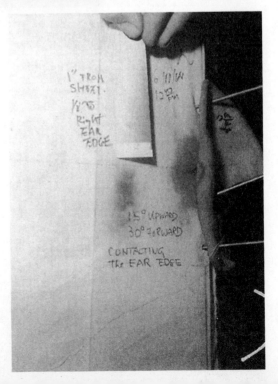

Muzzle distance test into pig's ear, showing that the fatal shot to Senator Kennedy head was fired from one inch or less *(California State Archives)*

Campaign worker Sandra Serrano, who claims to have seen and heard a girl in a polka-dot dress *(California State Archives)*

The LAPD-identified girl in the polka-dot dress: Valerie Schulte *(California State Archives)*

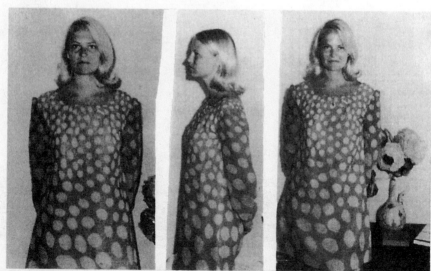

Above left: SUS member Manny Pena *(California State Archives)* **Center:** SUS member Gordon McDevitt *(California State Archives)* **Right:** SUS member James MacArthur *(California State Archives)*

Below left: SUS member Thomas J. Miller *(California State Archives)* **Right:** SUS member Michael M. Nielsen *(California State Archives)*

Sirhan: apprentice jockey
(California State Archives)

Innocent victim: Mary Sirhan *(California State Archives)*

May 18 9.45 AM - 68

my determination to eliminate R.F.K. is becoming more the more of an unshakable obsession

P please pay to the Order

plea port wine port wine port wine

R.F.K. must die- RFK must be killed Robert F. Kennedy must be assassinated R.F.K must be assassinated R.F.K. must be assassinated R.F.K must be assassinated R.F.K. must be assassinated R.F.K must be assassinated R.F.K. Must be assassinated assassinated Robert F. Kennedy Robert F. Kennedy Robert F. Kennedy must be assassinated assassinated Robert F. Kennedy must be assassinated assassinated assassinated assassinated Robert F. Kennedy must be assassinated Robert F. Kennedy must be assassinated before 5 June 68 Robert F. Kennedy must be assassinated I have never please pay to the order of of of of of of of of of this or that   HL

8 0 0 0 0 0 — ◻

Please pay to the order of

A page from Sirhan's notebooks: "R.F.K. must die"
(California State Archives)

Los Angeles district
attorney Evelle
Younger, who later
became California
attorney general
(State of California)

Defense attorneys
Russell Parsons and
Grant Cooper, with
pipe, flank Sirhan
*(California State
Archives)*

II. THE CONTROVERSIES

12. *Early Challenges*

arly on, the assumption that Sirhan alone killed Robert Kennedy aroused no public controversy, and thus his trial focused almost exclusively on the defendant's state of mind. Offering to concede that their client had fired the fatal shot, Sirhan's attorneys adopted a defense of "diminished capacity," attempting to show that his mental state precluded a first-degree conviction and death sentence. They failed on both counts, and Sirhan was sentenced to die in the gas chamber at San Quentin. Sirhan's defense team appealed on the basis of eighteen different grounds in its 740-page brief, claiming, in part, that Judge Walker had refused to accept Sirhan's guilty plea in return for a life sentence.[77]

[77] On October 9, 1969, Mary Sirhan, the convicted assassin's mother, went to the United Nations, pleading for help in obtaining clemency for her son.

Late the following month, Sirhan went on a hunger strike to protest his living

However, the order for Sirhan's execution would be voided in 1972 when the California supreme court revoked all pending death sentences in the state. In prison for "life," Sirhan could seek his freedom from the parole board as early as 1975.

Although Sirhan's guilt had been universally accepted, not everyone considered the case to be closed. Troubling questions about the number of bullets really fired at the crime scene of the Kennedy murder first surfaced immediately after Sirhan's conviction.

Deceptively simple and persuasive in its outline, the LAPD's accounting of Sirhan's eight shots is fundamental to the entire official theory of the assassination. But the seed of the budding controversies lay in the denial of criminalist DeWayne Wolfer of the LAPD/SID that any additional bullets had been found at the crime scene. During Sirhan's trial, no one, not even the defense, contested this denial.

On May 23, a month after Sirhan's April 17, 1969, conviction, a nearly unnoticed article appeared in the *Los Angeles Free Press,* an alternative newspaper. This story began to cast a large and growing shadow over the case. Written by local researchers Lillian Castellano and Floyd B. Nelson, the article, entitled "Truth Committee Releases Conspiracy Evidence," became the first to argue that overlooked evidence in the Sirhan case strongly suggested that another gunman had been firing when Robert F. Kennedy was shot.

The evidence revealed by Castellano and Nelson included a photograph of what appeared to be bullet holes in the center divider between the two swinging doors at the west end of the kitchen pantry. Kennedy had walked through these doors en route to his victory speech and then again moments before he was shot while walking toward the Colonial Room. The swinging doors were behind him when Sirhan, approaching from the opposite direction, opened fire.

The picture was taken on June 6, the day after the shooting and

---

conditions on death row at San Quentin. However, he ended it after thirteen days, on hearing pleas from his mother to give it up.

In September 1970, a group of terrorists hijacked a plane, holding 180 passengers as hostages and offering to exchange them for Sirhan. Mrs. Sirhan pleaded with the guerrillas to release the hostages.

Mary Sirhan, a fine and hardworking woman, suffered perhaps as much as anyone after Senator Kennedy's murder. But she always remained loyal to her son.

just a few hours after Kennedy was pronounced dead. John R. Clemente, an amateur photographer, snapped the photograph, not immediately grasping its significance.

The *Free Press* article also included a March 23, 1969, affidavit by Clemente's companion, John Shirley, who described what he had seen: "In the wooden jamb of the center divider were two bullet holes surrounded by inked circles which contained some numbers and letters. . . . It appeared that an attempt had been made to dig the bullets out from the surface. However, the center divider jamb was loose, and it appeared to have been removed from the framework so that the bullets might be extracted from behind. It was then replaced but not firmly affixed."

Castellano and Nelson also found CBS radio reporter Bob Ferris, who had reported seeing the same circled holes in the center divider on June 8, 1968, three days after the shooting. Like Clemente and Shirley, Ferris did not realize what it meant if these circled holes were indeed bullet holes.

Floyd Nelson explains, "We were aware of what was going on in the Robert Kennedy case by following Sirhan's trial. Lillian was a gangbuster researcher. We got the Clemente photo first, and then John Shirley sent the affidavit. When we added up how many people were hit and how many shots Sirhan could fire, we started to wonder about the two 'bullet' holes circled in that Clemente picture. We knew Sirhan had eight shots, and, according to the official investigation, they had all been expended shooting people. Now we had possible evidence of two extra bullets. So we started to wonder: Where did these two bullet holes come from? He didn't reload.

"We had decided not to come out with our story until there was a verdict in Sirhan's trial. We thought that maybe our questions would be answered during the trial—but they weren't."

Incredibly, no detailed evidence of the crime scene bullet flight path was ever presented at Sirhan's trial. But Nelson and Castellano knew that none of the bullets booked as evidence for the trial were recovered at the crime scene: seven of the slugs recovered were removed from the six victims; one had been lost in the ceiling space, according to the LAPD.

The *Free Press* article also cited a startling Associated Press wire-photo of a unidentified LAPD "police technician" and his unnamed partner, as well as its caption, which had been discovered by Castellano while she was poring over AP records. Headlined "Bullet Found near Kennedy Shooting Scene," the June 5 caption stated, "A police technician inspects a bullet hole discovered in a door frame in a kitchen corridor of the Ambassador Hotel in Los Angeles near where Sen. Robert F. Kennedy was shot and critically wounded early today. Bullet is still in the wood."

The *Free Press* article and related photographs generated little controversy at first. When a television reporter asked District Attorney Evelle Younger about the sighting of possible extra bullets at the crime scene, Younger dismissed the whole matter. The reporter, Robert Dornan, later a U.S. congressman, asked Younger about "ten bullets out of an eight [shot] revolver." Younger replied, "[T]here [is] tons of information over at the LAPD that's going to be made available, and not once was there any evidence to indicate that there was more than one person involved in this thing." Dornan didn't challenge Younger.

The "tons" of evidence alluded to by Younger included several items that were booked by Special Unit Senator (SUS)—the handpicked LAPD special task force assigned exclusively to investigate the Kennedy case. These materials constituted the only physical evidence listed in the LAPD's official booking records as having been recovered from the hotel crime scene.

In a June 28, 1968, LAPD booking report, the items recovered were described as "2 pieces of wood, from door frame at crime scene, both contain numerous holes," and "2 pieces of ceiling insulation taken from kitchen near where Kennedy was shot." The ceiling tiles were later identified by LAPD records as those containing the three bullet holes identified by Wolfer, two of entry and one of exit.

Did the two pieces of wood also contain bullet holes? Were they the two wooden jambs referred to in the Clemente and AP photographs and the Shirley affidavit? If no bullets were discovered, why were these pieces of wood booked as evidence in the first place? And what kinds of analyses were done on them?

Available LAPD records of DeWayne Wolfer and SID's work answer none of these questions.

Also, LAPD chief of detectives Robert A. Houghton shed no

new light on any of these matters with the publication of his book, *Special Unit Senator: The Investigation of the Assassination of Senator Robert F. Kennedy,* in January 1970. Theodore Taylor, a former police reporter, assisted Houghton with writing the book.

In a later sworn affidavit, Houghton recounted, "[At] some point during the investigation I had an interview with Police Chief Tom Reddin. I told him, as I had previously, that it was my opinion that the Kennedy assassination investigation had considerable historic interest and that the potential for suspicion of conspiracies was great, and that in my opinion it would be valuable that some information regarding the effort and concern of the L.A.P.D., and the extent of the investigation, should be released for public consumption. I told him I felt that a book would be the best way to do this, that writing the book would require some information from L.A.P.D. files, and that in all probability I would have a co-author work to assist me. I received Chief Reddin's approval to go forward."

In the first book written about the murder, Houghton chronicled the process by which SUS had conducted its investigation, including "the girl in the polka-dot dress" inquiry and the other prominent conspiracy theories.

However, because Sirhan was in the midst of appealing his conviction, the LAPD and the district attorney's office did not appear to be thrilled with the upcoming publication of Houghton's book.

In a September 12, 1969, memorandum to Joseph P. Busch, the assistant district attorney, Acting District Attorney John Howard wrote, "The publication will not affect the appeal. . . . [But] legal position of Chief Houghton in publishing same is questionable. Additional facts as to manner, time and source material would determine and resolve publication rights. My opinion is insufficient factual grounds to enjoin publication; recovery of publication payment by L.A.P.D. probable. It is ethically improper for Chief Houghton to benefit financially from the efforts and work product produced and paid for by L.A.P.D."

Nevertheless, many book critics treated Houghton's work as the official and definitive story of the Robert Kennedy murder case.

However, nine months after its publication, the first book to challenge the official version was published, by E. P. Dutton: *"R.F.K.*

Must Die!", a brilliantly written inside story of Sirhan's defense team. Its author was former *Time* correspondent Robert Blair Kaiser, who had worked for Sirhan's defense as an investigator and knew the case better than anyone else. The book contained remarkable detail about Sirhan, based upon hundreds of hours of interviews with the convicted assassin.

In the course of researching and writing his book, Kaiser enjoyed absolute independence, guaranteed under the contract he signed with Sirhan and his attorneys. However, after the trial, Kaiser had to go to court to fight a proposed injunction filed by Sirhan, who wanted but did not receive any control over the book's contents.

Regarding his relationship with Sirhan, Kaiser explains, "I kept elaborate notebooks, and I tape-recorded meetings. But I never had Sirhan's complete trust. There were times when I would ask him questions, and he wouldn't give me the answer. And then he would confide in Russell Parsons. An example would be like Sirhan going to the Ambassador on June 2. I said to Sirhan, 'Hey, I think we have some movie footage that shows you on June 2.' He didn't tell me, 'Okay, you have me dead to rights.' Instead, he waited and told Parsons, 'Maybe I was there.'

"He constantly played a game with me. I kept trying to get him to reveal more and more. It was up and down. He told me a lot one day. I come back the next day, and he won't tell me anything."

Although Kaiser completely rejected the notion of the firing of a second gun at the crime scene, the book still generated considerable controversy. In the last chapter of his masterful work, Kaiser posed the possibility that Sirhan was, like the protagonist in John Frankenheimer's *The Manchurian Candidate*, "programmed to kill Bob Kennedy and was programmed to forget the fact of his programming."[78]

---

[78] Nine years after the release of Kaiser's book, the public-interest group American Citizens for Honesty in Government received once confidential files after a Freedom of Information Act request, revealing "Operation Artichoke." Operated by the Central Intelligence Agency, Artichoke was a twenty-three-year program of experimentation with drugs for use in mind and behavior control.

In one of the declassified memoranda, written in January 1954, a CIA official posed the question of whether "an individual [could] be induced under Artichoke to perform an act, involuntarily, of attempted assassination against a prominent . . . politician or if necessary, against an American official?"

Later in the same memo, the official concluded, "In answer to the hypothetical

---

Kaiser defends his theory—which includes the possible involvement of the Mafia, as well as "the girl in the polka-dot dress"—as follows: "Only in the final chapter do I list programming as one of a number of possible explanations. I tried to write the book as credibly as I could. Only in the last chapter did I allow myself to go outside the norms of objectivity and allowed myself to add things up.

"I think that Sirhan was put up to do it by others. I don't know who those others are. There are fingerprints of others all over him—which I saw mainly in his lies and evasions. Through the things he said and did under hypnosis, I would swear that there were others involved. Who these shadowy people were—say, the people he met through the horse ranch in Corona—I don't know."

Regarding Corona and the evidence of Sirhan's stalking Kennedy, Kaiser wrote in his last chapter, "[I]f Sirhan was after Kennedy on May 20 and May 24 and June 2, why not also on June 3? Sirhan changed his story three times about his movements on June 3. First, he said he was home all day. Then he admitted to me that he'd gone to Corona. Later still, he told me it wasn't Corona at all, but 'someplace in that direction.' And still later, he told investigator Michael McCowan with some satisfaction that he'd put 350 miles on his car June 3 and no one knew where he'd gone. . . . Maybe, as McCowan speculated, Sirhan drove to San Diego that afternoon. Driving from Pasadena to San Diego and back might explain the 350 miles. Why San Diego? That night at the El Cortez Hotel in San Diego, one of the candidates was scheduled to speak, but he begged off, overcome with exhaustion. The candidate was Senator Robert F. Kennedy."

---

question, can an individual . . . be made to perform an act of attempted assassination, involuntarily, under Artichoke . . . the answer in this case was probably 'No' because of the limitations imposed operationally. . . ."

However, in his book, Kaiser cited a Dutch case in which a man, Bjorn Nielsen, was convicted of "having planned and instigated by influence of various kinds, including suggestions of a hypnotic nature," two murders by another man, Palle Hardrup, whom Nielsen had programmed through hypnosis in 1951. Essentially, Hardrup had become Nielsen's robot.

The SUS's expert on hypnosis, Michael Nielsen, no relation to Bjorn, rejects all of this. He told me, "There is no such thing as mind control hypnosis. If a person were predisposed to do something like murder—well, you wouldn't even need hypnosis to convince him to do it. They would want to do it anyway. Say if I hypnotized you and gave you instructions that you were going to kill somebody, there's no way in the world you would do that."

---

13. *Assault on Wolfer*

Quickly becoming the lightning rod for critics of the LAPD's investigation of the Kennedy murder case, DeWayne Wolfer found himself under siege. A well-known criminalist, Wolfer joined the police department on June 1, 1950, and received his assignment in the crime laboratory six months later. After graduating from the University of Southern California with a bachelor's degree in zoology, he shifted gears dramatically and soon began to specialize in firearms identification for the LAPD. During the mid-1950s, Wolfer also became an instructor in criminalistics, eventually receiving an assistant professorship at California State College at Long Beach. A member of numerous professional societies, he also taught related courses at colleges and universities throughout California and published an important laboratory manual on criminalistics.

On May 28, 1971, after Wolfer was nominated for promotion as the chief forensic chemist of the LAPD/SID, Los Angeles attorney Barbara Warner Blehr, acting on her own behalf but with the support of several criminalists, initiated a city civil service complaint to block his promotion, alleging major errors by Wolfer during the Kennedy investigation and two other cases.[79] In doing so, she raised the possibility that a second gun had been fired in the kitchen pantry of the Ambassador Hotel on the night Senator Kennedy was shot.

In early June, Joseph P. Busch, Jr., the new district attorney of Los Angeles County, announced that his office would conduct an investigation of Blehr's charges: "As this office was responsible for the prosecution of Sirhan Sirhan . . . it is incumbent upon us to conduct the investigation so that there will be no loss of confidence on the part of the public as to whether the facts presented in the courtroom were correct."

Also, on July 23, Wolfer responded with a $2 million defamation suit against Blehr and others, which resulted in a sworn deposition being taken from Wolfer in September 1971 concerning his handling of the Kennedy murder case. Among the issues raised in the suit was Wolfer's bullet inventory from the crime scene.

"I went to the scene of the crime and I explored the trajectory of all of the holes in the wall, and the walls [*sic*] of victims," Wolfer said during his deposition. "I made up a basic plot plan, of all trajectories

---

[79] After the filing of Blehr's complaint against Wolfer, Evelle Younger, who had left as district attorney and become California's attorney general, received a June 26, 1971, letter from former FBI special agent Marshall Houts, the editor in chief of *Trauma*, a medical journal for emergency room physicians. Houts wrote, "I have no personal interest in this matter, but do have a deep academic and professional concern over Wolfer's horrendous blunders in the past and those he will commit in the future. . . . Wolfer suffers from a great inferiority complex for which he compensates by giving the police exactly what they need to obtain a conviction. He casts objectivity to the winds and violates every basic tenet of forensic science and proof by becoming a crusading advocate. This is rationalized as being entirely legitimate since the accused is guilty anyway which makes the social objective worthy of the means required to obtain it."

Houts's book *Where Death Delights* was the basis for the television series "Quincy, M.E.," about a crime-fighting medical examiner, portrayed by actor Jack Klugman.

and holes and the persons in there. I was there immediately after the [shooting] of the Senator. I retrieved and was in charge of the crime scene, and I recovered the bullets that were recovered [from the victims]. I checked all of the possibilities of holes, and I certainly feel that there were only eight shots fired and I accounted for all eight shots."

In short, Wolfer said, under oath, that no bullet holes were discovered in anything but ceiling tiles and the six victims.

Blehr's charges against Wolfer had been based on the private firearms identification and ballistics[80] investigation of William Wirick Harper, a sixty-eight-year-old Pasadena-based criminalist and firearms expert, whose testimony in hundreds of cases had been relied upon by prosecutors and defense attorneys for nearly four decades. He had become interested in the Kennedy murder case after reading Chief Robert Houghton's book, *Special Unit Senator,* and then discovering problems with the handling of the crime scene evidence by Wolfer, Harper's longtime nemesis.[81]

In late 1970, Harper was authorized by Sirhan's attorneys to examine the bullets and other firearms evidence entered at Sirhan's trial. Using photographic enlargements of the bullets recovered from the shooting victims,[82] Harper was stunned by his findings, which cast doubt on the grand jury and trial testimony of police criminalist Wolfer.

For one thing, Harper claimed that the characteristics of the Kennedy neck bullet could not be matched with the bullet that struck

[80] Very simply, *ballistics* is the study of the characteristics of a bullet in flight, from the instant of firing to the moment it comes to rest in its target. *Firearms identification* is the process of tracing a fired bullet or cartridge to a suspect weapon by microscopic comparison. These two terms are often misused.

[81] Wolfer and Harper had clashed several times in court. Before the Robert Kennedy case, their most celebrated dispute came during their opposing testimonies in the highly publicized 1967 murder case *People* v. *Jack Kirschke.* Harper had testified for the defense.

[82] Harper used a Hycon Balliscan camera, which permits a bullet to be pictured while in rotation, leaving a photograph of its path and characteristics to be examined. Firearms examiners tend to agree that this camera can be a valuable diagnostic tool. However, the most effective means of bullet examination is with a basic comparison microscope.

victim William Weisel; thus, the two bullets could not have come from the same gun.[83] Coupled with the muzzle distance problems cited by eyewitnesses to the shooting and the question of unaccounted-for bullet holes at the crime scene, this claim left open the possibility that a second gunman had been present at the crime scene.

Furthermore, Harper could not confirm Wolfer's match of the test bullets entered in evidence with the intact bullet reportedly recovered from Senator Kennedy's neck. Harper discovered that three packaged test bullets entered into evidence at the June 7, 1968, grand jury hearing were identified as having been fired by an Iver Johnson .22 revolver with the serial number H18602. The serial number of Sirhan's Iver Johnson was H53725.

In other words, it appeared as though Wolfer claimed to have positively matched the bullets recovered from three victims with bullets fired from a gun that Sirhan didn't use.

Remarkably, neither the prosecution nor the defense discovered this apparent error prior to Sirhan's trial. In response to Harper, Wolfer described this discrepancy as simply a "clerical error" he had made while labeling the evidence.

This became one of the most critical mistakes made by the LAPD in the Kennedy case, provoking considerable skepticism of the entire investigation.

However, piecing together evidence from a variety of sources, one can see how the mistake occurred:

On June 6, 1968, after Senator Kennedy died and Dr. Noguchi conducted the autopsy, Wolfer received an intact bullet removed from Kennedy's neck. Wolfer immediately began his analysis of the slug.

Also, Wolfer briefly had possession of Sirhan's H53725—before submitting it as evidence to the grand jury—and fired eight test shots into a water tank at the SID's crime laboratory, which is consistent with standard operating procedure for obtaining test bullets from a gun for comparison purposes. (Somehow, one of the eight bullets

---

[83] At Sirhan's trial, the Kennedy neck bullet was People's Exhibit 47; the Goldstein bullet was People's Exhibit 52; the Weisel bullet was People's Exhibit 54. Sirhan's gun was People's Exhibit 6.

became lost during the test, leaving only seven test bullets to compare with the victim bullets.)

Using his comparison microscope, Wolfer claimed to have matched the bullet recovered from Kennedy's neck with one of the test bullets that had been fired from Sirhan's H53725.

Wolfer presented the seven test bullets to the grand jury on June 7, 1968, along with Sirhan's H53725. Wolfer testified that he had made a positive match between the Kennedy neck bullet and the test bullets with his comparison microscope. Wolfer concluded that Sirhan's gun, and "no other gun," fired the neck shot that hit Senator Kennedy. Also, during his testimony, Wolfer claimed to have positively matched the bullets removed from two other shooting victims.[84]

Because Wolfer wanted to compare the slugs removed from the other victims with the test bullets, he asked the district attorney's office to allow him to keep three of the seven test bullets from H53725. Permission granted, Wolfer wrapped the three test bullets in a piece of paper and put the paper in his shirt pocket. At his office, he placed the three test bullets in his desk drawer and locked it.

As Sirhan's gun was in the custody of the grand jury and no longer available to him, Wolfer used a similar Iver Johnson .22-caliber revolver, with the serial number H18602—which had been borrowed from the LAPD's Property Division on June 10, 1968[85]—for the purpose of conducting a sound test[86] and a powder pattern test to

---

[84] The four remaining victim bullets were too badly damaged for conclusive firearms identification analysis. However, the damaged bullets—with the exception of the one that killed Senator Kennedy—were determined to have come from a gun with the same rifling specifications as Sirhan's Iver Johnson revolver. The bullet that killed Kennedy was too badly fragmented for such analysis.

[85] According to an LAPD property card, the Iver Johnson revolver H18602 was originally booked as evidence for an earlier robbery case on March 18, 1967, over a year before the murder of Senator Kennedy. It was test-fired on March 22, 1967, by the LAPD in connection with that prior investigation.

On June 10, 1968, Wolfer sent his partner, William Lee, to the Property Division to obtain a gun similar to Sirhan's H53725.

[86] Wolfer conducted a "firing for sound" test at the Ambassador Hotel on June 20, 1968—using the H18602 as his test weapon. The purpose of this test was to find out whether Sandra Serrano, the Kennedy campaign worker, could possibly have heard the sound of gunfire from where she was sitting outside the

determine the distance from the gun's muzzle to Kennedy's body and clothing.

Wolfer insists that he didn't keep *any* bullets from those two tests conducted with the H18602. However, while preparing for Sirhan's trial, Wolfer placed the three remaining test bullets fired from Sirhan's H53725 into an evidence envelope.[87] And Wolfer mistakenly noted on the envelope—which he dated June 6, 1968—that it contained three bullets fired from Iver Johnson H18602, instead of Sirhan's Iver Johnson H53725.

No one—not even Sirhan's attorneys—noticed the error during the trial. In a November 3, 1972, affidavit, Sirhan's trial attorney, Grant Cooper, stated, "Because DeWayne Wolfer's testimony under oath corroborated the facts learned through my investigation and preparation, I did not retain an independent ballistics expert to analyze the slugs removed from the deceased's body. Had I any feeling that in a case of this importance, Mr. Wolfer either willfully falsified his ballistics analysis or negligently, improperly or otherwise arrived at his conclusions, I would have had an independent ballistics expert or experts study the bullets."

Immediately after Wolfer's "clerical error" was discovered, his critics demanded a reexamination of the H18602. However, requests to refire the H18602 to determine if it was, in fact, used to fire the test shots had to be denied. The reason? The test gun, Iver Johnson H18602, had been destroyed, a routine procedure covered under California law. To add to the confusion, the date of the gun's destruction, first listed as July 1968, was later changed to July 1969—again because of a "clerical error."[88]

---

hotel—just before the girl in the polka-dot dress and her alleged male accomplice ran past her, claiming credit for killing Kennedy. According to LAPD investigators, Serrano had said in her original police statement to have heard "six quick backfires."

[87] The envelope containing these three test bullets was People's Exhibit 55 at Sirhan's trial.

[88] Actually, this clerical error is easily understood. The H18602 was originally scheduled for destruction in July 1968, a year after the gun had been booked as evidence in the 1967 robbery case, as per standard operating procedure. However, after the gun was used as a test weapon in the Kennedy case and returned to the Property Division, a new date for destruction, superseding the former, was im-

The controversy over the H18602 aside, after his study of the firearms evidence in the Kennedy case, Harper shocked everyone by offering the following conclusion, based upon his own work, the autopsy report, and the eyewitness statements: "[T]wo guns were being fired concurrently in the kitchen pantry of the Ambassador Hotel at the time of the shooting. . . . It is extremely unlikely that any of the bullets fired by the Sirhan gun ever struck the body of Kennedy."

Harper's conclusion immediately triggered more independent investigations and conspiracy theories about the Robert Kennedy murder case.

While publicly sloughing off Harper's declaration and evidence, the prosecutor's office mounted its own countercampaign. And the fall guy became the Los Angeles County Clerk's Office.

According to a July 28, 1971, confidential memorandum to Los Angeles district attorney Joseph P. Busch from Richard W. Hecht, "the extent of the violation focuses upon the activities of the Criminalist William Harper who was given unlimited access to the original exhibits in the case, and, in particular, the [firearms] evidence on at least nine separate occasions."

On the basis of the district attorney's probe of the clerk's office, the Los Angeles County Grand Jury investigation began on August 16. In an August 24 letter from the foreman of the grand jury to the county's board of supervisors, the grand jury announced, among its other findings, that there was evidence that the Los Angeles County Clerk's Office had been irresponsible in its handling of Sirhan's gun and bullets by allowing unauthorized people to tamper with these exhibits.

County Clerk William G. Sharp angrily denied this, insisting that his office had followed all proper procedures. He later charged that he

---

posed. The problem was that no one bothered to change the original date of destruction on the property report.

Interestingly, rumors persist that the H18602 was never really destroyed after all and is now a prize in the gun collection of an unknown party.

was being used by the district attorney's office and had become a "victim of a political play just to provide an excuse not to refire the Sirhan gun."

In fact, little evidence, and no proof, was ever presented that exhibits from Sirhan's trial had been tampered with while in the custody of the clerk's office. Nevertheless, the LAPD and the district attorney's office continued to blame the clerk's office whenever an evidence discrepancy arose in the future.[89]

Meantime, on October 18, the district attorney's investigation of Blehr's charges exonerated Wolfer, clearing the way for his promotion.[90] Also, Judge David Eagleson of the Los Angeles Superior Court later dismissed Wolfer's defamation suit against Blehr.

On the basis, in part, of Blehr's lawsuit against Wolfer, another complaint had been filed on June 25, 1971, by Los Angeles attorney Godfrey Isaac—an associate of Luke McKissack, a new attorney for Sirhan—and independent journalist Theodore Charach. The two men charged that the LAPD and other law enforcement officials had suppressed key evidence that would have proved serious deficien-

---

[89] An investigation by the Los Angeles Board of Supervisors in 1974, headed by Supervisor Baxter Ward, insisted that the integrity of physical evidence in the Robert Kennedy murder case had been maintained by the clerk's office.

[90] Wolfer did not appear to fare much better after he received his promotion. In 1974, he was reprimanded for alleged improper conduct and disqualified from serving on civil service interview boards. In 1975, the state court of appeals cited him for testimony in the 1967 Jack Kirschke murder case that "borders on perjury" and that was "given with a reckless disregard for the truth."

The Kranz Report, the last major official defense of the LAPD's handling of the probe, would in 1977 attack Wolfer's record keeping in the Kennedy murder case. It charged, "The apparent lack of reports, both written and photographic, either made by Wolfer and destroyed, or never in existence, raised serious doubts as to the substance and credibility of the ballistics evidence presented in the original Sirhan trial."

On May 23, 1980, Wolfer was temporarily suspended from his post for other infractions. It had been determined that he had "failed to provide proper storage and analysis of bullets and other evidence and had improperly supervised firearms and explosives investigators," according to a May 31, 1980, article in the *Los Angeles Times*.

cies and outright errors during the Robert Kennedy murder investigation. Consequently, Isaac and Charach demanded that the city of Los Angeles release all of the LAPD's investigative files in the case. Their arguments were unsuccessful; their case was later dismissed.[91]

[91] In or about July 1970, Charach had provided Sirhan's attorney Grant Cooper with information about the possibility that at least two guns had been fired at the crime scene. Cooper referred Charach to criminalist William Harper, who had just begun his own independent probe of the firearms evidence in the Kennedy case. However, after the events of 1971—the Blehr complaint, the DA's probe, and the grand jury investigation—Cooper had apparently soured on Charach. Indeed, on January 23, 1974, Cooper wrote a letter to District Attorney Joseph Busch, stating, "I am only sorry that the waters had been muddied by the passage of time and the doings of Theodore Charach and others of his ilk. . . . I can see from your point of view where reopening the case would add fuel to his fires."

14. Pointing the Finger at Cesar

Because the case against Sirhan was considered open-and-shut from the outset, the question of whether or not there were other guns in the pantry at the time of the shooting, and who had them, had never really been raised before Sirhan's trial. But at least one other gun was drawn in the room that night. It belonged to part-time security guard Thane Eugene Cesar, who had been walking to Kennedy's right rear, the point of entry of all four bullets that hit either his body or clothing.

Television producer Richard Lubic, an eyewitness to the shooting, says, "I was there next to Senator Kennedy's right side after he hit the floor. While I was kneeling, I looked up and saw a guy in a security guard's uniform a few feet to my left, standing behind Senator Kennedy. He had his weapon in his hand and was pointing it down in Kennedy's general direction." Lubic insists that he had given this information to the police after the shooting, but he was never asked about it during his testimony in court.

Lubic is not the only person who saw Cesar with a gun. Kennedy's official bodyguard, former FBI agent Bill Barry, reportedly saw him holding his gun after Kennedy had fallen. Barry told him to put it back in his holster. Karl Uecker also saw Cesar with a gun in his hand and said that he was relieved that Cesar had not fired at Sirhan—in which case Uecker might have been hit.

One eyewitness even claimed to have seen a security guard standing directly behind Kennedy draw his gun and shoot it. On the night of the murder, just moments after the shooting, Don Schulman, a runner for KNXT-TV, gave an interview to reporter Jeff Brent of Continental News Service. Schulman told Brent that he had seen Kennedy hit three times, adding that he had also witnessed a security guard standing in back of the senator draw his gun and fire it. At the time, Schulman assumed that the guard was returning Sirhan's fire in retaliation—although it is not clear from this interview who Schulman claimed actually shot Kennedy, Sirhan or the security guard.[92]

The LAPD claims that Schulman equivocated on his story during an interview with LAPD sergeant Paul E. O'Steen in August 1968. Schulman told O'Steen that he was outside the pantry at the time of the shooting and had made no reference to a security guard's drawing his weapon.[93] There is, however, a transcript of a 1971 interview

---

[92] Minutes after the shooting of Senator Kennedy, Phil Cogin of KLA radio breathlessly broadcast a report, stating, "Don Schulman, an employee of television station KNXT said Kennedy was walking to the kitchen when he was shot three times by a gunman who stepped out of the crowd. Schulman, who witnessed the shooting, said the gunman was shot by Kennedy's bodyguards. He was then taken into custody. Repeating that, Schulman, KNXT employee, said the gunman was shot by Kennedy's bodyguards."

Schulman's story that he had seen a guard returning fire was also reported in *France Soir,* on European radio stations, and in the *Boston Record-American* immediately after the shooting.

[93] According to a confidential 1971 LAPD memorandum, "Schulman was interviewed on August 9, 1968, by Sgt. O'Steen. He stated he was outside of the kitchen when he heard noises like firecrackers. He did not see the actual shooting or suspect due to the crowd. Mr. Schulman was reinterviewed on July 23, 1971. He stated during this interview that he was in the pantry about twelve feet from Senator

Schulman had with the LAPD. A reading of it shows him
nervous—not surprising, given his earlier statements that he
life was in danger. Here is a portion of the transcript:

> LAPD: You say you saw the security men pull out their weapons.
> Do you recall seeing more than one security man?
>
> SCHULMAN: No, I don't.
>
> LAPD: Then—then what you—is it fair to say that what you did
> see was one security man pull out his weapon?
>
> SCHULMAN: Well, I did see one. I don't know if there were any
> more at this time.
>
> LAPD: I see. And you did see him raise his weapon?
>
> SCHULMAN: Yes.
>
> LAPD: All right. Now did you observe him fire the weapon?
>
> SCHULMAN: As I recall—as I said there—he pulled it out and
> fired.
>
> LAPD: Did you see a flash come out of the muzzle?
>
> SCHULMAN: That I don't remember.
>
> LAPD: Did you hear a sound?
>
> SCHULMAN: Well, there were so many—it was like firecrackers
> going off.
>
> LAPD: Can you—can you say with certainty in your own mind
> that that particular security guard fired a weapon at that time.
>
> SCHULMAN: Well, as I said in the past, I can be pretty sure that he
> pulled out the weapon and fired.

The transcript of the recorded interview goes on for eighty-seven
pages, with Schulman becoming further unnerved by the sharp questioning and unsure about what he had actually seen. He continued to
insist that he had actually seen bullets hitting Kennedy, but he could
not determine who had fired the shots.[94]

Kennedy when the shots were fired. . . . Why Mr. Schulman has changed his mind
or why his memory which he describes as poor, has improved since August 9, 1968,
is subject to scrutiny."

Journalist Robert Blair Kaiser has stated that two other KNXT-TV employees,
Frank Raciti and Dick Gaither, claimed to have been standing with Schulman in the
Embassy Room at the moment of the shooting.

[94] Another eyewitness, citizen-activist Booker Griffin, claimed, during a 1987
interview with author Philip Melanson, to have seen a second gunman at the

When critics of the Robert Kennedy murder investigation discuss the possibility of a second gunman, the name most often raised is that of security guard Thane Eugene Cesar. They theorize that he could have crouched down behind and to the right of Kennedy and then pumped several shots into his back at point-blank range while Sirhan fired wildly into the crowd behind the senator, drawing all the attention of the witnesses in the pantry.

Within minutes of the shooting of Senator Kennedy, John Marshall, a reporter from the local radio station KFWB, cornered Cesar and interviewed him. Marshall asked, "Officer, can you confirm the fact that the Senator has been shot?"

"Yes," Cesar replied. "I was there holding his arm when they shot him."

"What happened?"

"I don't know. . . . As he [Kennedy] walked up, the guy pulled a gun and shot at him."

"Was it just one man?"

"No. Yeah, one man."

"And what sort of wound did the senator receive?"

"Well, from where I could see, it looked like he was shot in the head and the chest and shoulder. . . ."

Soon thereafter, police officers questioned Cesar, along with numerous other witnesses, at Rampart Station. Cesar told the police during the tape recorded interview, "[J]ust as he [Kennedy] got to the steam table, I was up to him where I had ahold of his arm here. I was pushing people away from the other arm."

"You were on which side of him?" An officer asked.

"I was on his right side."

"His right side?"

"Yes. And at that moment when we got on the edge of the steam

---

Kennedy crime scene. However, there is no record of Griffin's making this claim in any of his interviews with either the LAPD or the FBI. He did tell the LAPD during a taped interview that "it sounded as if there was more than one gun being used."

An officer then asked Griffin, "Did you have any reason to believe, other than the fact that you heard the shots, there was more than one person shooting?"

Griffin replied, "No reason."

table, he had reached out and sort of turned to shake hands with somebody."

"Turned to his left?"

"Well, he was walking this way [east], and he turned just like this [north], just his body. Because when he did, my hand broke loose, sort of broke loose away from his arm. And, of course, I grabbed it again, because people were all over the place."

"People were pressing in pretty close?"

"Right. Now, at that time, I just happened to look up, and that's when I seen—all I could see was an arm and a gun. And I reached for mine, but it was too late. He [the shooter] had done fired five shots. And when he did, I ducked, because I was as close as Kennedy was. And—from what I can remember, from what I did—I . . . fell back. When I ducked, I threw myself off balance and fell back [against the ice machine]. . . . And then the senator fell right in front of me. And then I turned around [and saw] blood coming down this [right] side of his face. . . ."

"Did you get a look at the gun?"

"I really didn't get a real good look at it. I knew it wasn't a .38 when it went off, because I've shot a .38 and a .22, and I can tell the difference."

Cesar told the police that after the shooting, another security guard asked him to assist with crowd control. Cesar and the other guard then left the kitchen pantry.

At no point during the interview did the police examine Cesar's gun to determine whether it had been fired.

Six days after the shooting, on June 11, an FBI agent interviewed Cesar at Lockheed Aircraft. According to the FBI report of the interview, "As Kennedy was shaking hands with a busboy, Cesar looked up and suddenly saw a hand sticking out of the crowd between two camera men and the hand was holding a gun. . . . Just as Cesar started to move to jump on the gun, he saw the red flash come from the muzzle. At the same time, Cesar was shoved by an unknown individual, and the next thing he remembered he was on the floor against the ice machine. Cesar stated he was approximately four feet from the gun when it went off and that Senator Kennedy was approximately two feet from the gun.

"Cesar scrambled to his feet, drew his gun, and moved to the Senator. At this time, Cesar stated there were several men on top of the assassin trying to get the gun from his grasp. Cesar stated he took a position next to the Senator's body to protect him from further attack. . . ."[95]

On June 24, 1968, LAPD sergeant P. E. O'Steen visited Cesar at his home and taped a brief, twenty-minute interview. Essentially, Cesar repeated his version of events, but O'Steen's questions were not very penetrating. During the interview, Cesar even showed O'-Steen his Harrington & Richardson .22 revolver, which he had given to his wife for "home protection." Nothing Cesar had said up to that point was being challenged.

Not called to testify at the grand jury or against Sirhan at his 1969 trial, Cesar faded into oblivion. Then Los Angeles freelance journalist Theodore Charach, who had talked to Cesar in early October 1969, rediscovered him.

After his interview with Cesar, Charach charged, "The presidential candidate was murdered by a Second Gun—a uniformed unidentified gunman, firing four distinct shots from the rear at contact range. . . . The Second Gunman was a professional, functioning at the time as a private guard. . . . He fell down backwards, simultaneously with Kennedy, his double-action revolver out of his holster even as they fell."[96]

During Charach's brief interview with the former security guard, Cesar admitted that, at the time of the Kennedy murder, he had been a 1968 supporter of George Wallace who hated the Kennedys and was predicting a race war.

Cesar told Charach, "I definitely wouldn't have voted for Bobby Kennedy. His brother John sold us down the river. He literally gave it [the country] to the Commies, the minorities, the blacks. . . . I voted for George Wallace's ideals."[97]

---

[95] The FBI again interviewed Cesar on June 15, 1968. Only a cursory outline of the interview exists.

[96] Charach, "Why Sirhan Could Not Have Killed Robert F. Kennedy: Part 1," *Knave*, March 1976.

[97] Charach, "Why Sirhan Could Not Have Killed Robert F. Kennedy: Part 2," *Knave*, April 1976.

When Charach asked him whether he fired his gun, Cesar insisted that he did not.

Charach has stated that he commissioned a voice stress test, using his taped interview with Cesar. According to Charach, the test revealed that "Cesar was far from telling the whole truth" when asked whether he had fired his gun in the kitchen pantry.[98]

Charach also learned that the H & R .22 revolver Cesar showed Sergeant O'Steen on June 24, 1968, had been sold three months after the Kennedy shooting to Jim Yoder, a friend of Cesar's, who had moved to Blue Mountain, Arkansas.

In a receipt for the sale that Yoder provided to Charach, Cesar misspelled Yoder's name. "On the day of Sept 6, 1968," Cesar wrote on the signed receipt, "I received $15.00 from Jim Yolder. The item involved is a H & R .22 pistol 9 shot serial No. Y13332." When contacted, Yoder told Charach that the gun had been stolen during a burglary in October 1969, the month of Charach's interview with Cesar. The gun had not been recovered.[99] Yoder also said to Charach that Cesar had allegedly told him that he was in trouble because of that revolver.[100]

In the wake of the 1971 litigation that challenged the competence of DeWayne Wolfer—as well as of Charach's revelations about the security guard—the LAPD contacted Cesar and asked for another official interview, to which he agreed. This interview took place in the district attorney's office in downtown Los Angeles on July 14, 1971.

According to the official transcript of the meeting, there was a discussion about the .38 Rohm revolver Cesar reportedly had in his holster on the night of the shooting. After some preliminary ques-

---

[98] Ibid.

[99] LAPD investigator Gordon McDevitt, a former member of SUS, interviewed Deputy Penn Smith of the Logan County Sheriff's Department in Arkansas, on December 24, 1974. Smith told McDevitt that all sheriff's department records had been "purged" from the files prior to January 1973 by the previous sheriff, who left office that month. "There was nothing in the office but paint," Smith said.

[100] Charach and French journalist Gerard Alcan co-produced the 1973 film *The Second Gun*, about the Robert Kennedy murder case, which was screened by the American Academy of Forensic Sciences, prompting the academy's own investigation of the killing. American Films, Ltd., released the film; National General distributed it. Clearly, Charach portrays Cesar as the top suspect in the murder.

tioning, he was then asked whether he owned any other handguns. "Yeah," Cesar replied, "I owned a .22 pistol at one time."

"How long ago was this?" a police officer asked.

"Oh, it's been over two years ago. I—a friend of mine working at Lockheed retired and moved to Arkansas. He asked me if I had any handguns. He wanted one for his house, so I sold it to him."

"How long ago did you sell it?"

"Oh, it's been—well, he retired in February '68, I think. Yes, '68, somewhere around in that period of time."

As he had done three years earlier for Sergeant O'Steen, Cesar identified the gun as an H & R nine-shot .22 revolver with a two-inch barrel. Cesar said that he had originally purchased the gun from a friend in 1961 and used it exclusively for home protection. Cesar identified Jim Yoder as the man to whom he had sold the gun, and he gave the police his address.

Cesar then referred to the fact that he had mentioned the .22 when he was interviewed by the police sergeant. "Did you own that .22 on the night of the Kennedy assassination?" a police officer asked.

"No," Cesar replied.

"Well, how did you show it [the H & R .22] to the sergeant the night he came out to interview you?"

"No, I didn't. That's what I said. I just told him about it, and I wanted, you know, I was telling him what it was. I wanted to show it to him, you know, what kind of gun it was."

"But you didn't have it available that night—"

"No."

"—to show it to him?"

"No, no. In fact, I don't remember whether Jim [Yoder] had left the state or not for Arkansas, but I had already sold it to him for [$15.00]."

Cesar had been either grossly mistaken or less than truthful with the police. He had sold the gun to Yoder three months *after* the murder, not several months before. And he had clearly shown his .22 to Sergeant O'Steen on June 24, 1968. But law enforcement authorities accepted Cesar's account. When Los Angeles district attorney Joseph Busch was questioned by reporters about Cesar's .22, he told them that it had been sold *prior* to Kennedy's murder.

At the end of the July 1971 interview with Cesar, a deputy district attorney asked him if he would agree to take a polygraph test.

Cesar calmly replied, "Anytime you want me to come down. I don't have anything to hide."

For reasons unknown, no law enforcement agency took Cesar up on his offer.

15. *The Ward Hearing*

Further complications in the Kennedy murder case resulted from the release of the March 9, 1973, affidavit executed by Dr. Eduard Simson, a clinical psychologist, who had worked with inmates at San Quentin. "During the summer of 1969," Simson stated, "I interviewed and tested extensively and repeatedly during approximately twenty weekly visits, one particular inmate on Death Row, Sirhan Sirhan."

Simson went on the criticize the psychologists working with Sirhan's defense team, specifically Dr. Bernard Diamond and Dr. Martin Schorr. Simson wrote, "Reading and studying carefully the transcript of Sirhan's trial, there is a dominant impression that the psychiatric-psychological team, largely made up of Jewish doctors, pooled their efforts to prove that Sirhan, the hated Arab, was guilty and insane, a paranoid schizophrenic. Subsequent studies I have done in a more neutral, trusting relationship at San Quentin clearly point out the simple truth: *Sirhan is not and was never a paranoid schizophrenic.* The jury was fed pooled information, the main author of the defense strategy being Dr. Diamond. . . . [Sirhan] was the center of a drama, the true center of which probably still lies very much concealed and unknown to the general public. Was he merely a double, a stand-in, sent there to draw attention? Was he at the scene to replace someone else? Did he actually kill Robert Kennedy? Whatever the full truth of the Robert F. Kennedy assassination might be, it still remains locked in Sirhan's mind and in other, still anonymous minds."

Appearing to challenge Sirhan's guilty verdict, Simson zeroed in on the prosecution's explanation of motive, which relied on Sirhan's notebooks, in which he repeated over and over that "R.F.K. must die!" Simson stated, "The handwriting of Sirhan in his notebooks [differs], often drastically, from the handwriting on numerous test materials I obtained from Sirhan at San Quentin. Whether someone else wrote the notebooks or whether they were written under some special influence, such as hypnosis, is entirely unsolved. If someone hypnotized him when the notebooks were written, who was it? Unfortunately, the defense failed to bring in a handwriting expert. . . .

"At no time did Sirhan offer the admission that he wrote the notebooks; yet the notebooks were one of the most important parts of evidence leading to his conviction. Sirhan rejected and disowned the notebooks. . . . I strongly suspect the notebooks are a forgery, for the thinking reflected in them is foreign to the Sirhan I carefully studied."

Concluding his affidavit, which clearly implied that Sirhan did not receive a fair trial, Simson again criticized Sirhan's psychological team: "Most of the doctors testifying saw their role in proving why Sirhan killed Kennedy. . . . They failed to consider the real facts in a more objective light and failed to consider the possibility clearly suggested by the ballistic testimony and Sirhan's own testimony under close scrutiny that perhaps Sirhan did not kill Robert F. Kennedy."

Simson stated that he had wanted to "unlock" Sirhan's mind. However, his "visits with Sirhan were abruptly terminated by San Quentin's Associate Warden James Park."[101]

Because of the lingering doubts about the Kennedy murder case, Los Angeles county supervisor Baxter Ward, a former KHJ-TV news reporter who was elected to the board of supervisors in 1972, conducted a hearing about the firearms issues. As a journalist, Ward had run a three-month series of reports in 1971, highlighting the discrepancies in the Robert Kennedy murder case. Criminalist William Harper had convinced Ward that evidence existed to show that two guns might have been fired on the night of the shooting.

Like Harper, Ward, who had announced his candidacy for the governorship in February 1974, targeted Wolfer's work. He declared that he would hold a hearing about the crime scene evidence in the case on May 13, 1974.

However, with the support of LAPD chief of police Ed Davis, Wolfer refused to cooperate or to testify. District Attorney Joseph Busch—with whom Ward clashed during his 1971 series of reports—also refused to appear, charging that Ward was using the Kennedy case as a forum to promote his campaign for governor.

Actually, Busch was livid over the Ward hearing. On June 10, 1974, he fired off a lengthy letter to Peter F. Schabarum, another member of the Los Angeles County Board of Supervisors. Busch stated, "I can illustrate to you how any person motivated to create the illusion of the possibility of a second gun could have succeeded in such a mission.

"The obvious starting point is to create a conflict between eyewitness accounts and physical evidence regarding muzzle distance. Whenever a number of persons see an event, it is axiomatic that there

---

[101] On September 24, 1969, San Quentin associate warden James W. L. Park wrote a letter to Dr. D. G. Schmidt, the prison's chief psychiatrist, saying, "I am concerned that Dr. Simson appears to be making a career out of seeing Sirhan. I think contact should be limited to those strictly necessary to accomplish the official purpose of psychiatric examination and should not be grossly in excess of the services offered other Condemned prisoners."

After Simon's visits with Sirhan were stopped, Simson met with criminalist William Harper, who encouraged him to get involved in the case.

will be different accounts in regard to different details. . . . The next step for anyone who seeks to raise questions would be to point out what the prosecution failed to do with respect to its investigations of the physical evidence relating to the number of guns involved. Although such a technique may have the purpose of disclosing ineptitude, it is also consistent with unnecessarily raising questions when no questions in fact exist."

But Busch was wrong. Serious questions did exist, mostly because of continued secrecy concerning the LAPD's investigation of the murder case. And Baxter Ward was demanding some answers, calling an impressive list of witnesses to provide them.

Among others, firearms identification experts Professor Herbert L. MacDonell and Lowell W. Bradford, as well as Los Angeles county coroner Thomas Noguchi, testified at the Ward hearing. MacDonell was the director of the Laboratory of Forensic Science, in Corning, New York; Bradford had headed the Santa Clara County Laboratory of Criminalistics, in San Jose, California. Noguchi, of course, had conducted the highly praised autopsy on Senator Kennedy.

William Harper could not appear at the Ward hearing. But in a sworn affidavit, he again, flat-out, insisted that the bullets that struck Kennedy and the other victims could not all have been fired from the same gun.[102]

Seeming to confirm Harper's finding that the Kennedy neck bullet (Exhibit 47) and the Weisel bullet (Exhibit 54) could not have been fired from the same gun, MacDonell, who used Harper's original photomicrographs,[103] said in an affidavit that the bullet removed from Kennedy's neck could not have come from Sirhan's revolver.

MacDonell's conclusion was derived primarily from his analysis of the cannelures—the concentric rings formed on a bullet's surface and running around its circumference—on the bullets recovered from

---

[102] Harper had also maintained that the rifling angles of the bullets that hit Kennedy and Weisel differed by twenty-three "minutes." The rifling of a gun barrel, according to firearms experts, causes the bullets' spin and raised grooves as they are fired through the barrel of a gun. The steepness of the grooves is the rifling angle. The same gun should produce the same rifling angles.

[103] Another set of photomicrographs, using the Hycon Balliscan camera, was authorized for the Ward hearing.

Kennedy and Weisel. MacDonell determined that the Weisel bullet had two cannelures, while the Kennedy bullet had only one.

MacDonell also discovered that the empty shell casings taken from Sirhan's gun were manufactured by the Cascade Cartridge Company of Lewiston, Idaho—which had *never* made bullets with only one cannelure. Thus, he claimed, the bullet that struck Kennedy could not have come from Sirhan's gun.

The LAPD responded that the number of cannelures is not universally accepted as scientific evidence, because they can be "erased" during routine firings. MacDonell replied that if Sirhan's gun erased one of the cannelures on the Kennedy bullet, then the same gun should have done the same with the Weisel bullet.

When asked during his testimony whether he was claiming, as he had stated in his affidavit, that the bullets were *not* fired by the same gun, MacDonell replied, "I am suggesting that they were not fired from the same gun based upon the photographic evidence."

Although firearms examiner Lowell Bradford said during his testimony that he could not match the Kennedy neck bullet and Weisel bullet either—on the basis of Harper's photographs—he did not go as far as MacDonell in claiming that they could not have come from the same gun. Instead, Bradford advocated a refiring of Sirhan's gun to lay all controversies to rest.

Dr. Vincent P. Guinn, a Harvard-trained chemist who was a professor at the University of California at Irvine, also testified at the Ward hearing. Guinn stated that two days after the Kennedy shooting, he had been contacted by Noguchi, who asked him to conduct a neutron activation analysis of the crime scene bullets. The analysis, Guinn explained, could determine whether all of the bullets came from the same "batch" of ammunition. However, just before Guinn's analysis began, Noguchi said that he was contacted by Wolfer, who stopped it. Wolfer said that he feared that the analysis might be inconclusive and, thus, complicate matters. Noguchi yielded to Wolfer's judgment.

Noguchi, Ward's final witness, became the star of the hearing. His testimony rocked not only Wolfer and the LAPD but the district attorney's office as well, by acknowledging other "clerical errors" in the handling of the physical evidence in the Kennedy case. First, he expressed his regret at not having challenged Wolfer's 1968 decision not to conduct a neutron activation analysis.

And then, with the aid of charts and diagrams, Noguchi revealed that the LAPD never had a single credible eyewitness who could testify that Sirhan shot Senator Kennedy from point-blank range, a foot or less away.

Also, Noguchi used the Ward hearing to reveal the incident involving the deputy district attorney who gingerly approached him during a recess at the June 7, 1968, grand jury hearing and asked him to reconsider his testimony about the distance from the muzzle of Sirhan's revolver to Senator Kennedy's head. Noguchi still stuck to his findings that the shots fired were from contact or near-contact range, which were based on his very thorough autopsy and even confirmed by the LAPD's own muzzle distance tests.

However, Noguchi also admitted that he had committed a glaring error. Firearms identification demonstrated that the bullets fired from Sirhan's Iver Johnson had six grooves. During the autopsy, Noguchi removed the Kennedy neck bullet and examined it. During this examination, Noguchi mistakenly counted five, not six, grooves on the bullet and noted this on the evidence envelope.

Of course, this mistake, left uncorrected, could have led a reasonable person to speculate that at least one bullet that hit Senator Kennedy was not fired from Sirhan's gun—since the other analyzed bullets had six grooves.

In a June 6, 1974, memorandum to Busch, Deputy District Attorney Dinko J. Bozanich grudgingly conceded, "The testimony of Noguchi before Ward regarding the wounds sustained by Kennedy, including opinions regarding cause of death, muzzle distance, and paths of the various gunshot wounds, was the same as his testimony in *People v. Sirhan*. But Noguchi also testified before Ward to certain matters never elicited in *People v. Sirhan*. . . . The corollary of such hypothesis is that the District Attorney has been either derelict in investigation or engaged in a 'cover up' since Ward's prospective findings establish such a conflict still exists."

This battle between Noguchi and the Los Angeles law enforcement community was not the first. Beginning in August 1968, two months after the Kennedy murder, Noguchi became the target of a variety of attacks. These ranged from charges of assorted minor "deficiencies" to a bizarre and unfounded charge that he had gleefully exclaimed while Kennedy lay dying in Good Samaritan Hospital, "I hope he dies, because if he dies, then my international reputation will be established!"

Three days before Noguchi's scheduled February 26, 1969, testimony at Sirhan's trial—which would include his anticipated discussion of the controversial muzzle distance problems—a rumor sped around Los Angeles that Noguchi would be facing a dismissal hearing before the Los Angeles County Board of Supervisors. Despite the obvious pressure being applied to Noguchi, he nevertheless testified at Sirhan's trial. His testimony included the statement "When I said 'very close,' we are talking about the term of either contact or a half-inch or one inch in distance [from Kennedy's right ear]." However, when Grant Cooper had the opportunity to zero in on this problem, he relented, telling Noguchi he didn't want the "gory details."

On March 4, Noguchi received a suspension from the board of supervisors; he was fired two weeks later. With other charges piling up, Noguchi was charged with "erratic behavior" during the Kennedy autopsy, specifically that he had "danced" around Kennedy's body. He had also been charged with illegally using drugs. All of these charges were groundless.

Instead of capitulating to the growing list of false charges, Noguchi decided to fight them. In July, the Los Angeles County Civil Service Commission, which had conducted a thorough investigation of the matter, cleared Noguchi of all charges and reinstated him as county coroner.

Noguchi says, "Some people believe that the problems I had resulted from my work on the Kennedy case. One of the charges was that the Kennedy autopsy was 'botched up.' The first thing they did was withdraw that particular charge. There were sixty-four charges in all. They were prepared to show a shock value. They didn't expect me to fight back. And I was fully vindicated in the end."[104]

[104] Noguchi also told me that his difficulties apparently stemmed from charges filed by an informer in his office. "He was hired with the understanding that he was a licensed physician. Somehow, he felt that he needed to testify about some things.

Godfrey Isaac represented Noguchi during his battle; Isaac later became Sirhan's attorney. Both Noguchi and Isaac had cheered Baxter Ward's investigation on.

But not everyone outside of the LAPD and the district attorney's office welcomed Ward's actions. Three days after the May 13 hearing, the *Los Angeles Times* published an editorial, "A Strange and Ghoulish Inquiry," attacking Ward's probe. "Ward's ghoulish revival of the Kennedy assassination is gaining national attention, which he may think will help his campaign for the Democratic gubernatorial nomination," the *Times* wrote. "But any serious reopening of the inquiry belongs not before the Board of Supervisors, but in the courts, where the responsibility properly lies."

In a letter to the *Times,* published on May 30, District Attorney Busch agreed with the editorial: "[I]f any new evidence exists, it should be presented to the courts in a full hearing under rules of legal evidence, not before a public hearing chaired by a political candidate who is neither judge nor attorney. . . . Ward's attempt to capitalize politically on a national tragedy smacks of cheap sensationalism."

Perhaps prompted by such attacks, Ward on June 18 proposed to the five-member Los Angeles County Board of Supervisors that the body petition the district attorney to request the court to order a refiring of Sirhan's weapon by an independent firearms panel. However, the motion, fiercely resisted by Busch and the LAPD, failed. That same month, Ward also lost his party's nomination for governor.

With the Ward hearing seemingly disposed of, the LAPD, the Los Angeles District Attorney's Office, and the California Attorney General's Office specifically blamed William Harper for the renewed interest in reopening the Kennedy murder case. As part of the effort to discredit him, a "confidential" probe of his background showed that

---

I don't know why he did it. When I returned, I made sure that every physician was licensed. We ran a check on him, and he was the only one who wasn't licensed. He claimed to have been a graduate of the University of London. He attended the school but did not complete his studies and did not receive a degree."

he had misrepresented his educational and work experiences.[105]

Further, according to the investigation, Harper had claimed under oath during the 1967 Jack Kirschke murder case—in which he served as an expert witness for the defense—that he "took charge of the police laboratory for the Pasadena Police . . . [for] seven years." However, the prosecutor during the trial never brought out the fact that Harper had merely served "as an advisor to that department's Records and Fingerprint Section" from June 1935 to October 1939 and then "signed a contract with the City of Pasadena to act in a traffic advisory capacity for the Pasadena Police Department. . . . Letters written by the Chief of Police of Pasadena during the tenure of subject's contract refer to him as 'our traffic engineer.' "

The investigation of Harper continued, "Subject's contract with the City of Pasadena did not prohibit his doing outside work which enabled him to become a 'self made expert.' He did in fact testify in many criminal cases on behalf of the prosecution while under contract . . . and apparently no one investigated his qualifications to any great degree."

The probe concluded "that criminalists with recognized qualifications do not consider subject to be one of their peers. The consensus of opinion in this field is that subject is a 'tire skid mark' and 'broken glass' expert as a result of his 'evaluating and equating' evidence in traffic accident cases."

Adding more doubts about the seventy-one-year-old Harper, the *Washington Post* published an article about the Robert Kennedy murder case on December 19, 1974. The story, by staff reporter Ronald Kessler, who interviewed Harper, stated, "The nationally recognized ballistics expert whose claim gave rise to a theory that Robert F.

---

[105] According to the investigation, Harper's claim "that he has completed certain technical training at U.S.C., U.C.L.A., California Institute of Technology" was contradicted. Records at the University of Southern California indicated that Harper had never even been enrolled at the school. Although Harper studied mathematics and physics at UCLA for two years and at Caltech for two years, and did physics research at Caltech for two additional years, he never received a degree from either UCLA or Caltech.

Harper's detractors based this information on a May 17, 1955, letter from Harvey M. French, special agent for the National Board of Fire Underwriters, to a colleague, Special Agent R. Bruce Ryder.

Kennedy was not killed by Sirhan Bishara Sirhan this week admitted that there is no evidence to support his contention."

Kessler quoted Harper as saying that his 1970 affidavit had been prepared on behalf of Sirhan's attorney. "I didn't think he would do anything with it. . . . I didn't have any plans to have it publicized. It was supposed to be held in confidence."

Despite Harper's insistence that he did not make any statements to Kessler that could even be interpreted as repudiating his long-standing position on the case—that Sirhan did not shoot Kennedy—the *Post* refused to give Harper the space to rebut the article.[106]

Nevertheless, the *Post* continued to tout Kessler's story. In the April 24, 1975, issue of *Rolling Stone*, Ben Bradlee, the executive editor of the *Post*, told a reporter, "Ron Kessler did a recent story knocking down the second gun theory in the Robert Kennedy assassination and nuts from both coasts were all over me. Letters, telegrams, phone calls, personal visits. I've been up to my ass in lunatics."[107]

However, on May 20, the *Post* did publish a letter from Lester S. Hyman, a close friend of Senator Kennedy, who protested the newspaper's entire handling of the Kennedy investigation, especially its treatment of Harper. Hyman wrote, "I have been troubled by the fact that immediately after a *Post* reporter wrote that William Harper had backed down on his affidavit that the bullets probably came from

---

[106] The article also stated that Vincent DiPierro had again changed his version of the events. DiPierro, according to Kessler, was now saying that Sirhan had "lunged" forward at Kennedy, managing to fire at the senator's head at point-blank range. This was contrary to what DiPierro had said during his earlier grand jury testimony. There, he stated that Sirhan "looked like he was on his tiptoes because he wasn't that tall." In that testimony, DiPierro mentioned nothing about Sirhan's lunging.

[107] On June 6, 1976, the eighth anniversary of Robert Kennedy's death, actor Robert Vaughn, a Kennedy friend and supporter, challenged Bradlee during their appearance on the "Merv Griffin Show." "There were many bullets in excess of the eight in Sirhan's gun found at the scene of the crime," Vaughn argued. "Why aren't these questions being answered? I do not know. We have endeavored to work with the *Washington Post* on this on a number of occasions."

Griffin turned to Bradlee and asked, "Why won't you work on it?"

Bradlee replied to Vaughn, "Well, we have worked on it. Every time we've worked on it, it breaks down in the most fantastic personality fights with people that I've ever seen. And, I mean, you are the first person who appears to be absolutely calm about this."

different guns, Mr. Harper wrote to the *Post* and vehemently denied that he had in any way changed his position; yet nothing has been done to bring Mr. Harper's denial to the attention of your readers."

Regarding the handling of the Kennedy murder case by Wolfer, Dave Butler, another LAPD/SID firearms expert and one of Wolfer's strongest defenders, says, "I know there's been criticism of the way the evidence was handled—but that criticism was coming from people that have probably never been in a major crime scene—and had all of the weight of all of the responsibility of that crime scene on his shoulders. The manual of the department gives exclusive authority to the technician. It gives us sole jurisdiction to exceed the chief of police. And that is an awesome responsibility, because if you do something wrong, it's going to affect the whole investigation.

"Witnesses lie, witnesses can't remember, witnesses are [biased] by prejudice—but physical evidence is not. That's as close to pure as you can get. Of course, the fault comes with the interpretation. The collection, the preservation, and the interpretation of that evidence. That's a subjective analysis. And that's where the problem comes in; and that's where the dispute between various examiners and experts arise on these issues. But, as to his handling of it, I don't think that I could have done any better. And I don't know of anybody else that would've done things differently or better."

16. *The Schrade-Lowenstein Initiatives*

Regardless of the debate over Wolfer's performance and the setbacks suffered by those who wanted to reopen the case, the controversy over the LAPD's investigation of the Robert Kennedy murder case continued to gain momentum. It did so in a political, social, and cultural climate infected by the distrust and disillusionment created by the Vietnam War, Watergate, and the secret wars of the CIA and the FBI.

On December 15, 1974, former Kennedy aide Paul Schrade, wounded on the night of the shooting, and former New York congressman Allard K. Lowenstein held a press conference in New York to demand a reopening of the Robert Kennedy murder case.

Lowenstein had first become concerned about the discrepancies in the case during a trip to Los Angeles in 1973, just after being revealed as a member of President Richard Nixon's notorious "enemies list."[108] Paul Schrade explains, "Lowenstein got directly involved after talking to Robert Vaughn, the actor. Vaughn was a real zealot on this case."

Interested in the claims presented to him by Vaughn and other critics, Lowenstein, then a private attorney, had a series of meetings with Los Angeles law enforcement officials. He was startled by the misstatements and evasions by LAPD and district attorney officials when they were confronted with fundamental questions about the Kennedy investigation. To clarify matters, Lowenstein and Schrade submitted a list of questions about the Kennedy shooting and proposed evidence tests to LAPD chief Edward Davis, who appeared, at first, to be receptive and promised to reply to their concerns.

Among these were the whereabouts and condition of the following: "Ceiling tiles with bullet holes to determine their location in the pantry and the angle of entry and exit of the bullets . . . [and] the divider between the swinging doors and the two boards taken from the door frame."

Lowenstein and Schrade never received a reply to any of their questions.[109]

Schrade explains, "Lowenstein convinced me that getting involved was the responsible thing to do. I became part of the planning operation after reading a lot of materials, talking to him, talking to Lillian Castellano [who had co-written the May 1969 article in the *Los*

[108] A Yale Law School graduate, Lowenstein had been elected to Congress from the Fifth District, on Long Island, in 1968. He was defeated for reelection in 1970 after the gerrymandering of his district.

[109] The LAPD later revealed that within a week after the Lowenstein-Schrade press conference on December 15, 1974, the LAPD had compiled a secret seventy-six-page internal memorandum in response to Lowenstein's questions. But the LAPD never released it.

According to the LAPD's cover sheet, the anonymous author wrote, "This separate addenda contains confidential information relative to the questions submitted by Allard Lowenstein. The information has not been revealed prior to this report and may conflict with previous statements made by the Chief of Police and other officials.

"Serious consideration should be given to the release of this information."

Angeles Free Press], and talking to my wife. I agonized over the decision, but I decided that he was right. I jumped in."

A protégé of UAW president Walter Reuther, the tall and distinguished-looking Schrade became politically active while at Yale. He left college in 1947 and went to work for North American Aviation in Los Angeles. Later, deeply involved in UAW politics, he became a top assistant to Reuther in Detroit.

An anti–Vietnam War activist who had also marched with Martin Luther King, Schrade became an articulate spokesman for a variety of social causes, ranging from justice for the United Farm Workers Union to work with the ACLU and to organizing community unions in Watts and East Los Angeles. A friend of both John and Robert Kennedy, Schrade continued to work hard to promote their idealism and programs. And Robert Kennedy recognized Schrade's sincerity. In fact, as he lay on the floor of the kitchen pantry after being shot three times, Robert Kennedy, according to United Press International, quietly asked, "Is everybody okay? Is Paul all right?"

After the murder of Bob Kennedy, Schrade's life changed. "I had a very difficult time dealing with it for a long time," Schrade says painfully. "I was off work for three months and only part-time for another three. The head wound was patched up, but I had a bad case of whiplash. I had nightmares for months and months about it. Even though I was treated very well by a lot of people, most of them viewed me as a relic of that event. Then I had to decide what my future was going to be in the union. Since the shooting, my commitment had increased. I felt that much more strongly about the issues I was involved in. Knowing that anyone could die at any moment, I thought I might as well do what I had to do now."

However, after Reuther's tragic death in a 1970 plane crash, Schrade lost his political base and, in 1972, his UAW executive board seat. Nevertheless, he remained a committed activist.

In their joint statement to the media in December 1974, Schrade and Lowenstein said, "We offer no answers today—only questions. . . . The circumstances of the Robert Kennedy assassination must be re-examined by disinterested, qualified people if doubts raised by the hard evidence are ever to be resolved."[110] Though noting the existence of other issues in the case, Lowenstein and Schrade focused primarily on concrete and testable questions concerning the crime scene evidence, such as Sirhan's gun.

The day after the Schrade-Loweinstein press conference, Los Angeles district attorney Joe Busch held one of his own, at which he insisted, "In my mind, the refiring of the Sirhan gun would serve no useful purpose, and, in fact, the physical integrity of both the gun and the original bullets is now in question due to the lax handling by the Los Angeles County Clerk's Office and the access by unauthorized persons to these exhibits."

Clearly, Busch feared that an inability to match Sirhan's gun with the bullets recovered from the bodies of Kennedy and the other victims would create more speculation about a "second gunman" at the crime scene.

On a live broadcast on NBC's "Tomorrow" show four days after the press conference, Lowenstein confronted Busch with the evidence of two guns at the scene. Responding to the issue of possible extra bullets, Busch asserted, "There were eight bullets fired, seven recovered, and there were never any more shots fired. That's the fact. . . . Mr. Lowenstein will not accept the fact that that is what was established."

Host Tom Snyder then asked about the eyewitness statements regarding muzzle distance. He specifically mentioned that no one could place Sirhan's gun closer than a foot and a half away from Kennedy.

"Well, that's not true," Busch replied. "It was point-blank, right into the right ear of the Senator. The gun was right there. The bullet that killed him entered right there, and we can show it."

Lowenstein shot back, "Now who has said that they saw it? Just name one witness that said they saw a gun, point-blank, fired into Senator Kennedy's ear. . . ."

---

[110] Schrade and three of the other shooting victims—Ira Goldstein, Irwin Stroll, and William Weisel—also issued a separate joint statement: "Four of us who were wounded during the assassination of Robert Kennedy have become convinced of the need [for] a new investigation of this case. Until now, we have strongly resisted all efforts to question the obvious and official version that Kennedy's death and our wounds involved only one gunman."

Busch countered erroneously, "Would you like Mr. Uecker, the man that grabbed [Sirhan's] arm? Would you like any of the fifty-five [*sic*] witnesses . . . ?"[111]

Busch refused to concede that Uecker had said precisely the opposite.

Once again, the *Los Angeles Times* was quick to the punch, attacking Lowenstein and Schrade's effort to reopen the case. In a December 19 editorial, the *Times* wrote, "The evidence [they] presented is wispy and consists mainly of repetition of facts long known—disagreement over some ballistics tests, the citing of some discrepancies in the [statements] of witnesses and an old allegation that while Sirhan's gun held only eight bullets, more than eight bullets were fired, an assertion long since discounted by authorities."

Fueled by national news coverage—including a surprisingly sympathetic April 20, 1975, hearing on William F. Buckley's "Firing Line"—the effort to reexamine the basic crime scene evidence in the case began to gather steam.[112]

However, the Los Angeles District Attorney's Office continued to oppose new firearms or other tests, insisting that a legitimate reinquiry into the issues raised in the Kennedy murder case could properly be held only in a legal forum. "That's where you try a lawsuit: in court," said Assistant District Attorney John Howard. "You can't try it with Buckley."

On July 13, the *Los Angeles Times* published another long defense of the official version of the Robert Kennedy assassination. The story was written by William Farr and John Kendall. Accepting the LAPD's

[111] In the midst of the seemingly endless battles over the Kennedy case, Joe Busch died in his sleep on June 27, 1975, after suffering a heart attack. He was forty-nine.

The Los Angeles County Board of Supervisors selected John Van de Kamp to succeed Busch as DA. John Howard served during the interim; Howard assigned Deputy District Attorney Dinko Bozanich the task of handling the continuing controversy over the Kennedy case.

[112] Sirhan's attorneys followed these activities closely. They had filed a writ of habeas corpus and a writ of error *coram nobis* with the California State Supreme Court in January 1975, claiming that existing firearms evidence demonstrated that at least two guns were fired at the crime scene. However, the court rejected these writs the following month.

and DA's office's explanations right down the line for nearly every controversy, the reporters asked, "So what, authorities may well ask now, are media types, conspiracy buffs and publicity seekers talking about? It's simply ridiculous to say that anyone but Sirhan was firing in that pantry."

On the day of the *Times* article, Robert J. Joling, the president of the American Academy of Forensic Sciences, announced the conclusion of the academy's executive committee that "a reexamination of the physical evidence in the case would provide additional information which could be of value in clarifying the circumstances of the death of Robert F. Kennedy."[113]

Together, Lowenstein and Schrade concluded that the only way to get serious answers to the unresolved issues in the case was to file suit in order to air their concerns, hoping to use the court as a means of investigation and discovery.

On August 4, 1975, Schrade, whom no one could accuse of playing politics with the murder of Robert Kennedy, filed the first of two lawsuits. Schrade recalls, "First, I filed suit against Sirhan and fifty John Does.[114] It was a personal injury suit. By suing Sirhan and any others who may have been involved—which was part of our legal strategy—we were trying to get at any new information we could. The second suit was under the Public Records Act of California. We were specifically after the evidence files that were held by the Los Angeles Police Department: all of the evidence not used in the trial. We also wanted a panel of firearms experts to refire Sirhan's gun and reexamine the firearms evidence."[115]

---

[113] The American Academy of Forensic Sciences had become interested in the Robert Kennedy murder case after receiving a private screening of Ted Charach's documentary *The Second Gun.*

[114] Schrade's principal attorneys were Geoffrey Cowan, Mel Levine, and Leonard Unger, all of Los Angeles.

[115] Meantime, in February 1975, Congressman Henry Gonzalez (Democrat of Texas) and thirty-nine cosponsors introduced a resolution in the U.S. House of Representatives, calling for a reopening of the John Kennedy, Martin Luther King, and Robert Kennedy murder cases. Soon afterward, a modified resolution passed, and the U.S. House Select Committee on Assassinations was created. Later, however, because of budgetary problems, the committee dropped its plans to reopen the Robert Kennedy murder investigation.

Filing its own petition with the court, CBS News joined Schrade in his demand to resolve the firearms issues in the case, including a refiring of Sirhan's gun.[116] CBS claimed—through its firearms expert, Lowell Bradford—that the firearms evidence in the case had never been challenged at Sirhan's trial. Specifically, Bradford charged that within "the public record, there [are] no examiner's notes, no pretrial discovery information, no demonstrative exhibits, no explanation of the exact examination methodology used in the case, no statement of the basis for the opinions rendered that give an indication of identification."

Meantime, internal LAPD data about its investigation of the Robert Kennedy murder case started to leak out of the department in the form of a LAPD property disposition card dated June 27, 1969—which was less than three weeks after Evelle Younger, the district attorney at the time, had pledged to release the case file. The disposition card noted that SUS had destroyed pieces of wood from the door frames and the ceiling insulation recovered from the Kennedy crime scene![117]

News of the disposal of these items taken from the crime scene immediately became a national story. Attempting to explain the destruction, Dion Morrow, a spokesman for the Los Angeles City Attorney's Office said, "There was no place to keep them. You can't fit ceiling panels into a card file."

---

[116] In a September 22, 1975, letter to Sam Williams, the president of the Board of Police Commissioners, CBS News producer Lee Townsend asked for answers to fourteen principal questions and follow-ups. Several were specifically about the known movements of security guard Thane Eugene Cesar.

On January 5, 1976, CBS News aired part 4 of its four-part series "The American Assassins," co-produced by Townsend and reported by correspondent Dan Rather, which, in part, examined the issues in the Robert Kennedy murder case.

During this broadcast, Rather discussed Cesar in some detail, raising suspicions about his actions, dispelling them, raising them again, and then dispelling them again.

Also, Sirhan agreed to be interviewed by Rather but denied him authorization to record the interview.

[117] The destruction occurred a month after Lillian Castellano and Floyd Nelson's article in the *Los Angeles Free Press,* alleging the presence of extra bullets in the center divider.

Because of the news of the destruction of evidence, the Los Angeles City Council summoned Assistant Police Chief Daryl Gates to provide the LAPD's explanation. Gates acknowledged that the materials had been destroyed, but he was unrepentant, stating that the piece of wood and ceiling tiles "proved absolutely nothing." When asked whether the SID had made X rays of the door frames before they were destroyed, Gates replied that X rays had been made. However, he added, "The records of the X rays and the X rays themselves are not in existence."

California attorney general Evelle Younger's response was to argue against a motion to restudy the crime scene filed by Schrade in his civil suit. Younger's brief characterized ceiling panels and door frames as "crucial." It went on to say, "Without these items, it will be impossible to compute angles of flight for a number of the bullets. Thus, it appears that petitioner Schrade is asking this court to embark on an exercise in futility."[118]

LAPD criminalist David Butler of the SID, who assisted Wolfer in the Kennedy case, explains, "I understand that a certain amount of the evidence had been destroyed. And that's a matter of routine. What happens is that when a case is adjudicated and the DA doesn't submit the evidence, it doesn't go into court evidence. It's the responsibility of the investigating officers to have that evidence disposed of.

"In other words, if it were your personal belongings and your family wanted them, they would be turned over to the next of kin. If it was an inanimate object, like a door jamb, stuff like that, we would have no knowledge of when the evidence was destroyed in the laboratory. It's a matter of routine, because you cannot physically hold all the evidence that the department takes in."

The SUS officer who signed the original June 28, 1968, LAPD property report, transferring the door panels and ceiling tiles to the SUS, as well as the June 27, 1969, "property disposition card,"

---

[118] In response to a similar statement, Vincent Bugliosi, who joined Schrade's legal team, later stated, "That reminds me of the story of the young man who murdered his parents and then begged the court for mercy because he was an orphan."

which authorized their destruction, was Thomas J. Miller.

Asked about the disposal of these items, Miller replies, "We determined through SID that the holes in those items were not bullet holes. So when it was time to dispose of them, we put a disposal card through."

When later asked about the destruction of the physical evidence from the crime scene, Robert Houghton, the LAPD's chief of detectives and the founder of Special Unit Senator, says angrily, "Do you want to grill me about the bullets supposedly imbedded in the door frames? I'm the one who said okay to the disposal—a year after the trial—as long as they had been screened by our lab officers. As far as I knew, those frames had been tested. None of the holes, I was told, were bullet holes. They asked me, 'Can we get rid of them because there is not enough room in that locker?' And I said yes. In hindsight, that's the one regret that I have. At the time, there was no controversy. The panels [and door frames] had no evidentiary value. I said that as long as the records were in the file that was good enough for me."

However, all of the records of these tests—if they ever existed—are also missing from the LAPD's files.

17. *The Firearms Panel*

fter considerable legal maneuvering, Paul Schrade's demand for a court-authorized, independent study by firearms examiners prevailed. On September 18, 1975, Judge
Robert A. Wenke ordered a refiring of Sirhan's gun, as well as a
reexamination of all bullet evidence by a seven-member panel of respected firearms experts.[119]

In its review, the firearms panel found that only three of the
original bullets recovered from the victims were in sufficiently good
condition for *conclusive* microscopic comparison—the Kennedy neck

[119] The seven firearms experts were Stanton O. Berg, Alfred A. Biasotti, Lowell
W. Bradford, Cortlandt Cunningham, Patrick Garland, Charles V. Morton, and
Ralph Turner.

bullet, the Weisel bullet, and the Goldstein bullet.[120] The others were too badly fragmented to be used for conclusive firearms identification analysis, which each expert would conduct with his own comparison microscope.

The panel's final report, which was signed by the examiners on October 4, 1975, documented a number of alleged errors by police criminalist Wolfer. For example, *none* of the seven examiners could confirm Wolfer's sworn testimony that three of the bullets recovered from the victims—including the one reportedly taken from Kennedy's neck—could be matched with Sirhan's gun. Some of the examiners determined that they could match the three victims' bullets with each other—that is, to show that they had come from "the same" gun. But whether that was Sirhan's gun, they could not say

[120] In order to assist the firearms examiners with their upcoming tests, DeWayne Wolfer was called to testify. Judge Wenke insisted that the purpose of Wolfer's appearance was "not to impeach or vindicate the witness." The only major surprise during his testimony was his revelation that he had taken his own photomicrograph, consisting of two separate negatives of the Kennedy neck bullet and a test bullet on June 6, 1968. (Actually, the firearms panel later determined that this photomicrograph was a comparison of the Kennedy neck and the Goldstein bullets. Wolfer produced the photograph during the hearing. Not even the district attorney's office had realized that this picture existed.)

According to the LAPD in an undated and never sent reply to written questions raised by Allard Lowenstein, "[T]here were no photomicrographs taken for comparison purposes. . . . Comparison photographs are not taken in Los Angeles Police Department cases. In this case photographs would not show an accurate representation of what a comparison is based upon. The District Attorney and Investigators were informed that unless they so desired there would be no comparison photographs."

However, a separate, undated LAPD report refers to Wolfer's photomicrograph and makes the same mistake as Wolfer in his testimony. The report states, "There exists a photograph of the Kennedy bullet and a test bullet taken through a comparison microscope showing one Land comparison. It is *not* intended to be a bullet striation identification comparison because the lighting and details of the bullet are not displayed in the proper position. . . .

"The existence of this photograph is believed to be unknown by anyone outside of this Department. It should be effective rebuttal evidence were this case ever to be retried. However, the release of this information at this time would be susceptible to criticism because lay people would in all probability have difficulty deciphering the photograph. The issue as to its not being revealed at an earlier time may further make its authenticity suspect, particularly to the avid, exact assassination buff."

conclusively.[121] This finding effectively overturned a basic pillar of the case against Sirhan.[122]

However, the examiners also found no proof that specifically supported the second-gun theory. They added that specific issues previously raised by firearms experts William Harper and Herbert MacDonell—especially regarding the number of cannelures on the victim bullets—had been discredited. The analyzed bullets viewed through a comparison microscope, not just through photomicrographs, showed conclusively that all of them—including the Kennedy neck bullet—had *two* cannelures.[123]

In other words, the firearms examiners had three bullets that matched each other, but no one knew for sure whose gun they came from.

Even though the evidence was *inconclusive,* the statement that there was no *conclusive* proof of a second gunman was immediately seized upon by the LAPD, the district attorney's office, and, surprisingly, the national press, as a vindication of the original police investigation.

---

[121] The panel specifically stated, "It cannot be concluded that Exhibits 47 [Kennedy neck], 52 [Goldstein], and 54 [Weisel] were fired from the Sirhan revolver. The reasons for this are that there are insufficient corresponding individual characteristics to make an identification. The poor reproducability [*sic*] of striae left on consecutively fired test bullets may be attributed to the following factors: a. barrel fouling; b. copper alloy coating; c. impact damage and distortion; d. cylinder alignment; e. possible loss of fine detail over intervening years."

[122] Another pillar was shaken: the examiners could not match any of the original test bullets reportedly fired on June 6, 1968, by the SID with the new test bullets fired by the 1975 panel from Sirhan's Iver Johnson H53725 or with any of the victims' bullets. Once again, this gave rise to speculation that the test bullets had been mistakenly fired by the H18602.

[123] The firearms panel also examined the bullets that mysteriously contained traces of wood, which were found in Sirhan's car on June 5, 1968. The experts concluded that these bullets had the same general characteristics as the analyzed bullets. However, no one could explain the traces of wood in the bullets, nor could anyone match them with any of the other bullets.

When asked why he would place spent slugs in his car, Sirhan told me, "Why would I do that?" Sirhan has no memory of doing this; thus, he said he has no idea of how the bits of wood got into the slugs.

Some critics have suggested that these slugs had actually been recovered from the door frames in the kitchen pantry and then placed in Sirhan's car. There is no evidence that this occurred, but the source of these traces of wood has never been determined.

The *Los Angeles Times* published yet another editorial, insisting that the panel had simply concluded that there was no second gun and calling for an end to all of the conspiracy nonsense. The *Times* stated on October 8, "Seven experts, all conducting separate studies of the ballistics evidence, have come up with an identical conclusion: There was no second gun in the assassination of Sen. Robert F. Kennedy in the pantry of the Ambassador Hotel on June 5, 1968. . . . That should put to rest, once and for all, the theory that Sirhan had an accomplice in the pantry and that Kennedy's murder was the culmination of a conspiracy."

The media's reaction to the firearms examiners' report prompted Lowell Bradford, one of the experts, to issue a statement on October 7. It noted, "The findings of the firearms examiners [are] being improperly interpreted by the news media:

"1. The examiners found that the Sirhan gun *cannot* be identified with the bullets from the crime scene.
"2. The firearms evidence does not in and of itself establish a basis for a two-gun proposition; likewise, this same proposition, on the basis of *other* evidence, is *not* precluded either.

"The other evidence is as follows:

"A. [Witnesses'] statements that another gun was being fired at the scene;
"B. Bullet pathways contradictory to a direction from which Sirhan was firing;
"C. Evidence of more than eight fired bullets. . . .

"The firearms examination simply closes one episode of evidence evaluation and should not constrain further efforts to resolve valid questions concerning the possibility of the firing of a second gun at the assassination scene."

When questioned in court, all of the examiners agreed with Bradford that the evidence of more than eight bullets merited further careful study. But that subject had been outside the panel's mandate.

Reacting to the mix-up over the firearms identification tests, Sergeant James MacArthur, a top official at the crime scene, observes,

"As I recall, yeah, there was something where they couldn't positively identify the bullets that were recovered as being fired from the same gun—in other words, from Sirhan's gun. If somebody goofed up, it was the SID."

Former Los Angeles prosecutor Vincent Bugliosi, the attorney who represented Schrade during the firearms panel's inquiry, explains, "With firearms identification, it's very common to get positive IDs between guns and their bullets. It's like fingerprints: the signature of a gun. When these guns are being manufactured, the barrels, etc., you can take one gun following the next, one rifle barrel following the next, and they are not identical, because they have these random marks, these striations. Same manufacturing company, two rifle barrels—they are different. So it's not uncommon for your firearms guys to give positive 100 percent IDs, as they do in fingerprints.

"During my cross-examination of the firearms experts, not one of them said that they could give a positive, 100 percent identification of the crime scene bullets matching up with the test-fired bullets.

"They test-fired Sirhan's gun into water tanks. They got those bullets and compared them with the evidence bullets under a comparison microscope. The experts said, we believe these evidence bullets came from Sirhan's gun, but we can't give you a positive identification. Why? There were some dissimilarities that they could not account for. The experts did say that three of the victim bullets were fired from the same gun.

"However, they also rebutted Wolfer, who wrote a report of a positive ID: that the bullets from the victims came from Sirhan's gun 'to the exclusion of all other weapons.'

"The seven experts said there was 'no evidence of a second gun based on what we've seen thus far.' Five of the seven recommended further examinations, such as ballistics studies. They could not exclude the existence of a second gun. This case cried out for a further ballistics examination, a study of the paths the bullets took in flight."

Although Bugliosi had no question of Sirhan's guilt, that did not necessarily preclude the involvement of others.

On December 4, 1975, in a petition to compel the testimony of witnesses and to examine public records, Bugliosi, on behalf of Schrade, wrote, "We might add that Thane Cesar, the guard from the Ace Guard Service who was employed by the Ambassador Hotel to guard Senator Kennedy on the evening in question was, by his own admission, to Senator Kennedy's right rear immediately prior to Senator Kennedy's being shot. The flight paths of the bullets entering Senator Kennedy's body and clothing were therefore compatible and consistent with the location of Mr. Cesar vis-a-vis Senator Kennedy.... Although Cesar was one of the most likely witnesses and/or suspects in the assassination of Senator Kennedy ... unbelievably, 1.) The District Attorney's Office never called him as a witness before the Grand Jury or at the trial, 2.) Although the Los Angeles Police Department saw fit to give a considerable number of polygraph tests in this case, they never gave Cesar such a test, and 3.) His gun was never test fired!

"Mr. Cesar literally vanished a few months ago and his present whereabouts are unknown."

18. *Bugliosi's Affidavits and the Kranz Report*

s a result of Paul Schrade's 1975 civil suit to open the
LAPD's case file on the Kennedy murder, several LAPD
photographs were released showing that the police had
photographed the same bullet holes shown in the John Clemente and
the AP photographs, which were revealed in 1969 by the *Los Angeles
Free Press*. In fact, the LAPD appeared to have taken the exact same
two pictures.

In a third LAPD photograph, Coroner Noguchi is shown pointing to apparent bullet holes in the center divider. In a fourth, he is
measuring the distance between two holes in the door frame. In an
affidavit dated December 1, 1975, Noguchi wrote, "I asked Mr.
Wolfer where he had found bullet holes at the scene. I forget what he

said, but when I asked him this question, he pointed, as I recall, to one hole in a ceiling panel above, and an indentation in the cement ceiling. He also pointed to several holes in the door frames of the [west] swinging doors leading into the pantry. I directed that photographs be taken of me pointing to these holes. I got the impression that a drill had been placed through the holes. I do not know whether or not these were bullet holes, but I got the distinct impression from him that he suspected that the holes may have been caused by bullets.

"If there are discrepancies as to the number of bullets fired in the pantry or the number of bullet holes, I would recommend, as I would do in any criminal case, further studies by an impartial panel of experts to resolve this matter."

The search for and documentation of bullet holes and extra bullets had suddenly become the focus of attempts to determine whether a second gun had been fired the night of the murder. The man behind the new evidence, such as the Noguchi affidavit, was Vincent Bugliosi.

Famous and respected for his prosecution of the Charles Manson case, Bugliosi, by then in private practice and acting on Paul Schrade's behalf, had sprung into action—first with his cross-examination of the firearms panel and then with an effort to find the police officers pictured in the AP photograph. Schrade explains, "Vince came in at a very crucial time after the experts had rendered their decision. We wanted to continue in court, raising questions about the seven experts' reports which were problematic. So we asked Vince to get involved in this case and question the firearms experts in court."

Bugliosi explains his subsequent actions in the Schrade case as follows: "The appellate court had affirmed Sirhan's conviction. Where does another judge—on his own—say I want to reopen this case and call in some independent experts, re-test-fire the gun, and see whether the slugs came from Sirhan's gun. Where was the jurisdiction? It was extrajudicial; it was outside the normal judicial procedure. In any event, the judge had appropriated jurisdiction of the matter, and I conducted a cross-examination of the firearms experts.

"But also, Allard [Lowenstein], who got me involved in this case, showed me an AP photo of these two officers and told me that they had been looking for these two guys for years. And they had gone to

Joe Busch and the police, and they wouldn't tell who these guys are. So I told Allard, 'It shouldn't be too hard to find out who they are. I'll just take the photos down to the Rampart Division of the LAPD, which has jurisdiction over the Ambassador Hotel, and the Wilshire and Metro divisions, which are nearby. Undoubtedly, these guys come from one of these divisions.' A sergeant at Wilshire identified the two officers for me."[124]

The first officer Bugliosi found was LAPD sergeant Robert Rozzi, one of the officers in the AP photo published six years earlier by the *Los Angeles Free Press*, who was now at the Hollywood Division of the LAPD. Rozzi stated in his November 15, 1975, affidavit, executed at Bugliosi's request, "Sometime during the evening when we were looking for evidence, someone discovered what appeared to be a bullet a foot and a half or so from the bottom of the floor in a door jamb on the door behind the stage. I also personally observed what I believed to be a bullet in the place just mentioned."

A second affidavit, signed on November 17, 1975, was from Bugliosi himself, describing the obstacles he had encountered in attempting to take evidence from Sergeant Charles Wright, whom he had identified as the other police officer shown in the AP picture with Rozzi.

Bugliosi described this comedy as follows: "I . . . had placed a phone call with the Watch Commander of the West Los Angeles Division, requesting that [he] have Sgt. Wright call me at my home. Sgt. Wright called me at approximately 7:00 P.M. on the evening of November 16, 1975. I related to him what Sgt. Rozzi had told me and he told me unequivocally that it was a bullet in the hole and when I told him that Sgt. Rozzi had informed me that he was pretty sure

---

[124] Unimpressed, the *Los Angeles Times* employed the same tactic it had used against Baxter Ward a year earlier before the Ward hearing. The *Times* wrote, "Former prosecutor Vincent T. Bugliosi claims to have 'vital new data' that 'pertains to the possible existence of a conspiracy' in the June, 1968, assassination of Sen. Robert F. Kennedy.

"Maybe he does—maybe he doesn't.

"But it strikes us as more than coincidence that Bugliosi's announcement comes at a time when he is actively lobbying the Los Angeles County Board of Supervisors for appointment as district attorney to succeed the late Joseph P. Busch. . . ."

that the bullet was removed from the hole, Sgt. Wright replied, 'There is no pretty sure about it. It definitely was removed from the hole, but I don't know who did it.'

"I set up a meeting with Sgt. Wright at the W.L.A. Division for the following day at 6:00 P.M. At approximately 3:00 P.M. on November 17, 1975 . . . Sgt. Phil Sartuche of the L.A.P.D. came up to me and asked, 'Do you have Rozzi's statement?' [and] I replied 'yes.' He asked me if he could read it but I told him I did not have the statement with me. Although my meeting with Sgt. Wright was scheduled for 6:00 P.M., when I learned that Sgt. Sartuche was aware of the fact that I had spoken to Sgt. Rozzi, I immediately raced out to the W.L.A. Division of the L.A.P.D. to get a statement from Sgt. Wright before anyone from the L.A.P.D. had the opportunity to get to him first.

"I was not quick enough. I arrived at the W.L.A. Division of the L.A.P.D. at approximately 3:40 P.M. and asked for Sgt. Wright. I was told that he was on the phone. Approximately 10 minutes later, Sgt. Wright appeared and he was holding a yellow piece of paper in his hand. I looked down on the paper and saw the name Sartuche.

"I said to Sgt. Wright words to the effect that 'old Sartuche really works fast. I guess you were just talking to him on the phone,' whereupon Sgt. Wright said yes. I told Sgt. Wright I wanted to take his statement on the door jamb incident, and he told me that he had just been instructed by Deputy City Attorney Larry Nagen not to give a statement.

"I got on the phone with Larry Nagen and told him that even if I did not get a written statement from Sgt. Wright, I could subpoena him and secure his testimony on the witness stand. Mr. Nagen told me to get a cup of coffee for a couple of minutes because he wanted to talk to Sgt. Wright. When I returned to Sgt. Wright, he put me on the phone again with Larry Nagen. Nagen informed me that it would be permissible for me to take a written statement from Sgt. Wright but he wanted to be present with Sgt. Sartuche. I agreed. . . ."

In talking to Wright immediately afterward, however, Bugliosi quickly realized that Wright was saying that he "thought" or "assumed" things that he had stated definitively the night before. Bugliosi wrote, "I told [Wright] that if that was going to be his written statement, it would not serve any purpose for me . . . and that we would proceed by way of a subpoena and would secure his testimony in court on this issue."

Soon thereafter, Bugliosi served a subpoena on Wright. But Bugliosi's attempt to secure Wright's testimony in court the following day was sharply opposed by attorneys representing Los Angeles district attorney John Van de Kamp and California attorney general Evelle Younger. During the hearing, Bugliosi also argued that the testimony of the police officers was "perishable," because of the clear possibility of official pressure on the witnesses. Judge Robert A. Wenke observed that if the testimony was perishable, the "perishing" had probably already occurred.

Undaunted, Bugliosi pressed forward on his own. Over the course of the following month, he managed to secure other significant affidavits.

On December 1, 1975, he took a statement from Angelo DiPierro, the Ambassador Hotel's maître d' at the time of the Kennedy murder. DiPierro said that following the shooting he had noticed "a small caliber bullet lodged about a quarter of an inch into the wood on the center divider of the two swinging doors." The door in question was at the west end of the kitchen, behind Kennedy, and therefore in Sirhan's line of fire. "I am quite familiar with guns and bullets," DiPierro stated, "having been in the Infantry for 3½ years. There is no question in my mind that this was a bullet and not a nail or any other object."

On December 12, 1975, Bugliosi took the statement of shooting eyewitness Martin Patrusky, who had testified for the prosecution at Sirhan's trial. A waiter at the hotel, Patrusky stated, in regard to the same crime scene reconstruction attended by Noguchi, "[O]ne of the officers pointed to two circled holes on the center divider of the swinging doors and told us that they dug two bullets out of the center divider. . . . I am absolutely sure that the police told us that two bullets were dug out of these holes . . . and I would be willing to testify to this under oath and under penalty of perjury."

Since giving this affidavit, Patrusky has not been called to testify in any reexamination hearing.

Of all the witnesses cited by Bugliosi at this stage of the Schrade case, only one, Angelo DiPierro, was questioned by the district attorney and attorney general's offices. A measure of the impartiality of this session is the fact that the LAPD told DiPierro prior to the session that the object he had seen was not a bullet. Nevertheless, DiPierro refused to change his story.

No official statements were taken from Rozzi, Wright, Patrusky, or Noguchi about possible bullet holes.

All of the firearms examiners had been asked by Bugliosi about the value of further inquiry if serious evidence existed that more than eight bullets were filed at the crime scene. They noted that such questions were beyond their original mandate, but each of them replied that such a study could indeed be of value. Nevertheless, the district attorney and the state attorney general continued to oppose any further inquiry.[125]

The district attorney's office also refused all requests for a transcript of the November and December legal proceedings, which included arguments about the crime scene issues and detailed formal testimony from the seven firearms examiners. Also, the court reporters' notes of those proceedings have been destroyed.

In early December 1975, on Schrade's behalf, Bugliosi incorporated the information from his affidavits and requested that an expert panel, comparable to the firearms panel, be convened to study the controversial flight path data relating to the number of bullets fired. Bugliosi also wanted to present the testimony of those from whom he had received affidavits or statements about possible extra bullets at the crime scene.[126]

[125] Senator Edward Kennedy, when asked by a reporter on August 14, 1975, about the renewed inquiries into the case, said, "It is painful to the members of the family, but that shouldn't be the consideration. It ought to be what evidence is before the duly constituted procedures of law. And if there is new information, new evidence, then that ought to be considered."

[126] When I asked Bugliosi in September 1993 whether he thought that two different guns had been fired in the kitchen pantry on the night of Kennedy's murder, Bugliosi replied, "Even assuming, for the sake of argument, that there are bullet holes and bullets in the center divider, that's only relevant in pointing toward a second gun *if* you assume the premise that the July 8, 1968, LAPD ballistics [and bullet inventory] report is correct.

"See, according to his ballistics report, there were seven bullets physically

This motion was again opposed by District Attorney Van de Kamp and California Attorney General Younger. "Selected and partial testimony regarding trajectory and ballistics will only lead to public confusion rather than a determination of the truth," the district attorney's brief observed. "[T]here is no justifiable basis for further expenditure of taxpayer funds to conduct a mere 'fishing expedition.' "

Nevertheless, LAPD officials and members of the district attorney's office decided to reassure the public that the fix was not in by returning to the kitchen pantry for a highly publicized seven-and-a-half-hour search for bullet holes on December 18, 1975. Deputy District Attorney Stephen Trott insisted, "The significance of the examination, as far as I am concerned, is the fact that it again shows that we are taking every step to unturn . . . every stone in this case to get to whatever bottom there may be."

Of course, this photo opportunity yielded no additional bullets, since the door frames, center divider, and the ceiling tiles—which, according to numerous witnesses, contained bullet holes—had been destroyed six years earlier in 1969.[127]

---

removed from six of the victims—and one was lost in the ceiling interspace. Supposedly, no bullets were found at the scene and there were no bullet holes—with the exception of the three in the ceiling tiles. If Wolfer's report is correct, then it gives eminent significance to finding bullets and bullet holes elsewhere in addition to the eight physically accounted for by the LAPD. But you're starting out with the assumption that his report is correct.

"If his report is in error, for whatever reason, then there might be an explanation for some of these things: ricochets, parts of bullets, fragments. This whole notion of the second gun is premised on the assumption that his report is correct.

"But even if you come up with more than eight bullets, it still doesn't necessarily mean a conspiracy. Someone could have fired in retaliation."

When I asked Bugliosi if he believed there was a conspiracy in the Robert Kennedy murder, he replied, "I've never had any doubt about Sirhan's guilt, but, on the issue of conspiracy, I don't have a strong feeling one way or the other. If I were pressed to the wall, I'd probably say there was not—that there is an explanation for everything.

"But I think there are enough substantial, unanswered questions in this case that the House Select Committee on Assassinations should have reinvestigated this case in 1977 and 1978 along with the assassinations of John F. Kennedy and Martin Luther King."

[127] The door jamb in the backstage area with a bullet hole, identified in the famous AP wirephoto, was also examined. During the "Pantry Raid," LAPD crimi-

"The Great Pantry Raid," as it became known, was nothing less than another very seriously played-out farce. Had the tests and measurements conducted on the physical evidence collected during the pantry raid actually occurred in 1968, the issue of extra bullets could have been put to rest once and for all. Instead, because of the LAPD's poor record keeping and its cavalier handling of the materials originally recovered from the pantry, the Kennedy murder case continued to linger.

In oral arguments in December, Lowenstein, acting as Schrade's co-counsel, emphasized the national importance of determining the unresolved issues in the Robert Kennedy assassination. However, these considerations did not prevail in court.

On February 5, 1976, Judge Wenke acceded to the jurisdictional arguments of the district attorney and attorney general, extinguishing the renewed court inquires into the murder case. In his decision, Wenke concluded, "This has been an unusual proceeding. . . . Throughout, there appears to have been a misconception about the court's role. It has been stated that the court was conducting an investigation. This was and is not the fact. . . . Investigations are conducted by police, district attorneys, grand juries, and other agencies, but not by the courts."

Once again, the Robert Kennedy murder case appeared to be closed—this time because of legitimate concerns over judicial jurisdiction. Also, the case file of the Kennedy murder investigation remained sealed; it reportedly included police reports about the official search for bullets and bullet holes at the crime scene in June 1968.

In March 1977, the LAPD and the district attorney's office tried to ram a stake through the heart of the critics' case against the official probe with the publication of the so-called Kranz Report. Authorized by the Los Angeles County Board of Supervisors and written by Special Counsel Thomas Kranz, a private attorney who had been on special assignment for the Los Angeles District Attorney's Office since August 1975, the report marked a blatant attempt by official

---

nalists said they found a nail in the hole. However, according to Sergeants Rozzi and Wright, the object they were examining in the AP photo had been removed on June 5, 1968.

Los Angeles to dismiss the obvious inconsistencies in the LAPD's official version of the RFK murder. It remains the final formal defense of the work of those law enforcement agencies involved in the investigation.

Kranz had worked as a volunteer during Robert Kennedy's campaign for the presidency and was in the Embassy Room at the time that Kennedy was shot in the kitchen pantry. He also had served as the district attorney's representative for the firearms court proceedings.

From the outset of his personal probe, Kranz insisted that he wanted "to insure a fresh independent look at the entire matter and controversy surrounding the death of Senator Kennedy."

However, in the end, the Kranz Report contained an array of factual errors and misrepresented the significance of certain pieces of physical evidence and eyewitness testimony.

What was supposed to be the final word on security guard Gene Cesar also appeared in the report. Kranz attempted to minimize the controversy surrounding Cesar but actually accomplished the opposite, raising more doubts about the police investigation of Cesar's possible role in Kennedy's murder.

Kranz wrote that he had interviewed Cesar in November 1975,[128] and he had a number of surprising things to say about him. For example, he said that Cesar had denied ever having held extreme right-wing views on racial issues, ever having canvassed for George Wallace, or ever having professed hatred for the Kennedys.

In spite of reports and transcripts that show that Cesar told the police that he drew his gun *before* falling to the floor behind Senator Kennedy the night of the shooting, Kranz absolved Cesar of that admission as well.

In one of the most blatant errors in his report, Kranz wrote, "Cesar states, and the L.A.P.D. orally verifies, but have no documents to substantiate, the fact that the .38 caliber weapon Cesar had on his person that night as part of his Ace Guard Service assignment was examined by an unnamed L.A.P.D. officer." The official interviews with Cesar contradict that point as well.

And Kranz barely touched on one of the most troublesome issues

---

[128] Sirhan refused to speak with Kranz.

of all—why Cesar told police that he sold his H & R .22 four months *before* the murder when, in fact, he sold it several months *after* it. Kranz simply says that Cesar was "somewhat vague" about the timing of the transaction.

The Kranz Report received a blistering response at a county board of supervisors hearing on May 17, 1977, from Allard Lowenstein, Paul Schrade, and Robert Joling, former president of the American Academy of Forensic Sciences. Three months later, on July 27, 1977, at the request of the board of supervisors, Lowenstein and his aide Gregory Stone submitted a lengthy memorandum detailing seventy-five major errors of fact in the Kranz Report. Nevertheless, the LAPD and Los Angeles District Attorney's Office would continue to cite the report as the final statement of its position on the case.

The Kranz Report effectively quashed the Schrade-Lowenstein-Bugliosi effort to resolve the lingering issues in the case.

The only major question Kranz raised dealt with evidence of apparent tampering with the barrel of Sirhan's gun, which the firearms panel found to have been heavily coated with lead. Kranz suggested that it had been sabotaged while in the custody of the county clerk's office, and he asked the district attorney to investigate.

Locked up in Soledad Penitentiary, Sirhan Sirhan had his own theory, expressing it in a handwritten letter to Judge Wenke, which he received on January 20, 1976. Sirhan wrote, "I suspect that after the discovery of all the physical discrepancies and inconsistencies now known in my case, that the prosecution had fired my gun, exhibit #6, anew, without the knowledge of anyone but themselves, and substituted the bullets recovered from this firing, for the original disputed bullets in evidence at trial, in order to produce consistent results ballistically with the bullets that will have been recovered from a Court ordered test firing of my gun."[129]

However, it was not until 1985 that another coordinated attempt to reopen the Robert Kennedy murder case was made.

[129] Judge Wenke sent copies of Sirhan's letter to all of the principal attorneys involved in the Kennedy murder case, saying, "I do not intend to reply to this letter."

19. *The Push for the Case File*

During the summer of 1985, while living in Los Angeles and working on my third book, *Dark Victory: Ronald Reagan, MCA, and the Mob,* I met Greg Stone, a former aide to by then deceased Allard Lowenstein,[130] and Dr. Philip Melanson, a political science professor at Southeastern Massachusetts University. Both were in the midst of a public crusade to reopen the investigation of the Robert F. Kennedy assassination.

During our meeting, Stone summed up their stance on the con-

---

[130] A crazed former colleague shot Lowenstein five times and killed him on March 14, 1980. The fifty-one-year-old Lowenstein left behind three children. In a column published two days after Lowenstein's death, *Washington Post* reporter Richard Cohen said of him, "He mattered."

troversies involving muzzle distance and extra bullets. "Consider this," he told me: "the existing crime scene evidence supports the probability that more than eight shots were fired from more than one gun and that the three shots that struck Kennedy were fired from point-blank range—no more than three inches from the senator's body. A fourth shot passed through Kennedy's jacket but did not hit him. No one but the police, who were not present at the time of the shooting, claimed that the barrel of Sirhan's gun was any closer than a foot and a half from Kennedy, who was shot from the right rear at a leftward and steeply upward angle. Eyewitnesses stated that the senator was moving toward Sirhan, shaking hands, when the assassin opened fire. They also claimed that Sirhan, whose arm was grabbed after the second shot, never had an opportunity to shoot Kennedy in the back once—let alone four times—at point-blank range."

Overwhelmingly, Stone insisted, the eyewitnesses' versions of events directly contradicted the official police reconstruction of the murder. When confronted with this point, LAPD officials had referred instead to the panic and confusion that broke loose inside the pantry while Sirhan was emptying his .22 revolver into the crowd. In essence, the police had said, the eyewitnesses lacked the training and experience necessary to make their stories credible.

The only hope for learning the full truth, Stone and Melanson told me, was to expand responsible efforts at independent investigation. And they wanted me to try to break new ground in the case.

This was not my first contact with an assassination conspiracy. Since 1974, I had been an independent journalist who concentrated on organized crime investigations. As a mob reporter, I constantly investigated conspiracies. (After all, any reasonable definition of "organized crime" must include that it is "conspiracy crime.")

Also, I have always greatly admired Robert Kennedy, especially for his roles as chief counsel of the Senate Rackets Committee from 1957 to 1960 and as U.S. attorney general from 1961 to 1964.

In my first book, *The Hoffa Wars: Teamsters, Rebels, Politicians and the Mob,* a 1978 chronicle of the rise and fall of former Teamsters boss Jimmy Hoffa, I published new evidence showing that Hoffa and two Mafia figures—Carlos Marcello of New Orleans and Santo Trafficante of Tampa—may have played a role in the events leading to

President John F. Kennedy's murder. The following summer, the U.S. House Select Committee on Assassinations released its final report. Without making a formal charge, it concluded that Marcello, Trafficante, and Hoffa had "the motive, means and opportunity" to have John Kennedy killed. Speaking for himself, G. Robert Blakey, the chief counsel of the committee, stated flatly, "The mob did it. It's a historical fact."[131]

Still, considering the flak I had initially taken for getting involved in a probe of John Kennedy's murder, I would have to be convinced the Robert Kennedy murder merited further study. But the evidence Stone and Melanson provided me was extremely persuasive.

When I finally began to read the limited number of available documents concerning this 1968 murder, I was shocked by what I saw. Without question, the case I had assumed was open-and-shut had been badly mishandled by the Los Angeles Police Department, particularly with regard to physical evidence. It was clear that law enforcement officials had misrepresented key facts in the case, destroyed material evidence, and obstructed independent attempts to resolve the critical issues surrounding the case. Evidence that had not been tampered with made it seem unlikely that Sirhan was the only person to fire a gun that night.

I began to wonder: Did the Mafia have Robert Kennedy killed?

Many factors separated the two Kennedy murder cases from each other, but one stood out. In President Kennedy's murder, according to the official version, the suspect perched unseen on the sixth floor of the Texas School Book Depository in Dallas and fired his rifle from concealment at the president's motorcade as it passed on the street below.

During Senator Kennedy's shooting, however, the accused fired his weapon in the midst of no fewer than seventy-seven people crowded inside the narrow kitchen pantry at the Ambassador Hotel in Los Angeles. Sirhan fired in open view, Kennedy fell mortally

---

[131] Tampa attorney Frank Ragano—who had represented Hoffa, Marcello, and Trafficante—confessed in January 1992 that Hoffa requested a contract on President Kennedy's life. Ragano admitted having carried the contract to the two mobsters. He believes that Marcello and Trafficante engineered the murder. See also Ragano's book *Mob Lawyer* (New York: Charles Scribner's Sons, 1994).

wounded, and the shooter was immediately restrained by bystanders.

There was, though, another scenario that would account for the problems posed by the crime scene evidence, and that scenario required a second gunman in the room, who fired his weapon as well.

As Stone told me, "The evidence we have makes the case for a second gun. We neither attempt to deny Sirhan Sirhan's role in the shooting, nor do we try to establish any particular conspiracy theory. We deal strictly with the crime scene evidence present in the room where Kennedy was murdered and the inescapable conclusion to which that evidence leads."

Stone added, "The only leap of faith necessary to reach that conclusion is this: An eight-shot revolver cannot fire more than eight bullets."

What also helped to perpetuate the doubts about the investigation of Robert Kennedy's murder was the fact that the LAPD's case file of the investigation had remained hidden. When the Warren Commission completed its inquiry into the assassination of John Kennedy, its final report and twenty-six volumes of supporting evidence were promptly released for public review and criticism.

Promises to release the Robert Kennedy murder case files were made as early as the end of the Sirhan trial, when District Attorney Evelle Younger said, "The Los Angeles Police Department has agreed without reservation that the interests of the public and law enforcement are best served by full disclosure of the results of the comprehensive investigation which they have conducted."

But full disclosure had never come.

The only way to resolve this problem, Stone and Melanson insisted, was to force the entire official case file to be released. And they pointed out a potential legal point of access: LAPD chief of detectives Robert Houghton had used the files to write *Special Unit Senator*, his own 1970 book on Robert Kennedy's assassination.

Indeed, Houghton wrote in the foreword to his book, "The material herein was drawn from the files of the Los Angeles Police Department, and particularly from the exhaustive work of Special Unit Senator, a unique task force created for the investigation."

In a sworn August 26, 1975, statement in connection with Paul

Schrade's civil suit, Houghton added, "I did write the book with the assistance of Theodore Taylor. I had no recollection of having shown the 10-volume Summary to Taylor, but I did show Taylor some items and some material from L.A.P.D. files. Much of the material I showed Taylor was material used in the trial of Sirhan, or held by the District Attorney. In showing this material to Taylor, it was not my intention or understanding that this amounted to any publication or release of confidential police information to the public, but was only shown to him as my agent for the purpose of putting together the background material for the book. . . . At no time did Taylor ever come to Parker Center and go into the police investigative files. Generally, Taylor received whatever information he had regarding the investigation from me."

Phil Melanson later corralled co-author Taylor and sat him down for a discussion about his book with Houghton. Melanson wrote, "Taylor says he picked up tapes and documents and transported them to his home, while the investigation was still ongoing: 'My car was parked outside of Parker Center and I kept loading this crap in there. I don't know, the guy helped me with a cart; he had a big cart. And I thought Jesus Christ, what really do I have here.' "[132]

Now, these same documents from these same files were being withheld from the public. After CBS withdrew from the fight for full disclosure, Paul Schrade, along with Greg Stone and Phil Melanson, continued to press for it.

On July 30, 1985, the Los Angeles Police Commission reluctantly agreed to release the LAPD's ten-volume, 1,453-page summary of its investigation of the Kennedy murder. However, the commission rejected demands to release the 50,000 documents and over 2,400 photographs that supported the summary and that were locked away in five steel file cabinets.

The commission also ordered LAPD personnel and the city attorney's office "to redact the ten volume summary in accordance with the following standard: remove items that are prohibited by law from being released, and those items which were to be held in confidence

[132] Philip H. Melanson, *The Robert F. Kennedy Assassination: New Revelations on the Conspiracy and Cover-up, 1968–1991* (New York: Shapolsky Publishers, 1991), p. 89.

per agreements with other public agencies and information from informants; with due respect to issues of privacy and national security and any other privileges not enumerated above." The commissioners expressed fear that the personal privacy of certain witnesses would be violated if the files were released unedited.

Greg Stone, who testified at the commission hearing, protested, "In complex matters of this kind—matters of supreme national importance relating to recent history and the public life of our country—the historical needs and the evidentiary needs simply cannot be addressed by the release of . . . minute materials from the entire body of evidence."

During another hearing of the police commission, on February 12, 1986, Schrade made an impassioned plea for the LAPD to release its files on the Kennedy case. He said, "I want [the documents] and other people want them because there are unanswered questions about the case. . . . You have been using every legal means to obstruct us in getting them. I have grave concerns about the intent of the commission." Barbara L. Schlei, a member of the commission, replied, "We have been too slow, but I would like to assure you that to the best of my knowledge there has been no coverup."

On March 4, the LAPD released its case summary, which was heavily censored, much of the material clearly blacked out with a felt-tipped pen. After the release, Stone told the *Los Angeles Herald-Examiner*, "The three percent summary of the file is not important. What is important is the 97 percent of the material which remains withheld."

Schrade, Stone, and Melanson led another round of bureaucratic deliberations and study committees featuring further demands that the LAPD release its *entire* case file. This time, the effort enlisted support from such prominent people as Arthur M. Schlesinger, Jr., former RFK press secretary Frank Mankiewicz, various university professors of history and political science, the Los Angeles County Board of Supervisors, and actors Paul Le Mat, Martin Sheen, and Robert Vaughn, among others. In particular, Schlesinger wrote, "Every consideration of scholarly and national interest calls for the disclosure of all information related to Robert Kennedy's death."

In April 1986, in response to public pressure and a recommendation from the police commission to consider a repository for the case file, Mayor Tom Bradley appointed twelve individuals, "representing the archival, library, and legal professions, and the academic and historical communities," to the Mayor's Advisory Committee regarding the Robert F. Kennedy Assassination Investigation Materials. Mayor Bradley stated, "[T]he tragedy which occurred and the subsequent investigation have immense historical significance. For that reason, I am determined to ensure that the public has quick access to as many of the underlying documents as the law permits."

The committee began its work on May 12 and completed it on October 30. The committee voted unanimously "that the California State Archives in Sacramento be selected as the repository for the Kennedy investigation materials."

Finally, on December 9, 1986, the Los Angeles City Council unanimously passed a resolution, prepared by the city attorney at Bradley's request, calling for "the transfer of the Robert F. Kennedy assassination investigation records from City Archives to the Public Archives of the State of California."[133]

[133] The full account of these proceedings and the considerations involved in the release of the materials by the California State Archives appears in Diane S. Nixon's article "Providing Access to Controversial Public Records: The Case of the Robert F. Kennedy Assassination Investigation Files," in *The Public Historian*, vol. 11, no. 3 (Summer 1989).

20. Rediscovering Cesar

My own investigation began in December 1986, the same month the Los Angeles City Council passed the resolution. I had been intrigued by the issues in the Robert Kennedy murder case that Stone and Melanson had laid out for me during our earlier meeting. They prompted me to research the Kennedy case and write an investigative piece about the unanswered crime scene questions. My work appeared as the cover story in the June 1987 issue of *Regardie's,* a Washington-based magazine. The article hit the newsstands in mid-May.

In addition to examining the inconsistencies in the official version of the killing—in which I relied heavily, probably too heavily, on eyewitness testimony—the story also contained my exclusive interview with Thane Eugene Cesar, the security guard who had been accused of behaving suspiciously before and after the shooting. He had already been prominently mentioned—even accused in some publications and specifically in the 1973 film *The Second Gun*—as the possible second gunman.

The evidence to support Cesar's alleged role in the shooting was extensive and clearly demonstrated motive, means, and opportunity. For instance:

- Cesar was standing directly behind Kennedy when Sirhan began firing and, according to his own statements, was in a position to shoot Kennedy at point-blank range.
- He was seen with a drawn gun by no fewer than four eyewitnesses and by another who claimed to have seen him fire the gun. He admitted to law enforcement authorities that he drew his gun after Sirhan began shooting, but gave contradictory statements to the police and to the FBI about exactly when he drew the weapon.
- He had repeatedly given different versions of his movements immediately after the shooting.
- Cesar owned a .22-caliber revolver similar to Sirhan's but gave false statements to the police about when he sold it. The gun had since disappeared; its new owner reported it stolen.
- Cesar was a supporter of 1968 American Independent Party presidential candidate George Wallace and made no secret of his hatred of the politics of both John and Robert Kennedy.
- He was on guard duty in the pantry at the time that Sirhan reportedly slipped into the area.

Despite these circumstances and the contradictory statements he had made to the police and the FBI, Cesar, by his own account,

- had no criminal record and claimed never to have been in trouble with the law
- was not scheduled to work as a security guard the night Kennedy was shot and was called in to work at the last minute
- volunteered to be questioned when no investigating officer approached him after the shooting

- offered to surrender the gun in his holster, a .38-caliber revolver, for police inspection during his questioning—an offer rejected by the police officers who conducted the interview
- voluntarily told the police that he owned the additional .22 revolver and gave them the name and address of the man to whom he had sold it
- apparently cooperated with the police and FBI and even agreed to take a polygraph test in regard to his actions that night—a test the police later decided not to administer
- was candid about his support for George Wallace in 1968 and his distaste for the Kennedys and has never tried to conceal these opinions

When I began my investigation, no one connected with the Kennedy case had seen or heard from Cesar since November 1975, when he was interviewed for the final time by the district attorney's office during its preparation of the Kranz Report. In fact, an assistant district attorney had put out the word that Cesar had since died. Los Angeles journalist Theodore Charach, the first investigator to reveal the evidence against Cesar, was the last reporter to interview him, in October 1969.

However, through a network of sources and public-records searches, I found Cesar, living in Simi Valley, California. My first interview with him was conducted on March 27, 1987; Cesar was accompanied by his attorney, Garland Weber.

The forty-five-year-old Cesar arrived for the interview on time. When he walked through the door, I was stunned by his appearance. I had expected a snarling, muscle-bound man wearing a red T-shirt with a pack of Marlboros rolled up in his sleeve, the kind of guy who slaps around the newspaper boy for throwing the morning edition in the bushes. Instead, Cesar turned out to be six feet tall but out of shape, weighing well over 250 pounds; his belly hung far over his belt. His attorney immediately kidded him about how poorly he carried his weight. When we shook hands, Cesar was friendly and smiling but a little nervous. He had a pudgy, boyish face and a pronounced overbite. The only features that gave away his age were the wrinkles around his brown eyes and two deep lines that fanned out from either side of his nose. He also sported a narrow, well-trimmed beard, and the dark brown hair on his head was short and pushed to the left side. He had just come from his job and wore a blue-and-white-checked shirt, tan work pants, and running shoes. Outside, in the parking lot of his attorney's office, he had a 1986 Corvette. He insisted almost immediately that he had had four traffic citations for driving too fast—but no criminal record.

Cesar was born on February 28, 1942, in Kansas City, Missouri. He is a mixture of English, French, and German stock. Both of his parents were deceased by the time I interviewed him. His mother, a housewife, died in 1985; his father, a dispatcher for Air Cargo, an air freight company, died the following year. He has two sisters, both of whom live in southern California.

Cesar played football in high school and attended Valley Junior College, in Los Angeles County, studying police science. He wanted to earn his associate's degree and become a police officer. However, because of an ulcer from which he had suffered since his teens, he was not permitted to attend the police academy. Also, Cesar was classified as 4-F because of a high blood sugar count and did not serve in the military.

After his rejection from the LAPD, he decided to become a plumber. Cesar said, "When I was in high school, I worked for a plumber. He always told me, 'If you ever want to get into the apprenticeship program, I'll get you in.' Well, when I didn't make it in the police department, I went down, and he put my name on a list. I went and took the entrance exam and passed it. They only take the top twenty-five; I scored number twelve. And the guy took twenty-five apprentices every six months. So I went into the apprenticeship program, and I stayed in that for five years. I was in construction for about a year after that. And then I went to work for Lockheed Aircraft in Burbank as a maintenance plumber in 1966, making $12,000 a year. I had to receive a security clearance from the Department of Defense. Also, I was a member of the International Association of Machinists and Aerospace Workers Local 727, and I did some free-lance plumbing work on the side."[134]

---

[134] Cesar later became a member of Local 761 of the United Association of Journeymen and Apprentices of the Plumbing and Pipe Fitting Industry.

On March 28, 1963, Cesar married Joyce Arlene in North Holly-wood. They lived in their own house on Morley Street in Simi Valley. His wife did not work outside the home. The couple had two chil-dren: a daughter, Teresa May, born in 1959; and a son, Gary Eugene, born in 1964.

Gene and Joyce Cesar legally separated on December 29, 1968, after Joyce fell in love with a clarinet player, whom she later married. Cesar said that the circumstances surrounding the Kennedy murder had no bearing on the breakup of his marriage. The divorce became final on October 21, 1969.

After Joyce and Cesar separated, Cesar moved into an apartment on Yucca Lane in Thousand Oaks. Soon thereafter, he moved into an apartment with his sister on Victory Boulevard in Reseda. While living there, he met Marlena Mae, whom he married on August 3, 1969. Like his first wife, Marlena did not have a job outside the home.

On April 21, 1971, Cesar lost his job at Lockheed, but within a couple of weeks he went to work for Viking Insulation and became a member of Local 1506 of the carpenters' union. He remained at Viking for about six months. On October 28, 1971, after leaving Viking, Cesar filed for personal bankruptcy.

Cesar, who has never been unemployed for longer than six weeks, went to work as a plumber for Riker Laboratories, a pharmaceutical company and a subsidiary of the 3-M Corporation. In 1973, after working for two years with Riker, Cesar was hired by Hughes Aircraft in its Canoga Park plant, where he remained for the next seven years. There, as at Lockheed, Cesar received a security clearance. At Hughes, according to Cesar, he had a "secret" clearance, the second-highest clearance at his plant—even though he was just a plumber. "A plumber had to have the clearance to go just about anywhere in the plant in order to make repairs," he told me.

Always looking for ways to make extra money legitimately, Cesar remained a part-time security guard until 1972. His last employer in the private security business was the Protecto Corporation of Wood-land Hills.[135]

---

[135] For years, numerous conspiracy theories have alleged that Cesar worked for the Mafia, the CIA, Howard Hughes, or even as a freelance bodyguard, leg breaker, and hit man.

There is no evidence to support any of these allegations.

In 1972, Cesar and his new wife bought their home on Plum Street in Simi Valley for $24,000. Because it had been a badly taken-care-of rental home, they bought it for $10,000 under market value and enjoyed fixing it up. When he and Marlena split up in 1980, Cesar had to pay her off in order to keep the house. So he took out a loan against the house. His mortgage soared to $88,000. In 1976, Cesar installed a swimming pool at his house, borrowing $13,800 from his credit union at Hughes Aircraft to complete the job.

Cesar has never been a wealthy man. At the time of my first interview with him, Cesar had only $2,500 in his bank account and still owed the bulk of the $88,000 mortgage on his house. He owed $8,000 on a truck and $5,000 for another personal loan. Also, on December 9, 1986, Cesar married his third wife, Eleanor, a Filipino woman, and began taking care of her and helping to support her family.

A social drinker at worst, Cesar had an allergic reaction when he did drink. He had never frequented bars or taken illegal drugs. He had never been in a fistfight, other than a couple of scuffles on the football field while in high school. However, he did admit to having a temper. "Certain things will set me off right away," Cesar explained. "Other things, you could probably crank on me all day long, and I won't get mad."

He has never traveled to the East Coast—not even to New York or Washington, D.C.—except for a trip to Florida to visit an aunt and uncle in 1985. He has never been out of the United States, except for two trips to the Philippines to visit his wife before she was naturalized in the United States.

He is a baptized Methodist who occasionally attends church. He has never had any interest in the occult. He has never been hypnotized. He has never had memorable dreams or nightmares. He has never been a part of any medical or psychological experimentation. He has never heard voices through the fillings of his teeth.

Cesar does like guns, and he enjoyed target-shooting in the desert. There is no evidence that Cesar, unlike Sirhan, had ever been to the San Gabriel Valley Gun Club or to a Corona gun range to practice; he has never purchased ammunition at the Lock, Stock 'N Barrel Gun Shop. Although he owned a .22 semiautomatic rifle, he has never had access to a .22 target revolver built in a .38 frame, as some who accuse Cesar have suggested.

When I told Cesar early in the interview that he had been reported dead, he laughed, "I know it. I want it that way." Asked how he felt about being suspected by some to be the second gunman in the Robert Kennedy murder, he replied, "I just learned to live with it. Basically, I ignore people like you."

Cesar said that he had never complained about the charges: "I just tried to keep quiet. I figured the less said that this would maybe die out and go away. And, at times, it did. We'd go, you know, a year, year and a half, two years, and you'd never hear nothing. Every anniversary of his assassination, they'd start this same crap over again. . . . It didn't bother me, because the police department, like they told me, 'There's no way we're going to prosecute you. We know you didn't do it. We've got the man that did it. We're happy with it.' In fact, they told me that they had to spend a lot of time and money to prove that I didn't. . . ."

"I have a very good friend who works for the FBI. And after the FBI interview [on June 11, 1968], I called him up, and he went and pulled the files to see exactly what they reported on me. They gave the same conclusions the LAPD did: that I wasn't a suspect."[136]

Telling me that back in the late 1960s he was still fuming over the Watts riots in Los Angeles, Cesar explained that he had contributed only five dollars to the Wallace presidential campaign and passed out his candidate's political literature at work. "There's nothing wrong that I liked Wallace. I still like Wallace. I'd still vote for Wallace." But Cesar insisted that he had never been a member of any right-wing extremist group. "Other than unions, I've never been a member of anything."[137]

---

[136] Cesar's FBI agent friend is a former neighbor. Nothing about the relationship appears to be nefarious, although the circumstances and timing of Cesar's call to the agent do seem a bit bizarre.

[137] Cesar was quick to blame reporter Theodore Charach for all the attention he had received. "I was honest and up-front with him," Cesar said of their 1969 interview. "He asked me a question, and I answered it. If I hadn't laid my soul out to Charach, I wouldn't be in the position I'm in today. And I really believe that." During my interview with Cesar, his attorney, Garland Weber, took the blame

Cesar insisted that he had mellowed, especially on the subject of race relations. A former Democrat turned Republican and a staunch supporter of then president Reagan, Cesar said, "In a lot of ways, Reagan reminded me of Wallace. He didn't take any shit from people."

Blaming his racism on his upbringing, Cesar explained, "My father worked with blacks, but he was from the old school. He had no use for blacks, you know. He was prejudiced. And I was raised prejudiced. And I'm probably prejudiced today. When I say I've changed, I respect anybody no matter what their color is."

And Cesar remained unabashed in his attitude toward the Kennedys. "I had no use for the Kennedy family. . . . I've read a lot of books on the Kennedy family. I think they're the biggest bunch of crooks that ever walked the earth. And I'm not ashamed to say it today. But I live in this country. I can say what I want, because that's what I feel. And what you say does not make you guilty of anything. It's what you do that counts."

Cesar laughed, adding, "Just because I don't like Democrats don't mean I go around shooting them."

Cesar told me that neither his personal life nor any of his jobs had been influenced by the publicity he had received from the Kennedy case. "The only thing that affected my life was just the harassment I got from people like Ted Charach, the press. . . . There were dozens of articles that have come out saying that I carried a second gun, and that I possibly could've been the person who shot Bobby Kennedy—because the bullet entered the back of his head. But I think that was more my problem than anything else—because of where I was standing. Everybody at work knew, of course, what had happened. But it was no big thing there."[138]

---

for introducing Charach to his client. In short, Charach had been introduced to Weber by a mutual friend, who had asked Weber to represent Charach in a legal matter. "And after it was done," Weber told me, "Charach called me . . . and wanted me to put [him] in touch with Gene. . . . I let Gene know that I had a client who wanted to talk to him."

[138] Cesar's attorney, Garland Weber, told me that he had received numerous crank calls over the years. One anonymous caller specifically told him, "I don't like people who represent assassins."

Cesar said that he had talked to two attorneys about possible libel action against those who have accused him of having played a role in the murder. He said that both attorneys told him that he had been libeled and slandered, but both refused to take his case, because there was no money in it. According to Cesar, one attorney told him, "The case you've got is with people who have no money. So you're wasting your time and my time, because there's nothing you can get out of it."

As we went through his background and Cesar gave me his shoot-from-the-hip impressions about his life and times, I kept thinking to myself, "Keep him talking. Keep him talking."

Sensing that he was comfortable with our interview, I then asked Cesar about that night at the Ambassador Hotel.

21. *Cesar on the Night of the Shooting*

At the time of Kennedy's murder, Cesar was working as a part-time security guard for Ace Guard Service.[139] He told me, "You know, the only reason I took those guard jobs was because I was in deep shit for money. I mean, I really needed money bad."

Cesar said that he applied for the job in early 1968 after he saw an ad in the newspaper. "I just happened to see it in the paper—'Earn extra money'—so I went down. And the guy says, 'Here is what you have to have.' He says, 'You got to buy a uniform. You got to have a gun.' I said, 'All right! If that's all it takes to make extra money, I'm your man!' "

[139] The owners of Ace Guard Service, Frank J. and Loretta M. Hendrix, registered their articles of incorporation with the California Secretary of State on January 2, 1968. The California Bureau of Collections and Investigative Services licensed Ace Guard Service in March 1968.

Cesar explained that becoming a guard required no particular training and no certification for the gun. He added that he generally worked weekends and made three dollars an hour.

During our interview, Cesar gave me his version of his role at the crime scene. As was recounted in Chapter 1, during the afternoon of June 4, 1968, Cesar received a last-minute request that he work security at the Ambassador. Reluctantly, he finally agreed to accept the job and arrived at the hotel at 6:05 P.M.

Soon after being told by Ace Guard commander Fred Murphy to patrol the Embassy Room, where the Kennedy campaign party was being held, Cesar struck up a conversation with another Ace Guard. "We had a discussion about Kennedy," Cesar remembered. "And he [the other guard] says, 'I wouldn't be a bit surprised if somebody didn't try to knock Bobby off.' "

When I asked if he had any reaction to that statement, Cesar replied no. He later added that he didn't recall whether he had ever reminded the other guard of what he said.

When asked whether he thought it ironic that he was going to be a bodyguard for Robert Kennedy, he quickly corrected me. "We weren't there [to be] his bodyguards. In fact, and this is a matter of record, he didn't want us. In fact, he was explicit that he didn't even want us in a picture where it showed us with him. And we were told we were there for one reason only: crowd control. Nothing else."

At 9:30, Cesar was reassigned from the Embassy Room to the kitchen. He positioned himself at the east door of the pantry, adjacent to the Colonial Room, where Kennedy was slated to hold a press conference. Cesar's job was to check passes and credentials. "It was mostly political people [walking in] that worked for him. Reporters, entertainers, you know, walking back and forth. And most of them had ID badges on. . . . Otherwise, I wouldn't let them through."

However, neither Cesar nor anyone else can explain how Sirhan managed to get into the kitchen pantry. Sirhan had been spotted there by several witnesses before Kennedy had delivered his victory speech. Cesar insisted, "I was the only guard in the pantry, and I just never noticed him." He added that during his time in the kitchen, he watched television with Roosevelt Grier and Rafer Johnson and listened to Milton Berle's jokes.

At 11:15 Murphy told Cesar that Kennedy would be coming

through the pantry en route to the Embassy Room for his speech, and then he would come through again on his way to the Colonial Room. On Murphy's orders, Cesar then moved from the east pantry door to the west pantry swinging doors, near the stage where Kennedy would be delivering his speech.[140] Cesar said that, soon thereafter, Ambassador security chief Gardner instructed him to accompany Kennedy through the pantry on his way to the press conference. "He just said, 'Keep the aisle clear. Make sure that everybody's out of the way, so that Kennedy's group can walk through freely.' "[141]

[140] At the moment of the shooting, according to a June 13, 1968, FBI interview report, Murphy, who had been with hotel security man Arthur Maddox, stationed himself "at the double doors between the Colonial and Embassy Rooms leading into the [east entrance of the] kitchen area . . . to prevent any of the crowd from coming into the kitchen which could impede the Senator's proceeding from the rear of the Embassy Room to the Colonial Room."

Murphy heard the gunshots from that location and immediately ran into the pantry. Murphy, the FBI report continued, "identified himself as a former lieutenant of the police department, and attempted to get the gun from Sirhan, but was pushed away, by whom he does not know. Immediately thereafter, Roosevelt Grier obtained the gun and passed it to Rafer Johnson. Mr. Murphy advised Johnson to put the gun in his, that is Johnson's, pocket."

[141] An August 19, 1968, FBI report of an interview with William F. Gardner stated, "During the height of the Senator Kennedy campaign party it was mentioned to Gardner by some of the hotel employees, identities not recalled, that bumper stickers were being passed out in the front lobby and in front of the Embassy Room which bore lettering about killing Kennedy. The persons reportedly passing out these bumper stickers were described as being young people, 'hippie type.'

"A hotel employee had furnished one of the stickers to Gardner who said that it was a reddish orange in color with black lettering. He did not recall the exact caption on the bumper sticker but in substance the wording justified the killing of John F. Kennedy and did not pertain to Senator Robert F. Kennedy. Gardner said that he had turned this bumper sticker over to the Los Angeles Police Department after the shooting of Senator Kennedy."

The FBI report on Gardner added that the bumper sticker simply contained the words "Kill Kennedy" and that Gardner showed the bumper sticker to Ace guard Elmer M. Boomhower, who also notified the FBI about the bumper sticker.

The first complaint about two people who were passing out the bumper stickers was registered by reporter Jimmy Breslin of the *New York Post*. Breslin believed that the bumper sticker read, "Expose the Kennedy Death Hoax." The LAPD never booked it as evidence, and its exact wording was never agreed upon by those who saw it.

I believe that this little-known report accounts for the anti-Kennedy presence at the hotel and *might* account for those who gleefully celebrated the Kennedy shooting later that night.

Kennedy passed through the pantry and walked to the Embassy Room. "When he came down there, through that area," Cesar told me, he knew that Kennedy didn't like uniformed officers around him, adding, "Well, I stayed anyway, because that's what I was told to do. I didn't give a shit whether it was Bobby or not. You know, they told me to stay there, so I stayed there."

Cesar told me, "I heard them say he was on his way down. Someone said, 'This way, Senator,' as he was walking off the back of the stage. So I moved out of the way of the door and moved up, letting him come by me."

The commotion and the density of the crowd increased as Kennedy came closer. Cesar said that in front of him there were only about twenty people in the pantry. Kennedy, who was coming up behind him, was in the midst of a group of about fifty people.

As Karl Uecker, the assistant maître d', passed through the swinging doors, holding Kennedy by the hand, Cesar moved directly beside the senator. "I'm on the [right] side of him. And what I'm doing is taking my hand and pushing people back, because Kennedy was having a hard time walking forward."

I asked Cesar to act it out with me. We both stood, and he told me to play Kennedy and walk west to east through the pantry. Cesar, playing himself, walked beside me. Pointing to the south where the ice machine would have been and to the north where the steam tables would have been, Cesar explained, "They're congested in here [just before the ice machine]; they're mauled right in here. . . . But when they get back in here [a narrow alcove just before the ice machine], you've got a small area. All you had was maybe three people wide: the cameraman, the guy with the lights, and maybe one [other] guy."

Just before they reached the ice machine, Cesar said, he went directly behind Kennedy and took the senator's right arm at the elbow with his left hand while Uecker was still ahead, holding Kennedy's right hand. Kennedy never said anything to Cesar.

Cesar told me that he let go of Kennedy just as the senator shook hands. "The busboy was there, and [Kennedy] went over to shake his

---

At the moment of the shooting, Gardner was with Willie S. Bell, another Ace guard, and Lloyd Curtis, an unarmed Ambassador guard, on the first floor of the hotel.

hand." Although Cesar said that he was "inches" away from Kennedy, he was uncertain whether he grabbed the senator's arm again. Cesar said that at that moment he looked at the watch on his left wrist. "I wanted to see if it was 12:00, because I was going to leave." The time was exactly 12:15 A.M.

Acting out the exact moment of the shooting, Cesar played Kennedy, I played Cesar, and Cesar's attorney played the busboy. With Cesar setting the scene, he positioned me against the ice machine, wedged in behind and to the right of Kennedy and almost touching his back. The distance between the ice machine and the steam table was a mere six feet, three inches.

Cesar said he was so close to Kennedy, who was still moving east, that the flashes from Sirhan's gun appeared to be fired at him. But Cesar claimed never to have seen Sirhan immediately before or during the shooting, because of the "bright floodlights" in front of him. All he saw was an extended arm, a gun, and the flash from the barrel of the weapon.

According to Cesar, the shots were fired east to west at Kennedy as the senator's body, or at least his head, turned completely north while he was shaking hands with the busboy. Cesar said that the barrel of Sirhan's gun was "perpendicular" to Kennedy's head. Consistent with the statements of other eyewitnesses, Cesar estimated the muzzle distance to be about two feet, although he could not be certain, again because of the television floodlights. However, he believed, at the time, that four shots had been fired.

Cesar said that he was certain he knew where Kennedy was standing in relation to Sirhan. "A lot of people testified that [Sirhan] was standing this way [with Kennedy facing him]. I know for a fact [that's wrong], because I saw him [Kennedy] reach out there [to shake hands with the busboy] and which way he turned. And I told the police department that."

Cesar told me that he saw no other guns around him. He didn't notice anyone reach into a coat or make any quick, deliberate motions before the shooting started. He insisted that no one physically came between him and Kennedy before the gunfire began.

As soon as Cesar saw the flash of the gun and heard the shots—which, at first, he thought were firecrackers—he ducked and tried to take cover, he recalled.

He added that he neither saw Kennedy fall nor saw him get hit, because as Cesar reacted to the gunfire, he stumbled and fell forward to the floor "instantaneously."

However, on the point of Kennedy's falling, too, Cesar has given conflicting versions. In later interviews with me, Cesar claimed to have seen Kennedy fall. In one version, Kennedy fell backwards about two feet to his left. In another version, Kennedy fell backwards right in front of him.

Cesar also told me that he was wearing a clip-on tie, which somehow came off his shirt; he does not know how. It was later photographed next to Kennedy's right arm as the senator lay spread-eagle on the floor, with busboy Juan Romero kneeling to his left. When I asked whether it was Kennedy who had pulled off his tie, Cesar replied, "If he did, that's something somebody saw that I didn't know."

Cesar told me that when he came up from the floor after a five-count, he pulled his .38 from its holster and held it in his hand with his arm cocked at a forty-five-degree angle. In previous statements, Cesar had told the police and reporter Charach that he had drawn his gun when he first heard the shots—before he fell down. He admitted to me that he had contradicted himself. He estimated that his gun was out of his holster no longer than thirty seconds.

"First of all," Cesar said, "what I did when I got up—as soon as I got to my feet—I did pull my revolver, because I didn't know what was going on. I didn't know what the deal was. When I did that, when I looked up, Rosey Grier and Rafer Johnson and a bunch of people were beating the shit out of this guy [Sirhan]. Well, I assumed that was the guy that done the shooting. With that, I put my gun back in my holster."

When I asked Cesar whether he threw back the hammer after drawing his gun, he replied, "I didn't, because as soon as I got my gun out and looked up, I could see the guy that had done it. There were more people on him than you could believe. What's the sense in cocking it?"

Cesar told me that after he tried to regain his composure, his "adrenalin was pumped up." He explained, "I was scared. I was shaking, you know, physically, actually shaking. It's like having an accident. You know how you feel after an accident? I really didn't think too much about the fact that he [Kennedy] was laying there—

other than the fact that I was still shook up and scared."

Cesar also complained of having powder burns in his eyes that caused a minor irritation. When I asked how he received those powder burns, he replied, "I know that anytime you fire a gun at as close range as he [Sirhan] did, whether it be a .22 or anything else, it puts out minute particles in a spray. And it can be dust in the air, or it can be particles from the powder. But I was close enough that I got sprayed with it."

Although Cesar's movements immediately after the shooting are still unclear—and he has given conflicting accounts to the LAPD and the FBI about what he did—Cesar told me that he immediately ran out of the pantry and returned minutes later. "I felt I kept a very cool head, you know, as far as going out and getting help, coming back in, trying to keep as much order as possible."

Cesar summoned other Ace guards to the kitchen, including Jack Merritt and Albert Stowers, who were in the Embassy Room at the moment of the shooting.[142] Merritt entered the pantry with his gun drawn.[143]

[142] One other security guard was in the pantry at the time of the shooting. According to a July 2, 1968, LAPD report of an interview with Ambassador Hotel guard Stanley S. Kawalec, who was unarmed, "Just prior to conclusion of speech he was instructed by another security guard, Tom Perez (works back gate at Ambassador from 330 pm to 1030 pm), to clear the crowd in the kitchen area as the Senator would be coming through. Kawalec recalled there were a lot of people in the kitchen as he walked ahead of the senator. . . . He was not sure where he was when he first heard the shots. However, he did recall having to turn around, as the shots came from his rear."

A source gave me Kawalec's telephone number on September 24, 1993, and I called him that same day. His daughter, Carol Stimka, informed me that her father had died in 1987. Stimka told me, "We have all of these clippings from *Life* magazine. We were checking it out, because he was holding people back in the crowd that night. I remember him calling my mother and me. He was crying, and he said, 'I looked down and there was Bobby Kennedy.' It was a pretty traumatic thing in his life."

At the moment of the shooting, Perez was in the backstage/anteroom area, along with Patrick Murphy, another Ambassador guard.

[143] The FBI interviewed Merritt on June 13, 1968. Its report of the meeting stated, "In the confusion he [Merritt] noticed, among others, two men and a woman leaving the kitchen through a back exit. He could not see the woman's face but believed that she was approximately 5'5" tall, with light colored hair, and

Cesar remained in the Embassy Room for more than an hour after the shooting as the throngs of uniformed and plainclothes police officers began their investigation. "I was getting ready to go home," Cesar told me, "and I thought to myself, 'I wonder why nobody's questioned me.' . . . I went to a police officer. I said, 'Don't you really think you need my statement?' He said, 'Why?' I said, 'Well, I was standing right by Kennedy when he got shot.' [He said,] 'Oh, well, yes. Come with me.' So they took me down to a room. And from there they put me in a police car and took me down to Rampart [Division].

"I thought it was a necessary thing. What a mistake that was! If I hadn't said anything to that one particular police officer, nobody would've known to this day that I was even there."

Cesar was interviewed at Rampart by two police sergeants. According to the transcript of the discussion, when Cesar told them he worked for Ace Guard Service, he added, "Retired after tonight. I like quiet jobs."

Cesar admitted to me that he had given the police and the FBI conflicting stories about when he had drawn his gun. "You see," he told me, "you've got to understand something. I was very young [twenty-six]. I'd never been shot at before. [If] you want to see somebody in shock, I was as much [in shock] as Kennedy was. I was the closest person to him."

Discussing the police interview on the night of the shooting, Cesar explained, "They asked me at the police station, 'What're you carrying?' I said, 'I'm carrying a .38 [Rohm]. Do you want to see it?' 'No,' [the police said]."

By refusing to check Cesar's side arm and to obtain the precise details of when he drew his gun—as well as the nature and cause of the powder burns on his face—the police contributed significantly to lingering doubts about the crime scene events, especially those that concerned Gene Cesar.

Cesar didn't return home until 5:00 A.M. His wife, Joyce, remem-

---

wearing a polka-dot dress. One of the men was about 6'2" tall with dark hair and wearing a dark suit. The other man was approximately 5'5" or 5'6" tall and also wearing a suit."

bers little about that night except that she waited up for him. Cesar did not go to work at Lockheed the following day.

I also asked Cesar about the controversy over the .22 H & R revolver he sold to Jim Yoder three months after the shooting. Cesar remembered that he had bought the gun from Bud Sutherland, a fellow worker at a company called Gordon Enterprises, in or around 1962. Primarily, he kept but never used the H & R for "home protection."

When I asked him to compare his Rohm .38 side arm with his H & R, he replied, "They're shaped the same. My .38 was about [eight inches]; and the little H & R is about [six inches]. You can hide an H & R in the palm of your hand. The .38 had a four-inch barrel; the .22 had a two-inch barrel."

I questioned Cesar as to whether he could have been carrying his .22 instead of his .38 on the night of the shooting. Cesar responded, "Only thing is: the gun [.38 Rohm] I had in my holster was the one I showed the police department. And you could not put a .22 in that holster." He also denied ever using his .22 as a backup gun.[144]

When I showed Cesar a copy of the receipt of the sale of the H & R to Yoder proving that he had sold it *after* the murder, Cesar confirmed that, unintentionally, some of his remarks to the police had been false, especially with regard to *when* he sold the gun. He in-

[144] On June 2, 1987, firearms expert Lowell Bradford wrote a letter to Greg Stone in response to a request for a comparison analysis between Cesar's Harrington & Richardson .22 and Sirhan's Iver Johnson. Bradford wrote, "I have reviewed my notes of the post trial examination of the bullet evidence and find that the bullets from all of the victims, Wolfer's test bullets and the panel's test bullets have rifling marks of the lands which measure 0.054". At the time of our examination, the Crime Laboratory Information Service data was examined for the presence of any H&R revolver bullets that were marked with six riflings, right hand twist and land width of 0.054". None were present. . . . Now I find that this was an incorrect understanding. . . .

"The problem was that in 1975, no laboratory measurement data had been entered into the data. The current CLIS data now lists that H&R Model 922 as having class characteristics of six riflings, right hand twist with 0.054" land width mark.

"In other words, identical with Iver Johnson Cadet model."

That being true, no one had been able to prove that Cesar had his H & R .22 with him on the night of the shooting—and Cesar vehemently insists that the only gun he carried was his Rohm .38.

sisted, however, that the proof of his good intentions was telling the LAPD whom he "sold it to and where he lived."[145]

Cesar told me that he was still willing to take a polygraph examination. "The only thing is," he said, "if I took one, I'd want to take it at an agency, like the police department."

Why didn't the police give him a lie detector test, after having routinely given them to others who were questioned during the investigation of Senator Kennedy's murder? Cesar shrugged, "They asked me if I would take it, and I said I would. Then they suddenly decided not to give me the polygraph."[146]

Cesar and I had several sharp, even heated, exchanges when I confronted him with evidence of more than one gun being fired in the pantry; the position of his body in relation to Kennedy and the senator's wounds; the fact that he had drawn his gun and was possibly carrying a second gun; and his false and contradictory statements to the police and the FBI about his actions and movements that night.

In the midst of one of these confrontations, I looked Cesar right

[145] Regarding LAPD sergeant Paul O'Steen of SUS and his interview with Cesar at his Simi Valley home on June 24, 1968, Cesar recalled, "When he came out, I even showed him my .22 pistol that I owned. Because we were talking in depth about how easy it is to conceal a weapon like that and how Sirhan did it—and how he could keep it in his hand, and nobody would see it. And so I brought my .22 out, and I said, 'His is just like mine, except for it was a different brand.' "

A source placed me in contact with O'Steen's son, Paul E. O'Steen, Jr., in October 1993. Young O'Steen told me that his father was dying of prostate cancer, but that he would try to get him to talk to me. The following month, Sergeant O'Steen died before I had the opportunity to speak with him. His son gave me a statement from his father in response to my question about whether he had any doubts about the official investigation of the case. Through his son, Sergeant O'Steen stated, "At that time [in 1968], there were so many investigations going on and so many investigators. I was just one of them. I talked to a lot of people, and I may have known something important but just didn't realize it. All of the investigators had a piece of the puzzle, but there weren't many of us who saw the whole puzzle. I do know that we didn't want another Dallas, and I'm sure that, for my part, Sirhan Sirhan acted alone."

[146] In an undated, never sent reply to written questions posed to the LAPD by Allard Lowenstein, the LAPD stated, "Since all questions were satisfactorily answered and the evidence given by Mr. Cesar coincided with other evidence received by investigators, it was decided that a polygraph examination would not add to the investigation."

in the eye and asked, "Okay, Gene," I said, "let me ask you this point-blank: Did you shoot Bobby Kennedy, intentionally or accidently?"

Cesar glared right back at me and simply replied, "No."

This is how Cesar saw his dilemma: "I got caught in a situation I can't get out of. But no matter what anybody says or any report they come up with, you know, I know I didn't do it. The police department knows I didn't do it. There're just a few people out there who want to make something out of something that isn't there—even though I know that some of the evidence makes me look bad."

I went through the evidence with him again: his ownership of the .22, his feelings about the Kennedys, the inconsistencies in his stories, the muzzle distance, the angles of the bullets, the extra bullets, and his position directly behind Kennedy. It made a strong circumstantial case. Looking at the evidence, I asked what his thoughts would be.

"Probably the same thing as yours," he replied with some frustration.

I concluded my *Regardie's* article with the following observation: "Gene Cesar may be the classic example of a man caught at the wrong time in the wrong place with a gun in his hand and powder burns on his face—an innocent bystander caught in the cross fire of history. However, considering the current state of evidence, a more sinister scenario cannot be dismissed. Until the City of Los Angeles complies with its repeated promises of full disclosure of the murder investigation, monumental questions about the most basic issues surrounding the case remain. And after 19 years these issues deserve to be resolved."

Officers Robert Rozzi and Charles Wright: The controversial
AP wirephoto and caption *(Associated Press)*

Researcher Floyd Nelson
(Floyd Nelson)

Author Robert Blair Kaiser
(Robert Blair Kaiser)

LOS ANGELES POLICE DEPT.
CRIME LAB TEST SHOT
NAME *Sirhan, S. B.* DATE *6-6-68*
ADDRESS
MAKE *I & J* CAL. *22* TYPE *Rev*
NO. *H18602* DR. *168-521 466*
CRIME *187 P.C* OFFICER

H - 18602 - CADET MODEL

Mislabeled LAPD evidence envelope that confused Sirhan's Iver-Johnson revolver H53725 with test gun H18602
(California State Archives)

WEISEL (54)

KENNEDY (47)

TEST (55)

William Harper's Hycon Balliscan bullet comparisons
(California State Archives)

Reporter Ted Charach
(California State Archives)

Los Angeles district attorney Joe Busch *(California State Archives)*

Security guard Thane Eugene Cesar and family, 1967 *(Thane Eugene Cesar)*

Jim Yoder holding Cesar's Harrington & Richardson .22 revolver *(Beaux Carson)*

Cesar's sales receipt to Jim Yoder *(Cesar Collection)*

On the day of Sept 6, 1968 I recieved $15.00 from Jim Yolder. The Item Involued is a H & R. 22 pistol 9 shot serial No. Y 13332

Tione Cesar

Paul Schrade and former
congressman Allard
Lowenstein *(United Press
International)*

Attorney Vincent Bugliosi
(W. W. Norton)

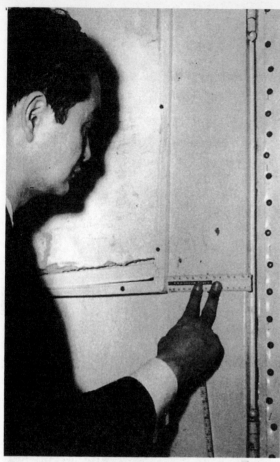

Thomas Noguchi examining alleged bullet holes, which are circled, in door frame *(California State Archives)*

Researcher Greg Stone *(Greg Stone)*

Professor Philip Melanson *(Philip Melanson)*

California state chief archivist John Burns *(California State Archives)*

The crime scene search: *left to right*, criminalist William Lee, Officer Kenneth Vogl, DeWayne Wolfer, Officer John Wilson (note: the center divider has been removed) *(California State Archives)*

Facing page, top left: FBI photo E-1, identifying two circled "bullet holes" in left door frame of the double swinging doors at the west end of the kitchen pantry *(FBI)*

Top right: FBI photo E-2, close-up view of identified circled bullet holes in E-1 *(FBI)*

Bottom left: FBI photo E-3, identifying two circled "bullet holes" in center divider *(FBI)*

Bottom right: FBI photo E-4, identifying reported "bullet mark" on door hinge *(FBI)*

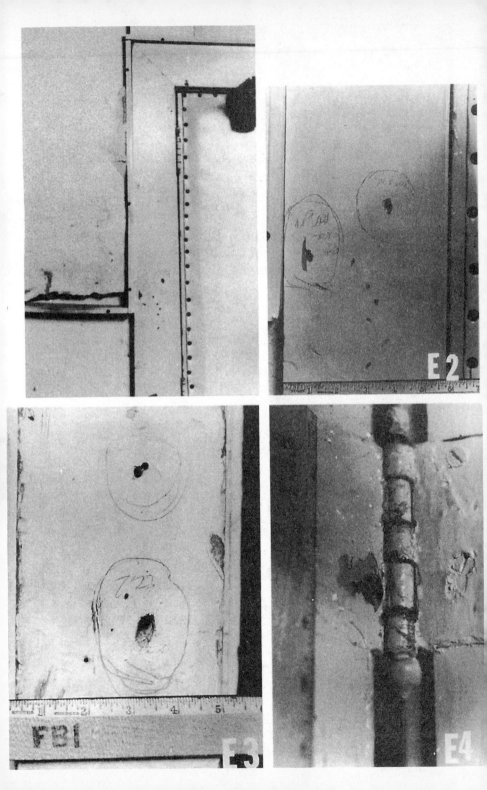

FBI special agent William
Bailey *(William Bailey)*

FBI special agent Roger
"Frenchy" LaJeunesse
(Roger LaJeunesse)

Author Dan E. Moldea
at the crime scene,
1987

III. THE CRIME SCENE REVISITED

22. The Release of the Official Files

At the time of my *Regardie's* article, it was clear that no thorough or adequate appraisal of crime scene issues would be possible as long as the LAPD continued to withhold its investigative files. Thus, after my interview with Gene Cesar, I simply concentrated on the crime scene issues, although Cesar continued to remain a suspect.

Playing off the release of *Regardie's*, Greg Stone pounced upon the nondisclosure theme in a sizzling June 3 press release, stating, "Nineteen years after the assassination of Senator Robert Kennedy, Los Angeles Mayor Tom Bradley was charged today with failure to implement the long-promised release of the primary investigative file on his death. . . . Approximately 95% of the police file . . . currently remains withheld, despite official promises for its release since 1969. The material contains 50,000 pages of documents, over 2,500 photographs and other evidence items."

Bolstering the impact of the *Regardie's* story and Stone's public lobbying campaign, surprisingly strong reviews supporting my article appeared in two unlikely publications, both of which had long defended the official version of the case: the *Los Angeles Times* and the *Washington Post.*[147]

The *Times* had called the LAPD for comment, reporting,

"[Commander] William Booth of the LAPD, who had not seen Moldea's piece, said that all the material that can be released has been released and that 'everyone has access to the same evidence and they can come up with their own theories.' The LAPD's position, he said, is summed up by the facts that Sirhan Sirhan was tried and convicted and is still in prison."

Booth's statement infuriated Greg Stone, because the LAPD appeared to have altered its position once again, now insisting that no more files would be released. But while the LAPD seemed to be backsliding, Stone and other advocates of full disclosure were buoyed by the sudden positive reaction to the possible release of the files. Stone, with the active support of Paul Schrade and Phil Melanson, immediately launched a full-scale attack on the LAPD and its continued efforts to conceal the files.

Then, suddenly, on June 26—while the *Regardie's* article was still on the newsstands—the city of Los Angeles reversed the LAPD's position, ordering the immediate release of the entire Robert Kennedy murder case file. Boxloads of documents began to be transported for permanent disposition to the California State Archives in Sacramento, where declassification commenced.

On October 28, 1987, while I was in Sacramento to lecture about the Mafia in America at the University of California at Davis, I stopped off at the state archives to pay my respects to John F. Burns, the state's chief archivist. He was principally responsible for cataloging, indexing, and preserving the Kennedy case file, which had offi-

---

[147] "Did Sirhan Act Alone?" *Washington Post,* May 26, 1987; "The Mystery Persists in R.F.K. Killing," *Los Angeles Times,* June 12, 1987.

cially been transferred by the city of Los Angeles on August 5.

A U.S. naval officer in 1968, who heard about the Kennedy shooting while standing watch on a ship returning from Vietnam, Burns had been the state archivist of California since 1981. He had been responsible for negotiating the transfer of the Kennedy documents from the city of Los Angeles to Sacramento.

True to the canons of archival practice during our conversation, Burns kept his silence about the files, pending a thorough assessment of what could be legally released. "We will be as open as possible," Burns told me, "and I will fight for the release of most of the material unredacted. Also, because of the volatile nature of the case, we won't discard anything. Even blank envelopes will be retained in order to allay any concerns by the research community."

Burns did inform me that all 50,000 documents, thirty-six cubic feet of material, would be released on twenty-four reels of microfilm, including reports of the 3,470 interviews conducted by the LAPD during its investigation. He added that several videotapes, 200 audio tapes, 230 items of evidence, and 3,400 photographs would also be available—along with a "finding aid" to help locate specific information. Sirhan's gun would be on display, too, as well as some of the physical evidence from the pantry.

Burns told me, "As a civil executive officer of the state of California, and personally, I have no feelings for or against Robert Kennedy, Sirhan Sirhan, the LAPD, or anyone else involved in this case. I just want to make sure that the record of this national tragedy be made available for historical scholarship. I'm just here to do what I do best."

Although I could not pry anything new out of Burns, I immediately took a liking to him, knowing that the fate of the files was in the hands of an honest and completely trustworthy person.

Indeed, with a minimum of censorship, the RFK case file was made public in a microfilm edition on April 19, 1988. However, on the day of the release, Burns announced that 2,410 photographs—with subjects unknown—from the case file had been inexplicably burned by the LAPD on August 21, 1968, just three months after the murder and nearly eight months before the conclusion of Sirhan's trial.

Furious over the news, Greg Stone told Linda Deutsch, an Associated Press reporter, "Someone should ask the police why they destroyed 2,400 photographs in the most important case they've ever examined. . . . We didn't know about that until today."

Stone also asked the Los Angeles Police Commission to investigate the destruction. In response, Robert Talcott, the president of the commission, replied, "From our viewpoint, the position of our investigation is exactly as it was: there was one person involved."

The LAPD spokesman, Commander William Booth, commented to the Associated Press, "It was 20 years ago and I certainly don't have any independent recollection. I don't know whether what was done here is routine or not because I don't know what was done here." After making inquiries within the department, Booth insisted that the 2,410 destroyed photographs were "superfluous" and non-coded duplicates of those already in the record.[148]

Also missing from the files were the taped statements of fifty-one key witnesses, including twenty-nine with accounts that "relate directly or indirectly to questions of conspiracy," Phil Melanson told reporters. He added, "LAPD conducted 3,470 interviews during its original investigation, yet only 211 witnesses and 301 interviews (some witnesses were interviewed more than once) were preserved on tape and released."

Melanson later executed an affidavit concerning the items missing from the LAPD release. He stated, "LAPD claimed to have performed several tests on the doorframes and ceiling tiles booked into evidence, in order to determine if the holes were, in fact, bullet holes.

[148] According to a May 16, 1969, memorandum from David Fitts to his file, 290 "post-mortem photographs of Senator Robert F. Kennedy" had been sealed by court order.

Regarding the photographs of Kennedy's autopsy, Schrade, Stone, Melanson, and all of the responsible critics *agreed* with the LAPD, the district attorney's office, and the state of California, which insisted that they not be released. (The autopsy photographs are absolutely precluded from release by a specific provision of California state law.)

There has never been a dispute about Dr. Thomas Noguchi's autopsy of Senator Kennedy; thus the photographs have no new evidentiary value.

During the course of my writing this book, a New York attorney, on behalf of his unnamed client, offered to sell me these autopsy photographs. When I refused, he offered to give them to me, for free, for publication in my book. I refused again.

"My complete examination of released LAPD files establishes that the substantive results of these tests are nowhere to be found in the preserved and released records. . . . The results of tests on the ceiling tiles and doorframes, tests described by an LAPD 'Work Log' as having been performed, were not present in released files. These tests (X-ray, chemical, and microscopic) were conducted to detect the presence of bullet holes or bullet materials. The files contain no explanation concerning the absence of these test results. . . . There is no explanation in released LAPD files concerning the description in an LAPD property report of 'numerous holes' in two pieces of wood from the pantry doorframe (pieces booked into evidence by LAPD)."

Regarding the destruction of the physical evidence that contained identified bullet holes, California archivist Burns later wrote to Melanson, "There is no information within the file concerning the destruction of the center divider, door frame, and ceiling tiles. After the records were opened, SUS leader Robert Houghton indicated that these materials were destroyed because they were 'bulky and difficult to store' and not needed for further investigatory purposes." Also confirming what Melanson claimed in his affidavit, Burns wrote, "Any tests performed on the ceiling panels and door frames are missing from the file."

After examining all of the available documents and noting the destruction of so many others, Burns told the Associated Press, "I've never seen a file quite this large. This is a very unusual murder file. I'm not absolutely satisfied that any questions [about the Kennedy murder case] are answered."

In a scathing April 22 editorial regarding the release of the case files three days earlier, the *Oakland Tribune* charged, "With its botched investigation and subsequent cover-up, the L.A. police department showed itself incompetent at best and guilty at worst of obstructing justice. Officials proved only what everyone knew: that Sirhan Sirhan fired shots at the senator on the night of his victory in the 1968 California presidential primary. But they suppressed a wealth of hard evidence that he did not act alone and, indeed, did not even fire the fatal shots. Their rush to judgment did justice a disservice and fed the public's unhealthy but understandable distrust of government."

However, the *Los Angeles Times,* after its supportive review of the *Regardie's* article, reverted to its former posture on the case, allowing it to be articulated by police reporter John Kendall, a longtime defender of the LAPD's Kennedy investigation, in his column, "My Beat," on April 30. Entitled "Die-Hards Are at It Again on Kennedy Death," Kendall's column defended the LAPD's investigation and even taunted assassination critics for their criticism of DeWayne Wolfer's work.

Then, in a misrepresentation of the 1975 firearms panel's examination, Kendall concluded, "For a second gunman to have shot Kennedy or the others, the invisible assassin would have had to fire a revolver exactly like Sirhan's . . . while using the same copper-coated, mini-mag, hollow-tip ammunition and shooting at the same time as Sirhan. And, without being seen by people closest to Kennedy in a pantry crowded with [seventy-seven] people.

"Now, what are the odds of a second gun? You'd have a better chance of winning the California Lottery."

The LAPD remained unrepentant and even defiant. Regarding release of the files, former LAPD chief of police Ed Davis told UPI, "It's like opening up a collection of pornography to a bunch of sex-hungry pornography addicts. They're going to fondle the gun, touch the wood, stick their fingers in the bullet holes, and read all the reports. But there isn't going to be much there."

Indeed, there wasn't. Many of the key materials had been destroyed already by the LAPD.

Watching Stone and Melanson wage their war, I stayed out of the fray over the release of the Kennedy files.[149] But, for me, the Robert

---

[149] By this time, I was back in Washington, D.C., and inundated with work for my fourth book, *Interference: How Organized Crime Influences Professional Football.* However, at Stone's request, I agreed to do interviews about the Robert Kennedy murder case on CBS's "Nightwatch," National Public Radio's "Weekend Edition," and a handful of other radio and television programs.

On April 22, 1988, I did a radio debate on KGIL in Los Angeles with Luke McKissack, Sirhan's attorney. In the midst of a discussion about whether one or two guns had been fired that night, McKissack stated, "There has been a suggestion about other bullets being fired. Remember, I've talked to some of these people, and I've heard conflicting statements. But, fundamentally, I think there is some evidence that a security guard by the name of Thane Eugene Cesar drew his weapon and may, in fact, have fired bullets. But there just doesn't appear to be any

Kennedy murder case just would not go away.

Although it was immediately evident that the LAPD files in the case were incomplete and that valuable evidence and records had been destroyed, Greg Stone convinced me in November 1989 that there was enough new information to draw me back into the investigation.

My first stop in Los Angeles was Parker Center, the downtown head-quarters for the LAPD. I had earlier given my *Regardie's* article to three homicide detectives, whom I had used as sources for my previous work on organized crime, and asked for their opinion of my article. One of them had actually played a minor role in the Kennedy murder investigation. The four of us met in a small interrogation room at the homicide division.

"Dan, I read your article," one of the detectives said, "and you don't have it."

"What do you mean I don't have it?" I asked defensively.

"You don't have it! You base nearly all of your research on eye-witness testimony. Eyewitness testimony? You talk about seventy-seven people in a room and twelve actual eyewitnesses to the shooting. These are people who were in the wrong place at the wrong time. You're expecting accuracy in their statements. Twelve different eye-witnesses will generally give you twelve different versions of a story."

"But in this case," I insisted, "especially with regard to muzzle distance, they're all saying the same thing: Sirhan never got off a single point-blank shot at Kennedy. There's no dispute here. There are not twelve different versions."

"Yeah, but eyewitnesses are not trained or experienced or qualified to make judgments about what they see in such situations. Don't get me wrong: eyewitness testimony occasionally makes convictions. But nothing beats physical evidence or a police official's expert testimony."

"So you're saying that only cops have the training, experience, and qualifications to know truly what they saw."

---

evidence that I've seen to suggest—he had a .38 revolver, for example, not a .22 Iver Johnson—that anything Thane Eugene Cesar had was used to kill Senator Kennedy."

"Essentially, yes, that's what I'm saying."

I started laughing out loud. And all three of the detectives looked puzzled at my reaction. One of them asked, "What's so funny, Dan?"

"I think I've just figured out how I'm going to approach the next phase of my research."

This time I decided not to rely on the supposedly shaky statements of eyewitnesses who found themselves thrust into a violent moment of American history. Instead, I decided to conduct a series of interviews over the next several months with the people whose training and experience would be beyond dispute: the officials, detectives, and patrolmen in the Los Angeles Police Department, the Los Angeles Sheriff's Department, the Los Angeles Fire Department, and the FBI, who performed their routine duties at the crime scene after the shooting. And the lists of those law enforcement personnel involved in the Robert Kennedy murder investigation were located at the California State Archives in Sacramento. They were now part of the public record.

Although I had access to both the active and the retired rosters of the LAPD, I found that my most difficult problem was identifying those officers and officials pictured in the captionless official and nonofficial LAPD photographs taken at the crime scene. Consequently—as Vincent Bugliosi had done before me with the controversial Associated Press photograph of Officers Rozzi and Wright—I began taking these pictures to the various divisions at Parker Center and to the LAPD's individual stations around the city.

Through my contacts, I was permitted to visit the various detectives' and patrolmen's offices. Upon my arrival at each location— where I was usually accompanied by one of my LAPD sources—I walked to the middle of their large group offices and held the photographs high in the air, shouting out, "Who wants to see some pictures of cops?"

Usually a party atmosphere quickly developed as LAPD officers and officials crowded around and gleefully identified their colleagues. Because of this enthusiastic cooperation, I was able to identify most of the LAPD personnel in the pictures.

Of the 187 principal law enforcement officials, detectives, and officers identified in LAPD records as having been involved in the

1968 Kennedy crime scene investigation, I was able to locate or learn the fate of 158. A total of 114 agreed to be interviewed and speak on the record. Another 26 refused to comment for various reasons; of that number, 8 refused to respond to written requests for interviews and 4 did not return my calls. Eighteen are known to have died since the murder. And I was simply unable to locate 29, many of whom are thought to be deceased.[150]

Virtually none of these law enforcement professionals had ever been interviewed about the Kennedy case. During my conversations with them, most were honest and unguarded in their responses to two basic questions about their work on the night of the RFK shooting: "What did you do?" and "What did you see?" Many officers had kept their field officer's notebooks, and some even referred to their notes during my interviews with them.

All but a small handful displayed a general lack of understanding regarding the significance of bullets recovered from the floor, the walls, and the door frames at the crime scene.

But before looking for the sources of the extra bullets controversy, I wanted to find out why the 2,410 photographs I would never have access to had been destroyed by the LAPD.

According to a August 21, 1968, "Employees Report," SUS member and LAPD lieutenant Roy Keene, now deceased, had signed off on the destruction of the photographs, which were burned in the incinerator at the County General Hospital. One of the two officers who carried out the assignment was SUS member Thomas J. Miller.

When I contacted Miller, he was very cooperative and told me,

---

[150] The preliminary results of this investigation are contained in my May 13, 1990, article in the *Washington Post*, "RFK's Murder: A Second Gun?: After 22 Years, the L.A. Police Talk about Extra Bullets." On May 16, NBC's "Unsolved Mysteries" featured a lengthy segment about the Kennedy case, based, in part, on the *Post* article—in which I advocated that an independent investigative body reopen the case. Also, during the NBC program, I was unbridled in my opinion that, on the basis of the existing crime scene evidence, two guns had been fired.

In the *Post* article, I concluded, "Theoretically, the firing of another gun besides Sirhan's at the Ambassador might have been accidental, defensive or sinister; it would be a mistake to rush to quick or simplistic judgments concerning the origin of additional assassination gunshots. The importance and complexity of this matter demand that it be examined impartially by a reconstituted official investigation."

"To control the confidentiality of or the security of documents, photos, reports, items of evidence and so forth, we tried to work with a minimum of, shall we say, copies. So that these things would not leak out to people who shouldn't have them or to—in cases we heard about in other major crime situations from other departments—they would not be souvenirs. And this has happened: scraps of clothing, threads of clothing, photographs ended up with souvenir hunters' collections. So in determining the exact number of sets of autopsy photos required for court preparation, we destroyed more than the copies necessary. That's all. That's all that was about."

I then asked, "But what about photographs taken at the crime scene? Were those destroyed?"

"For example, the Los Angeles Fire Department photographer [Harold Burba], who happened to be on the scene with a camera, doing his fire department crowd thing. He was just snapping as fast as he could snap, seeing what was going on in front of him. When we got the pictures, maybe we got twenty sets. . . . They were duplicate sets. There was no reason to have that many sets."

"What about the negatives? Were they destroyed too?"

"Oh, no, no. The negatives would initially go up to the photo lab. And eventually they came back down and were put in the office file set."

The photo negatives might have wound up in the files of SUS, but there was no record of their being in existence any longer. Apparently the negatives had been destroyed, too.

LAPD chief of detectives Robert Houghton, who put SUS together, told me, "There has been a lot of talk about photographers who took pictures and the pictures weren't returned to them. What I had done on that was—there were three assistant district attorneys assigned to this case by Evelle Younger: Dave Fitts, Buck Compton, and John Howard. I had those people sit down with my SUS investigators—the people who were most knowledgeable about the information coming in. One of the things the DA's people were told to do was to go through some two thousand photographs we had gotten from anybody we could. We screened out those that had no evidentiary value.

"A lot of the film we got was because we asked them to send it to us. I would assume that the investigators returned the photographs. If they had no value to us, we threw them away.

"If there was anything funny going on, those DA guys would have spotted it immediately."

23. *Bullet Damage*

Without question, the most controversial part of the LAPD's investigation of the Robert Kennedy murder case revolved around the crime scene search exclusively directed by Officer DeWayne Wolfer of the Criminalistics Section of the LAPD's Scientific Investigation Division (SID). For years, there had been claims that extra bullets had been found in the kitchen pantry by Wolfer. Some critics believed that he never reported them to his superiors or, if he did, he concealed their existence for unknown reasons. The discovery of even one extra bullet would prove that more than one gun had been fired, because Sirhan's Iver Johnson revolver could hold only eight bullets. Wolfer had always claimed that Sirhan fired all eight bullets and made good on each, hitting people with all eight shots.

From the outset, Wolfer had been adamant that he never confirmed bullet holes in anything but six people, as well as two entrance holes and one exit hole in the ceiling tiles suspended above the kitchen pantry. On September 20, 1971, in a sworn deposition for his defamation suit against Los Angeles attorney Barbara Blehr, which was later dismissed, he had the following verbatim exchange about bullet holes.

WOLFER: I went to the scene of the crime and I explored the trajectory of all of the holes in the wall, and the walls of victims. I interviewed several of the victims. I made up a basic plot plan, of all trajectories and holes and the persons in there. I was there immediately after the [shooting] of the Senator. I retrieved and was in charge of the crime scene and I recovered the bullets that were recovered. I checked all of the possibilities of holes, and I certainly feel that there were only eight shots fired and I accounted for all eight shots. . . .

QUESTION: And where did you find bullets holes?

WOLFER: Where did I find bullet holes?

QUESTION: Yes.

WOLFER: I made reports accounting for all bullet holes. I found them in the ceiling tiles, I found them in all bullet holes in the ceiling.

QUESTION: All of them were in the ceiling?

WOLFER: All holes, yes.

QUESTION: There weren't any in wood?

WOLFER: No.

QUESTION: None in—

WOLFER: If counsel is referring to what appeared in the newspapers showing it in wood, showing a hole, there were many holes and we explored all the holes in the door and were never able to find any bullets or even any indication that there was a bullet.

QUESTION: So, all of the bullets were in the ceiling as far as you know?

WOLFER: . . . Or in people.

QUESTION: . . . Was there a bullet hole in the woodwork between the swinging doors going to and from the kitchen?

WOLFER: No. There was not. I said this is a hole that I previously told you. There were many holes in the woodwork on the swinging doors that were caused by some other object. All of these holes were explored and no bullets were ever found.

QUESTION: What type of object was that particular hole caused by?

WOLFER: Well, these objects, the holes in this door, as I recall here today, were caused by something that went through and didn't spread them, but punched a hole there. You could see the impression of the wood pushed into the hole. It wasn't a typical bullet hole, but there were many of those holes in the door. In fact, when I arrived they had several of them circled.[151]

QUESTION: And what could they be caused by?

WOLFER: They were caused by some object poking the wood. A ramrod, a tray, a dish tray—there [were] many of those portable carts and [they] had a round area on it. That could have certainly caused it.

QUESTION: . . . Whatever became of that door frame?

WOLFER: I wouldn't recall, here today. I think that we even took portions of the door frame and x-rayed them and returned them to the Ambassador Hotel afterwards. As I recall, here today, but I am not sure.

In fact, there are *no* existing LAPD records of these scientific examinations of the suspected bullet holes. Also, LAPD records show that the door frames were *not* returned to the Ambassador Hotel after being booked on June 28, 1968. Instead, they were destroyed.

The first time the issue of extra bullets had come under public scrutiny was in May 1969, when the *Los Angeles Free Press* ran John Clemente's June 6, 1968, photograph showing suspected bullet holes

---

[151] The Kranz Report claimed, "Concerning the various circled holes in the pantry, particularly the circles on the wooden frames that had been removed, Wolfer replied that the police had circled every hole within the kitchen area as a matter of course."

However, according to all available photographs, eyewitness accounts, and police reports, the only holes circled were the four pictured in the left door frame and in the center divider.

in the center divider between two swinging doors at the west end of the kitchen pantry. These were the doors that Kennedy had just walked through after leaving the Embassy Room, en route to the Colonial Room. All of these reported bullet holes were directly in Sirhan's line of fire. The affidavit of Clemente's companion, John Shirley, stated that the divider "appeared to have been removed from the framework so that the bullets might be extracted from behind. It was then replaced but not firmly affixed."

Then there were the affidavits obtained by Vincent Bugliosi from three people who identified possible "bullet holes" in the center divider, including those from maître d' Angelo DiPierro and waiter Martin Patrusky. DiPierro, a former infantryman, had actually claimed to have seen the base of a .22-caliber bullet in one of the holes.

Bugliosi's third affidavit came from Los Angeles coroner Thomas Noguchi, who performed the autopsy on Senator Kennedy and also visited the crime scene a few days after the shooting to witness a re-creation of the shooting—which was photographed. In one picture, he is shown pointing to the alleged bullet holes in the center divider. In another photograph, he is seen measuring the distance between the two holes in the door frame. In his 1975 affidavit, Noguchi said, regarding the crime scene reconstruction, "I asked Mr. Wolfer where he had found bullet holes at the scene. . . . [He] pointed to several [circled] holes in the door frames of the swinging doors leading into the pantry. I directed that photographs be taken of me pointing to these holes. . . . I got the distinct impression from [Wolfer] that he suspected that the holes may have been caused by bullets."

And then, in May 1976, Greg Stone discovered the FBI's own official report that identified four bullet holes in the same locations, as well as a "suspected bullet hole" in a wall and a "suspected ricochet mark" on a door hinge at the crime scene.

Two of the identified bullet holes were in the center divider; the other two were in the frame of the left swinging door. All four holes were circled. Inside each circle was some scribbling, as well as what appeared to be the notation "LASO" and the number "723."

Since the night of the 1968 shooting, the author of those scribbled and indistinct letters around the holes had remained unknown to investigators of the murder. Acting on the premise that the man circling the holes was a Los Angeles Sheriff's Office (LASO) official with the badge number 723, I contacted one of my sources with the sheriff's department, former LASO deputy Dick Mardiros of Pasadena. Without giving Mardiros any details, I simply asked him to help me find out who wore LASO badge number 723 on June 5, 1968.

After a handful of telephone calls, we learned that LASO deputy Walter Tew of the Firestone Station had worn badge number 723. Upon receipt of Tew's name, it became easy to interpret the indistinct markings within three of the four circles as the letters "W Tew."

I obtained Tew's last known telephone number and called him.

Unfortunately, Tew, who retired in 1980, had died in June 1988, before I had a chance to speak with him. I did talk to his widow, Vivian Tew, but she sighed that her husband didn't like to discuss his work at home. And he kept no notes or journals about his life as a sheriff's deputy.

After Mrs. Tew provided me with some background information about her husband, I started to seek his former colleagues at the LASO.

Ex–LASO sergeant John C. Barber, now the chief of security at UCLA, also knew Tew, who was part of an LASO contingent of officers who had cleared people out the Kennedy crime scene before the LAPD finally secured it. Speaking of the circles Tew drew around the four bullet holes, Barber told me, "That would be the typical way a deputy sheriff in that era would mark his evidence. He would say, 'This is here.' You can't put a tag on it. And he would mark it, making sure that he didn't interfere with the hole. Mark it; put his name and badge number and LASO.

"Now, Walt [Tew] may have assumed that we [LASO] were going to take [the initial investigation], because we had control of the crime scene. There were so few blue suits [LAPD officers] there that we were really the only police in that area for the period of time of, I'd say, ten to fifteen minutes."

Tew's commander that night was Lieutenant Beto Kienast. When I asked Kienast whether he remembered receiving reports that bullet holes had been discovered by his men at the crime scene, he replied,

"I vaguely recall that, yes." He added that after marking the bullet holes, Tew would have jotted his actions down in his deputy's notebook. He would then have reported the discovery to Kienast, who in turn would have added the information to the report he later sent to the commander of his division. All of the sheriff's office reports from the evening would eventually be combined, according to Kienast, and turned over to the LAPD.

It was likely, then, that discoveries of apparent bullet holes at the crime scene by Tew and other LASO personnel would appear in the LAPD files now in Sacramento. In fact, the newly released files revealed that at least one LASO report had been received by the police.

An interview report numbered I-4411, describing an interview with LASO captain Paul Bratsch, states on page 1, "Captain Bratsch set up his command post on the 3rd floor of IBM at 1:30 A.M. He had Deputy T.J. Smith start a command post log. *(See attached log.)"* (emphasis added).

Regarding the log, Captain Bratsch told me, "It would include the times we received information, dispatched people over to the hotel, and the individuals in charge."

However, the log itself and the LASO's official reports from the night of the shooting were also missing from the LAPD's case files and, thus, were not included in the release to the California State Archives. (Deputy Smith did not return my calls.)

Astonishingly, even though LAPD records showed twenty-three interviews with LASO personnel, there was no record of an interview with Walter Tew. In fact, no known record of his presence in the pantry existed in the available LAPD investigative files—even though he is the only law enforcement official to have memorialized his presence at the crime scene by circling what the FBI and many others would later describe as "bullet holes."

Also not reported is a critical discovery by LASO deputy Tom Beringer, another member of the Lindblom wedge of deputies who had cleared out the crime scene on the night of the shooting. Beringer told me, almost matter-of-factly, concerning his presence in the kitchen pantry, "I remember one person trying to take a bullet out of the wall with a knife, a silver knife, for a souvenir." Beringer added that the man with the knife was wearing a tuxedo.

Startled by this information Beringer had just innocently volunteered, I asked, "Sir, just sort of think back for a second here when you saw this person digging in the hole. Was this person digging way below, down at the bottom of the door? Up above?"

"Probably middle," Beringer replied.

"At eye level then?"

"Yeah. He wasn't crouching and he wasn't reaching."

"And do you recall whether it was the edge of the door or in the middle of the door? Or whether there were two doors? And whether it was in the middle of two doors? Do you recall that?"

"There were two doors."

"And where was he digging?"

"On the edge."

"He was digging on the edge? Of both doors? Or in the middle of both doors?"

"Well, where the two came together. Would that be possible?" Beringer asked me.

I replied, "Sort of like a center divider, then?"

"Right."

"So he was digging in the center divider at eye level?"

"Yeah."

"And you stopped him from doing it?"

"Yeah."

"And did you report this to anybody?"

"The crime scene people. After we pushed all of the people out and all the exits [were] secured, the crime scene people came in. Then the LAPD people started posting their officers at the doors to secure it. . . ."

"Now, when you saw this person digging [the object] out, is there a possibility that he was digging out a nail? Or are you sure he was digging out a bullet?"

"It wasn't a nail. It was a definite bullet hole."

There is an official, though cursory, LASO report on Beringer's activities; but nothing is noted about the man in the tuxedo who was trying to dig a bullet out of the center divider.

After I began the second phase of my investigation in December 1989, identified Tew, and interviewed Beringer, several LAPD and

LASO officers told me that during the 105 minutes after the shooting, from 12:15 A.M. to 2:00 A.M., when the SID took control of the area, they saw what they believed to be bullet holes. Among these officers—all mentioned earlier in connection with the police response to the Kennedy shooting—were field commander James D. Jones, Edward W. Crosthwaite, and Albert L. Lamoreaux.

Other LAPD officials and officers, who were not part of the actual crime scene search but were present for part of the time while it was being conducted, also told me that they believed that they had seen or heard of bullet holes at the same location. They included:

- Lieutenant Albin S. Hegge, who then had over twenty years of experience with the LAPD and who coordinated and cataloged information coming into Rampart Station on the morning of the shooting. When I asked about bullets recovered at the crime scene, he told me that they were recovered from door panels: "I know there were some, because they took out the panels. I mean, they cut it out and saved it. . . . And they took them down to the lab so that they could examine the bullets."

- LAPD inspector Robert F. Rock, who later served as an interim chief of the LAPD. When I asked him whether he knew of any bullet damage in the pantry, he told me, "Yeah, in fact, I think they took a whole door frame to preserve it, as whatever evidence would be required." When I asked Rock whether investigators had dug out a couple of bullets from the door frame, he replied, "They did in the final analysis."

- Sergeant William R. Unland of the LAPD's Intelligence Division. "There were holes all over the kitchen," he told me. "You know, where the gun fired. All of them [the bullets] didn't hit somebody."

- Sergeant Raymond Rolon, the Rampart official who played a prominent coordinating role during the aftermath of the shooting. He told me that while the crime scene investigation was being conducted by the SID, he walked through the kitchen pantry. He recalled, "One of the investigators pointed to a hole in a door frame and said, 'We just pulled a bullet out of here.' "

- Sergeant James R. MacArthur, the Rampart detective responsible for the crime scene. MacArthur told me that he, too, had seen "quite a few" bullet holes at the scene.

However, like the others, MacArthur doesn't remember who took the actual bullets out of the holes. "Basically, that was up to the SID to locate [the bullet holes]," MacArthur said, pointing to a diagram of the kitchen. When I asked MacArthur why he didn't take the bullets out, he replied, "I worked homicide for a number of years, but we always left [that] up to [SID]. We would locate, basically, do the initial investigation, but then call them in. They had the expertise as to how to get them out."

· Officer Peter M. Despard of the Wilshire Division did assist the SID investigation. He told me, "I saw suspected bullet holes, but I never confirmed that they were bullet holes."

I also located several other LAPD officers who were posted at the doors of the kitchen pantry to guard the crime scene during the SID search. Officers Addison A. Arce, John H. Cronshaw, Anthony E. Davis, Thomas H. Dickson, Robert D. Hill, and Jeff A. Rogers all told me that during the course of the evening they had guard duty at the crime scene. They did not assist the SID in their crime scene search, and none of them remembered observing bullets holes in door frames.

However, several other officers also played an active role at the crime scene, including these:

· Officer John L. Wilson of Rampart, who spent nearly twelve hours at the crime scene, according to his LAPD report. He told me that he remembered seeing what he believed to be bullet holes in the pantry. During my interview with him, I showed him photographs and a diagram of the pantry. He couldn't remember their exact locations.

· Officer Kenneth E. Vogl, Wilson's partner, who also spent nearly twelve hours at the crime scene, according to his official LAPD report. Vogl told me that he didn't recall the specific locations of bullet holes other than those accounted for in the ceiling. However, he did discover two bullet fragments on the floor of the kitchen pantry near the west end of the ice machine. He identified one of the fragments as being nearly half a .22

bullet and the other as being "a shaving." When I asked Vogl to tell me on a scale of one to ten, with ten being absolute certainty, whether what he had seen were bullet fragments, Vogl replied, "Oh, it was a ten. There's no doubt. I saw fragments."

To my question whether he had marked or in any way identified the bullet fragments, Vogl replied that he reported his discovery to one of the SID officials at the scene. "For continuity of evidence," he told me, "you just show the guys doing the investigating so they can testify to it in court."

- Officer Robert G. Rozzi of the Hollywood Division, whom attorney Vincent Bugliosi had identified from an Associated Press wirephoto. Rozzi stated in his November 15, 1975, affidavit, "Sometime during the evening when we were looking for evidence, someone discovered what appeared to be a bullet a foot and a half or so from the bottom of the floor in a door jamb on the door behind the stage. I also personally observed what I believed to be a bullet in the place just mentioned."

Claiming that the bullet was actually a nail, the LAPD had scoffed at the AP picture that showed Officer Rozzi and his partner, Charles A. Wright, examining the object in Sirhan's line of fire that had lodged in the door jamb of the stage door. However, it is clear that the LAPD's own photographer had been instructed to take several shots of the same scene. One picture shows a close-up of the object, which, according to Rozzi, appeared to be the base of a bullet.

Standing by what he wrote in his affidavit in 1975, Rozzi told me, "I was just basically in there doing my job with the other guys. The only criticism I received was that I had talked to Bugliosi without first checking with the department. . . . What I said before has been documented. Whatever I told Bugliosi, that's what I had to say."

- Officer Charles A. Wright, who was with Rozzi and also part of the AP photo controversy. Wright told Bugliosi that he would cooperate with him, and then he balked, refusing to do so—after apparently being pressured not to cooperate by the city attorney's office. Bugliosi never received Wright's statement.

However, with Wright now retired, I found him more co-operative. He told me that he had balked with Bugliosi because he had been advised by his superiors not to say anything in the midst of the legal battle being waged by Bugliosi on behalf of Schrade.

When I asked Wright to tell me on a scale of one to ten, with ten being absolute certainty, that the object he had seen in the hole was a bullet, he replied, "You can never be 100 percent sure. But I would say that it would be as close to ten as I'd ever want to go without pulling it [the object in the hole] out." Wright added that he had never found out what happened to the object.

When I asked him why he or Rozzi didn't remove it himself, Wright replied, "You wouldn't take it out yourself, because you haven't got the proper equipment. If you try to pry it out with a pen-knife or a ball-point pen, you'll end up damaging the bullet and destroying any ballistic value."

Wright said that he had reported to the LAPD investigators in charge of the investigation that the object was, in fact, a bullet. However, in the official LAPD interview reports of Rozzi and Wright, there is no mention of their having examined a suspected bullet in the door jamb of the stage door—despite the existence of several official LAPD photographs of Rozzi and Wright examining the suspected bullet.[152]

---

[152] In an undated, never sent reply to a series of questions by Allard Lowenstein, the LAPD stated of Rozzi and Wright, "Neither officer was a qualified ballistics or firearms expert. They were not police technicians assisting the detectives.

"The officers were interviewed [by the LAPD] on the subject of the photograph. They stated that after the crowd partially dissipated, press photographers asked them to pose for photographs, pointing to the holes. The [AP] photograph was taken before the press was allowed to enter the shooting scene. The officers, keeping Chief Reddin's policy of full press cooperation in mind, posed to accommodate the press. The officers recalled that other holes were photographed, some of which had been circled by investigators.

"The photographers asked the officers if the holes were bullet holes. They replied, 'I don't know—could be.' They did not state that there was a bullet in the door frame."

Before seeing this document, I had already interviewed Wright, who told me that he and Rozzi had been posed and photographed by crime scene examiners for their police photographers—not for news photographers.

Nowhere in the LAPD files, in fact, is there any written reference to this examination, or to the recovery of any object from the location—although something was clearly recovered.[153]

[153] During my investigation of the suspected Rozzi/Wright bullet, I came across a statement by Richard Strobel, an editor at the Associated Press, who has been credited with writing the caption under the AP photograph of Rozzi and Wright, identifying the "object" as a "bullet." Strobel was interviewed in 1975 by official investigators and asked about the AP's picture of the alleged bullet hole found by Rozzi and Wright. Strobel said, "I couldn't possibly put out this picture without being told what the photographer said he shot." He added that the photographer had never reported any error in the caption.

Wally Fong was the AP photographer who snapped the picture. It was one among many that he shot the night of the shooting. Fong told me he realized that there was controversy over his photograph—but that he never bothered to learn why.

Fong was on assignment to cover the Kennedy victory party. He was in the Embassy Room at the time of the shooting, and he heard the shots. At first, he didn't know for sure that they were gunshots. When he realized that there had been a shooting, he tried to get into the pantry but was blocked by the push of the crowd storming out of the kitchen.

Fong said that he remained at the Ambassador for about an hour after the shooting without ever going into the pantry. He then went back to the AP office and then returned to the crime scene. That was when he took the picture of Rozzi and Wright. The two officers were in the midst of looking at the object in the door frame. *He did not pose them;* he did not ask them to do anything. He photographed them in the course of their natural routine.

I read Fong the caption as it went off the AP wire. Fong remembered that they were looking at an object in a hole. I informed him that the caption to his photograph had identified the object as a bullet.

When I asked Fong if he remembered this caption, he said that he did not. I told him that Richard Strobel had admitted writing the caption, insisting that he would have done so only after being told by the photographer.

Fong said that he never told Strobel that the object was a bullet. He said that he did not remember anyone's ever telling him that there was a bullet in the hole. He insisted that the police were not examining an object—instead, they were examining holes. "The word object never came up," Fong stated.

24. *The Untold Story of the Crime Scene Search I*

Obviously, the key to whether bullet holes, bullets, and bullet fragments had been found in the kitchen pantry rested with the crime scene search conducted by DeWayne Wolfer and the SID on the night of the Kennedy shooting. Thus, I focused my attention on the six hours between 2:00 A.M. and 8:00 A.M. on June 5, 1968, when Wolfer along with his partner, Sergeant William J. Lee, and their staff thoroughly examined the kitchen pantry of the Ambassador Hotel, searching for physical evidence, especially bullet holes.

As part of my research, I tracked down and interviewed nearly everyone alive who participated in the crime scene search.

Wolfer refused my repeated written requests for an interview. However, his recollections about that night are clearly memorialized in, among other places, his sworn statements at the June 1968 grand jury hearing, Sirhan's 1969 trial, the Board of Inquiry hearings in 1971, and the deposition in his defamation suit against Los Angeles attorney Barbara Blehr in 1971. Moreover, he had prepared a very sketchy log, a mere four pages long, of his personal activities from June 5 to June 19, 1968.

Lee also refused to be formally interviewed. However, I had a brief but pleasant conversation with him, during which he did provide me some background information.

At the time of the murder, Lieutenant Donald Mann served as the SID's administrator. Technically, he had been Wolfer's and Lee's supervisor and only had a peripheral role in the actual crime scene search. Mann agreed to a lengthy interview with me.

Also present during the crime scene search were photographer Charles Collier and surveyor Albert J. LaVallee. I had two long interviews with Collier. LaVallee had died several years before I began my investigation.[154]

Wolfer and Lee had two assistants that night at the kitchen pantry: Dave Butler and William E. O'Reilly, neither of whom is mentioned in any known official LAPD documents concerning the case. They spent nearly the entire night at the crime scene and performed a variety of tasks when ordered to do so by Wolfer. Both Butler and O'Reilly allowed me to interview them.

SID investigators Robert Druley and Danny J. Miller did not participate in the actual crime scene search. However, they did perform work on and with the physical evidence in the SID laboratory at Parker Center. Like Butler and O'Reilly, they are not mentioned in any official LAPD reports about the Kennedy probe. Druley and Miller also agreed to be interviewed.

Because of the lack of official LAPD documents regarding the SID's crime scene investigation, this chapter is based primarily upon the interviews I conducted with these SID personnel.

---

[154] LaVallee had created a blueprint and a scale model of the crime scene, which was placed in SUS headquarters, on the eighth floor at Parker Center.

At the time of the Kennedy murder, the SID's chief of criminalists was Lieutenant Donald W. Mann, who supervised ten employees in his unit, including DeWayne Wolfer. Explaining his operation to me, Mann said, "The SID included the bomb squad, ballistics, firearms in general, fingerprints, all photographic work, polygraph, and the Criminalistics Section. I was the officer in charge of the Criminalistics Section. That entailed firearms; and we called the section 'Comparative Analysis,' which also did hair analysis, alcohol testing, and fingerprints chemically through cloth. Narcotics analysis was a separate section in the criminalistics unit."

In his twenty-third year with the LAPD at the time of the Kennedy investigation, Mann, who had spent four years in the U.S. Army working on chemical warfare, said that he was at home when his wife informed him of the shooting. Soon thereafter, he received a telephone call from a superior, ordering him to report immediately to Parker Center. "I went to the police station, and everything was in an uproar. I remember going down to the detectives to see what they wanted done. Sirhan was sitting in a chair [in the detective bureau]. And there was nobody around him. I'll never forget that. So I stood by, just in case he decided to walk around or something. Pretty soon, an inspector came in. He said, 'Who's this?' And I said, 'This is the suspect.' And, boy, he hit the ceiling. 'Has he been booked?' 'No.' Oh, boy, things began to happen."

Mann said that he never went to the crime scene. But, speaking of his division's responsibility there, Mann explained, "If a SID man is out at the scene of a crime, he is to take orders from the detective, equal to his own supervisor, if there is one there. We are a support unit. The detectives—if something goes wrong or they miss some evidence—they have the final responsibility for it. The detective tells us what they want us to do. Of course, we make a lot of suggestions. But, in the final analysis, the detective has to say how they went about it."

Sergeant MacArthur, the detective in charge of the crime scene, agreed with Mann but added, "You can't be in two places at once, so we relied on what Wolfer was doing, and he was the expert in SID. . . . If somebody goofed up, it was the SID—because, actually, any evidence that was reported, there was complete follow-up."

Of course, the problem is that the records of this follow-up—especially regarding the search of the alleged bullet holes at the crime scene—no longer exist, assuming they ever did.

Although Mann supervised Wolfer, he appeared to resent his subordinate's independence. "Wolfer was a particularly strong individual," Mann said. "He was hard to supervise. He would go off by himself, and sometimes he would get himself in trouble and us, too. He would work with them [other LAPD divisions] without even me knowing it. It kind of burned me up at times. To keep the paperwork straight, I would sign off on some of the stuff. I would read it to know as much as possible as to what was going on, but I imagine that there was verbal communication that nobody ever signed for. It wasn't Wolfer's fault—well, partly, because he was that kind of person—but it was more upstairs [the LAPD's high command]."

I asked Mann what the SID's principal responsibility was at the crime scene. He replied, "We would start looking for shell casings, bullet holes, angles if there were bullets that went into the wall. We would try to make some kind of diagram as to where the bullets came from."

I then asked Mann if bullets were recovered from the walls in the kitchen pantry. Mann replied, "Well, I don't really know, because this was of such a big nature that I would just hear talk. I was responsible for Wayne and Bill. It was secret stuff from then on, because of the person [Wolfer] involved and so forth."

"So you never received reports about the bullets recovered at the scene?" I inquired.

"No. I didn't okay those reports. The chief told me, 'It's perfectly all right. You are relieved of responsibility.' "

"Did you find out about any bullets recovered from the crime scene?"

"You know, I found out more from the newspaper than I did [from Wolfer]. . . ."

"What would happen when you signed a report? Would they say, 'Here, Don, sign this?' "

"I'd look at it, and see if there was anything as far as my knowledge went. If it seemed okay to me, I would okay it. But in this case, as I recall, it was just kind of taken out of my hands."

Essentially, Mann's signature approval on Wolfer's reports was pro forma. "They had to have a name on there before they could file them," Mann said.[155]

Toward the end of the interview, I again asked Mann what he thought of Wolfer. This time, Mann replied, "I was neutral on him. He had a lot of ability. He saw some unique stuff. But, in my opinion, he was not afraid to go out on a limb over questionable evidence. Perhaps I shouldn't say that. I don't think he did that on this case, because it was straightforward. He's the sort of individual that your best deal is to appeal to his ego. He's quite egotistical. He was going to go his way, no matter what. You really didn't supervise him."

On the night of the shooting during the crime scene search, Wolfer had no supervision. He was the man in charge.

When Wolfer and his staff arrived at the Ambassador and took over the crime scene investigation, at 2:00 A.M., he assigned LAPD photographer Charles Collier the task of taking "orientation photos."

The fifty-one-year old Collier became a photographer at nineteen in Oklahoma City, primarily doing studio work for a commercial photographer. When World War II began, he was assigned to the Army's 101st Airborne Division and remained there for five years. A

---

[155] The known analyzed evidence reports signed by Lieutenant Mann were these, all from 1968: June 5 (clothing worn by Sirhan); June 6 (the Kennedy neck bullet and Sirhan's Iver Johnson revolver H53725); June 7 (Walker's H-Acid test on Kennedy's suit jacket, as well as other articles of Kennedy's clothing); June 11 (coroner's photos and X rays of Kennedy's wounds, the Iver Johnson test gun H18602, and CCI .22-caliber ammunition); June 19 (miscellaneous women's clothing and accessories found in "rear alley 1829 S. Crescent Heights"); June 20 (sound-level test results using a sound-level meter, an unidentified Iver Johnson revolver, and a box of mini-mag ammunition); June 24 (bullets and other materials found in Sirhan's car); June 28 (trace bullet trajectories and search for physical evidence, which included two ceiling panels, two boards from door frame, and a set of beads); July 8 (Wolfer's accounting of Sirhan's eight shots); July 8 (comparison of expended shell casings); July 15 (confirmation that the bullets removed from Kennedy's neck, Goldstein, and Weisel were fired from Iver Johnson revolver H53725 and that the remaining fragments of the other bullets removed from the other victims were too badly damaged for comparison purposes); August 12 (comparison of shells with "approximately 40 pounds [37,815] .22 caliber shell casings").

first lieutenant, he was among the team of photographers who chronicled the D-Day invasion of France in 1944.

After the war, he and his new wife moved to Los Angeles. He began working with the LAPD as a civilian employee photographer in 1952. He worked on the Black Dahlia case, the Marilyn Monroe suicide, the Charles Manson investigation, and the Hillside Strangler case, among many others famous investigations. He later became a supervisor in the LAPD/SID's photo lab in Parker Center before retiring in 1980.

Describing his job at a crime scene, Collier said, "Photography usually comes first. They [the SID] will want specific things, and they will tell me what they want. But then they let me record the scene. Everything. So I go around on my own, and take as many shots as I want to . . . and then of everything the investigators want me to photograph. I took both black and white and color. It's routine for a photographer to protect himself by maybe taking a second shot of something—or two or three shots from a different angle . . . before they disturb things. The same with something on the floor. It's usually not disturbed until you get a picture of it. And then they take up the evidence.

"Since I was a supervisor, I didn't do too much darkroom work. But, more often than not, I would develop the film, especially on the important cases." Collier told me that he developed some but not all of the pictures in the Kennedy case.

Collier explained that his photographs would be numbered in white ink by police investigators after they were developed. They would not be numbered as they were taken; instead, they were numbered in whatever sequence the investigator decided they should be in.

Regarding the destruction of photographs, Collier told me, "After the negatives are developed and the prints are printed, it's routine to throw away stuff that's already duplicated in some other picture. That's routine."

Collier added that he never kept any of the photographs he took while on the job. "They belong to the police department. No, no. I never kept negatives."

Speaking of the Kennedy investigation, Collier said that standard operating procedure was followed. "In a case like this, hundreds of pictures are taken. I wouldn't know how many. A rough estimate: two or three hundred. It was a famous case."

Collier said that he specifically took photographs of the route taken by Kennedy from his room to the Embassy Room, the podium in the Embassy Room where Kennedy gave his victory speech, the route taken by Kennedy from the Embassy Room to the kitchen, the kitchen pantry, suspected bullet holes, and the blood on the pantry floor.

Collier told me, "I remember spending the whole night there and taking lots of pictures. That's a vivid memory. I remember taking lots of pictures of bullet holes. I would estimate six or seven." When I asked where the bullet holes were, Collier replied, "In the walls in the pantry of the kitchen and in the doors, too." He added that he took some of these pictures on his own and was specifically ordered to take some of the pictures of these holes by Wolfer.

When I asked whether he actually saw the bullets, Collier replied, "No. You could just see the holes where they went in—but the investigators would dig out the bullets. I wouldn't normally be interested. The investigators would be. They dig them out. They're interested in the bullets."

When I challenged Collier as to how sure he was that what he had photographed were indeed bullet holes, he became defiant. "A bullet hole looks like a bullet hole—if you've photographed enough of them."

I had brought along all of the known photographs he had taken at the crime scene. Collier identified several circled holes in his pictures. With my tape recorder on, he specifically identified photographs 18, 18A, and 18B as showing bullet holes. All of these pictures were of the center divider.

"And so you could clearly identify these as bullet holes?" I asked.

"Oh, yes, yes," he replied. "I wouldn't doubt that they're bullet holes."

He added that they were clearly identified as bullet holes by the SID investigators, who posed for pictures, pointing at them.

"They ran strings from the bullet hole to [Sirhan's location to] determine the angle. And they would know where the gunman was standing. . . . They wait for the pictures to be taken. And then dig them [the bullets] out." However, he didn't recall photographing any slugs that had been specifically identified as having been removed from either the walls or the doors.

Consistent with what Officer Kenneth Vogl, a crime scene guard, told me, Collier also remembered taking pictures of bullets or bullet fragments on the floor of the kitchen pantry, as well as ricochet marks.

Although Collier estimated that he took 200 to 300 photographs at the crime scene, only 51 have been accounted for in official LAPD records. The numbering sequence assigned to his photographs runs as high as 98—an apparent indication that at least 47 pictures in the official police sequence are missing. Moreover, the LAPD has never released any captions for the crime scene photographs, including those that Collier said clearly pictured bullet holes.

In a 1971 deposition, Wolfer was asked about bullet holes and the photographs of them taken at the crime scene.

> WOLFER: Anything we found that looked like a bullet hole we explored. We went into and opened it up to see what was in it.
> QUESTION: Did you photograph it?
> WOLFER: Not all of that. We would have had too many photographs.
> QUESTION: How about the door jamb going into the kitchen where the swinging doors are?
> WOLFER: We did open up the holes that were circled and examined all other possibilities.
> QUESTION: How did you open them up?
> WOLFER: We took a knife and cut into the holes or whatever we had to do. We went into the holes and saw what was in it.
> QUESTION: You mean you probed the holes?
> WOLFER: We didn't probe, because if there [were] bullets I wouldn't want to scratch or damage the bullet to see what was in the back or what was in the hole.
> QUESTION: Was that photographed?
> WOLFER: No, because this is a negative type. If you don't find

a hole—if you don't find a bullet we wouldn't photograph just any hole. I mean there were too many holes to photograph. . . . I mean, if we had found something, naturally, we would have immediately photographed it.

Wolfer's statements contradict LAPD photographer Collier, who clearly remembers seeing bullet holes and being ordered to photograph them.

William E. O'Reilly, an officer in the SID's firearms unit and an assistant to Wolfer, said that he spent "a couple of hours" at the crime scene. The son of an officer in the SID's electronics unit, O'Reilly was in bed with his wife, watching the Kennedy victory celebration on television. He told me, "I was only twenty-three years old, so I was pretty impressionable. I wasn't naive, because my father had been a police officer for thirty years. I worked Watts after a couple of years. So I'd been a street cop and seen a lot of shootings and have been involved in shootings and things like that. But I just sat and just got tears in my eyes. Here is the man who is about to be the leader of our country. In my opinion, I thought he was going to win. Then, all of a sudden, someone has just killed him. And it's like, 'God, what's going on with our country? We're falling apart!' "

O'Reilly had earned his B.S. degree in forensic science at Long Beach State College before joining the LAPD and later received his master's degree. At Long Beach, Wolfer was one of his instructors. When O'Reilly joined the SID, Wolfer became his mentor. Speaking of Wolfer, O'Reilly told me, "He was probably one of the most recognized forensics men in the country. The man is a genius, and he knows what he's doing. He's taken a lot of heat over the years about different things, but there isn't anybody better in his field."

When O'Reilly arrived at the Ambassador Hotel to begin work, he took his orders from Wolfer. "In that situation, you basically let DeWayne do everything and just do what you're told. When you've got the master, you don't want to make a mistake, and screw something up. . . .

"It was amazing, because when it happened, it was one of those situations that everybody realized how serious it was. Nobody wanted to violate Sirhan's rights and to jeopardize the prosecution. Everyone was so cautious. It was not like a normal case."

Regarding his duties that night, O'Reilly explained, "I was just basically going back to the office with different things that we picked up and recovered. It wasn't a matter in my mind of whether he [Sirhan] did it or not. It was a matter of being able to show in a court of law to corroborate that he had done it.

"What I'm concerned about is, number one, I wanted to do everything and think of everything. Because once we leave, it will never be the same again. You only have one opportunity. And that's kind of the Golden Rule of the crime scene. That's why you photograph it first. Because once you pick up or move the very first piece of evidence, you've disturbed the crime scene forever."

O'Reilly recalled the search of the pantry. "I remember something about ceiling tiles. But, a lot of times, that doesn't mean that there was something there. I mean, remember, we're looking for bullets; we're scouring the whole thing for anything that could be. Like in a ceiling tile, it could have gone through. And you would have to be looking into the false ceiling and/or up above that—or also for a ricochet.

"I may have listened to television and watched it six times when they replayed it [the shooting], counting the shots and things like that.[156] But when I get there, I remember that I am trying to reenact that, independently, and corroborate what I already know. It's an unusual situation, because you already have seen what has happened. But what we're trying to do is corroborate exactly how many shots were fired. And to make sure that there isn't more than one individual or someone else in the heat of what had happened—who had also done something. What we have to do is show that [a specific] projectile went from [a certain] gun, from that direction, and that that gun was in the hand of that individual. We're only concerned about the projectiles exiting one particular firearm to the exclusion of any other firearms."

Speaking of the work done by the late Albert J. LaVallee, the

---

[156] Apparently, O'Reilly was not aware that the actual shooting had not been recorded from beginning to end.

SID's surveyor, O'Reilly told me, "You'd have a diagram of the whole premises to scale. . . . And after you take the bullet out—dig it out of the wall very carefully—you'd put a copper rod in there. And that would give you the angle and the trajectory of how the bullet entered the wall and from which direction."[157]

Upon hearing that, I asked O'Reilly where he and the SID found the bullet holes. He replied, "God, it's been so long, I don't even remember."

"Okay, but were you there when they were digging the bullets out? What's the process?"

"Well, really, it's a pretty simple process. You take a penknife, a crochet needle, or something like that—whatever you might have— and just carefully remove it, trying not to damage the bullet. You're going to want to do forensics on the bullet, and do a firearms comparison on the bullet with the weapon. It's really pretty simple, because the walls are malleable substances, so the bullet comes out pretty easily. . . . In some instances, you might want to cut a whole section out and take the section with you. . . . If it's a piece of molding, you might go to the backside, just dig a while if it hasn't gone all the way through, and then just push it on through from the back. Lead is a very soft substance, and you don't want to damage the lands and the grooves."

I asked, "Do you remember these bullets being dug out of the walls?"

"No," O'Reilly replied, "I didn't take care of that part. But I just know that it was being done. But I don't remember who did it. I think maybe DeWayne did it."

"That Wolfer was the one who dug the bullets out of the . . . ?"

"Wolfer. Wolfer would have done it."

The official LAPD report about William Lee's activities on the night of the shooting stated, "At 2 A.M. he arrived at the scene and assisted in searching for bullet holes and other physical evidence."

[157] The official LAPD account of an interview with LaVallee on September 27, 1968, stated, "Sgt. MacArthur instructed La Valle [*sic*] as to what areas he wanted surveyed and drawn. La Valle [*sic*] also assisted in measuring the location of the bullet holes, etc." Other than this one-page report, there are no other details of LaVallee's work in the LAPD's case files.

When I asked Bill Lee about whether he found bullet holes in the walls and the door frames during his search of the kitchen pantry, he referred me to the "paperwork" on the case. I replied, "Up in Sacramento, some of that paperwork is missing. And that's one of our concerns. We're trying to reconstruct this case."

Lee refused to say anything more about bullet holes. "I'm really not even interested in it after all these years, because I'm retired. I play golf now."

Interestingly, on December 15, 1975, Lee was interviewed by the LAPD prior to the district attorney's "Great Pantry Raid," which was conducted by the district attorney's office and the LAPD. According to the report of the interview, "In his capacity as a ballistics and firearms expert, [Lee] . . . had the opportunity of examining the two pantry doors which lead from the pantry to the rear stage area. Subject also examined the adjoining jambs and casings as well as the center post which divides the two doors. This examination was visually conducted and it was, and is, his opinion that there were no bullet holes. Subject does recall examining holes, but none of these in his expert opinion were caused by bullets."

However, when asked what he saw after the center divider was removed, Lee said that his recollection was "vague." He could not be sure what was or wasn't found.

Also interviewed during the pantry raid was Wolfer. According to the December 16, 1975, LAPD interview report with him, "[H]e performed an examination of the two pantry doors, the adjoining door casings, and jambs. This examination was conducted visually and with the aid of scientific instruments that are included in a portable kit. These instruments include, but are not limited to, microscope, probes, magnifying glass, etc. [Wolfer] recalls that portions of wood were removed from the right hand side of the doors. . . . Subject examined these pieces of wood at the scene and found no holes he could attribute to a bullet. The wood was taken to SID where it was further examined by fluoroscope. This examination determined there was no bullet in the examined wood. Subject recalls examining two separate pieces of wood, but is unable to identify either piece as having come from the center post of the doorway.

"The portions of wood that were removed were done so by carpenters employed by the Ambassador Hotel."

25. *The Untold Story of the Crime Scene Search II*

Dale L. Poore was one of the two carpenters who removed the center divider at the request of DeWayne Wolfer and the SID, and he, too, gave a statement to the LAPD on December 16, 1975. Poore recalled that on June 5, 1968, while working as a carpenter for the Ambassador Hotel, he "was requested by two police officers to remove the wooden facing, which was less than one inch in depth, from the center post of the double door area on the pantry side of the door located at the west end of the pantry. Before removing that material [Poore] noticed two apparent bullet holes on the east portion (pantry side) of that center post. These two holes were approximately four feet from ground level, with one about four inches higher than the other. After removing that material,

[Poore] does not recall looking to determine if the holes went through the material or looking at the underlying wood of the center post. The wood was turned over to the two police officers."

The now controversial center divider had been installed in the kitchen pantry of the Ambassador Hotel in 1962. Made of pine, a soft wood, with a "four by four" base and a three-fourths-inch facing, the center divider was supported by a fir wood base, which is much harder than pine. Constructed by another hotel carpenter, Wesley S. Harrington, the center divider had never been subjected to any firearms trauma. In other words, there had never been a known previous shooting in the kitchen pantry that could have caused the holes.[158]

The LAPD also interviewed Harrington on December 16, 1975, and he, too, recalled seeing what he believed to be bullet holes in the pine strip after the Kennedy shooting. However, the LAPD wrote,

---

[158] No one from the LAPD or the DA's office has ever suggested that the holes were caused by a previous shooting in the pantry.

In his continuing work to formulate as complete a record of the Kennedy case as possible, California state archivist John F. Burns conducted an interview with Karl Uecker, the Ambassador Hotel's assistant maître de', on April 13, 1990. Burns asked Uecker, "How many times a day do you think you passed through the pantry or were in the pantry normally?" Uecker replied, "Pantry? Oh, thirty times, forty times, fifty times. In out, in out, in out."

". . . Did you look around the pantry yourself?"

"Oh yeah, I did. Even the same night when it happened, I came back from the police, from Rampart Station there. I went back to the kitchen. That's why I noticed two shots [bullet holes], and I was looking a little more, but I didn't pay much attention.

"You noticed, though, something was different? Can you tell me a little more about that?"

Pointing to a diagram of the pantry and to the center divider between the two swinging doors at the west end of the pantry, Uecker replied, "Yeah, the two [circled] holes were by the, here by the door."

". . . Did you see any holes in that divider before the shooting?"

"No, I didn't."

"You're certain that you saw no holes in that divider?"

"No, I didn't."

"Because you used it all the time? You went through there all the time?"

"Yes, oh yes."

"Were you looking for holes?"

"You see, if you see a picture on a wall, you know, and all of a sudden it's hanging crooked, you see it, right? The same thing happened there. Somebody must be blind to use all the time this door, and you don't see the two holes there."

"He then looked at the opposite [side] of that center post to see if there were any corresponding or 'through and through' holes on that side and observed none."

The LAPD report also stated, "His recollection of the next time he observed that area was when unfinished wood facing was attached to the center post." In other words, the original center divider with the suspected bullet holes had been removed, analyzed by Wolfer, set back in its original position, removed again, analyzed again, and then finally destroyed.[159] A newly constructed piece of wood had replaced the old center divider.

At the conclusion of the official report on Poore and Harrington, the LAPD and the DA's office stated in a search warrant affidavit, "These statements, of officers Rozzi and Wright, Mr. DiPierro [all three obtained in 1975 by attorney Vincent Bugliosi], Mr. Poore, and Mr. Harrington, indicate the potential existence of four different bullet holes in the area of the shooting of Senator Kennedy and others."

With this justification, the pantry raid occurred—and the LAPD looked for bullet holes in pieces of wood that had been replaced in the pantry soon after the shooting had occurred. No one was surprised when no bullets or bullet holes were found. However, the DA's office and the LAPD have asserted that this examination provided "definitive" evidence that no additional bullets were found at the crime scene.

Neither SID man Bob Druley nor Danny Miller was present in the kitchen pantry during the crime scene search on the night of the shooting. They did their work in the laboratory at Parker Center. Miller told me, "The only place I would have gotten the bullets is from the coroner or from the on-scene crime guys who dug them out wherever they were and then booked them in as evidence. I would sign them out and make comparisons." He added that he had not heard of any bullets being removed from either the walls or the door frames of the kitchen pantry.

[159] The center divider was officially booked as evidence by the SID on June 28, 1968; it was destroyed on June 27, 1969.

I asked Miller why he didn't play a more prominent role in the investigation. He replied, "Wolfer was in charge of the section. Whenever anything big like this went down, Druley and I usually just followed orders, and let Wolfer take over."

During my interview with Druley, I asked, "Let me concentrate on the crime scene, because that's what you're going to be the expert in. Did you ever go to the hotel yourself?"

"Yeah, I did," Druley replied. "I went down and looked at the bullet holes, just out of curiosity. . . ."

"Can you recall where in the pantry—the kitchen area—where the bullets holes were?"

"Oh, lord, no. I know that there were holes there that people thought were bullets holes that were not. They were just places where somebody had driven a nail and pulled a nail out and chipped the plaster and then repainted over it. There was no wiping ring on the holes or anything. You know, when you shoot a bullet through something—lead or otherwise—the trash on the bullet wipes off on the entry where it goes through. It's called 'the wiping ring.' And it leaves a little dark area around the hole.

"They were just like in your home when you hang a picture and you take the picture down and you pull the nail out and chip it. The next time you paint, you don't putty it. You just paint over it."

SID officer David Butler, who has won the LAPD's Medal of Honor for bravery for disarming a bomb, is also one of Wolfer's former students at Long Beach State College. Butler told me that when he arrived at the Ambassador Hotel, "I was struck by the amount of people that were there. There were just droves of people. The ballroom was still crowded. There was a lot of confusion. . . .

"And that's what led to the difficulty of the re-creation of the shooting: that a lot of things had been moved, a lot of evidence that did not belong to the scene. . . . And we don't talk to the witnesses. We just basically isolate the physical evidence. We coordinate with the investigators. When they get information, we're both talking back and forth."

Of his boss and teacher, Butler said with great admiration, "Wolfer was very knowledgeable. I'd go through a crime scene, and he would see things that I couldn't see or didn't see. And this is where he became such an advantage. He would teach by example versus having you read books. . . .[160]

"He respected people who were qualified in their fields. That's the way to put it. When people would come in and try to BS him, he would cut them short in a heartbeat. He would not tolerate that. I think that's where he got into trouble with a lot of command staff in the department. They were making decisions that were affecting technical stuff in the laboratory. And that's where he got into a problem with the command staff. Ego. He would dent somebody's ego if he felt they were trying to BS him—in a minute. Hence, people would misread him a great deal. . . .

"We'd go to him, and we'd have arguments—knock-down, drag-out verbal arguments. But those were on a technical level. But there were no personal feelings involved. It was strictly professional."

Discussing Sergeant Lee, Butler said, "Bill, I had a lot of respect for. We didn't always get along, but Bill is a master locksmith. . . . He got called out a lot on narcotics busts to get into safes. There wasn't a safe this guy couldn't get into. He was very methodical, to the point that he would drive me crazy. I don't have the patience to stand there all day, because it is a subjective analysis. You are going to come to a point in your mind, based on your training and experience, when you are going to say, 'This is the same gun or it's not the same gun.' Or you are going to have to write it off and say, 'I can't tell.' "

On the night of the Kennedy shooting, Butler arrived at the Ambassador Hotel at about 2:00 A.M. and was present for much of the crime scene examination—though he, too, is not listed in any of the known LAPD's reports. At the time, he was a trainee and had

[160] Regarding Wolfer's teaching methods, Butler told me, "The way he would teach is: he would give you a project. And he wouldn't talk to you. He would have you do the project to the best of your ability. Then he would come back and pick it apart. He'd play devil's advocate. 'Why this? Why that? Why that conclusion?' And things of this nature. And that was his teaching . . . the way he taught. He'd give you an unusual gun, and just a box full of parts—and you had to put the gun back together. No manuals, no nothing. And when you got done—it would take you half a day—but when you got done, you knew that weapons system inside and out. . . ."

been assigned to the crime lab only the week before the Kennedy shooting.[161]

"This was my first major crime scene that I had ever been to," Butler explained. ". . . I had seen a couple of dead body calls, but I had never really seen a major homicide."

When I asked Butler what role he played that night at the crime scene, he replied, "Gofer. . . . Basically, Bill [O'Reilly, the other SID assistant,] and I were running to the main lab, getting equipment, bringing it back as DeWayne and Bill needed it. Lugging stuff back and forth. Packaging stuff."

During my interview with him, Butler gave me a briefing about bullet flight paths and the problem with the shots Sirhan fired that went through the ceiling tiles. I asked, "Well, who would be responsible for taking two bullets out of the wall?"

Butler replied, "We are. Our unit."

"Do you recall who took the two bullets out of the wall that night?"

"DeWayne Wolfer took the two bullets out of the wall. I know there was some controversy that developed later, regarding the holes in the wall. . . . We investigated that very deeply. And what we came to find out is that you have these pushcarts—which the busboys use to put dirty dishes in. And the brackets had broken. . . . So when they shoved the pushcart up against the wall . . ."

"How tall was this pushcart?"

"Oh, I forget how tall it was. But it exactly matched the same location, right near a door jamb."

"Down below?"

"Right. And then some uniformed officer says . . . got a picture of him, pointing his finger at those holes."

Referring to pictures of the center divider by the two swinging doors in the kitchen pantry, I wanted Butler to clarify the location of the reported bullet holes. I asked him, "So then the bullets that Wolfer took out of the wall would be just like the ones in the center divider there?"

[161] At the time of my interview, Butler was still active as a top firearms examiner in the SID.

"Yes."

"Those are the ones he took out?"

"And we did investigate those other holes. Okay?"

"The other holes what? In the frame and in the walls?"

"Right."

"But it was the center divider holes where he took out the bullets?"

"Right."

"Were you there when he took those bullets out?" I asked.

"Yes."

". . . Were you there when he took the bullets right out of the center divider? What did he do? Just tear it out? Because we have pictures of it torn out."

"Yeah."

"What did he do? Just tear it out and lay it down?"

"Tear it out. We had to disassemble it to find the bullets."

"So you disassembled it and found the bullets?"

"Right."

". . . And you were there when they ripped the center divider out?"

"Yes."

"And what did they do? Lay it across, like, the steam table or something?"

"Right. And then dissect it to get the projectiles out."

". . . Let me ask you a question, just procedure: How are things booked? What do you do? Say, you get the eight-foot strip of this center divider here. You lay it across the steam table, Wolfer digs the bullets out. What does he do then? He puts it in a bag or something? A plastic bag?"

"Photographed, labeled, packaged, then it will be booked within a couple of days."

"Did you ever handle the bullets or were you just there watching?"

"No, I really didn't handle the bullets."

Significantly, like Officer Kenneth Vogl and photographer Charles Collier, Butler told me that he was aware that bullet fragments had been found at the crime scene. He even identified possible fragments in a picture taken by Collier of a location on the floor near the pantry steam tables. He said that they were "packaged, labeled 'bullet fragments,' [with] an item number." However, according to official LAPD records, no bullet fragments of any kind were ever booked or even reported at the crime scene. Police spokesmen have repeatedly denied that any were recovered, insisting that the only bullets removed were from the six shooting victims.

In fact, *no* specific written account of the LAPD crime scene examination exists in the available records at all—other than the officers' own brief and cursory reports. In other words, regardless of whatever the LAPD did do at the crime scene, its job of documenting its tasks and managing its records was atrocious.

Thus, the importance of these statements made by Butler regarding the removal of bullets, if correct, cannot be overstated. But Butler attempted to alter his story during our second interview.

During that second lengthy interview, Butler changed his story about having seen bullets removed from the center divider—*after* he finally realized that I was accounting for more bullets than Sirhan's gun could hold. He said that he saw only what he believed were bullets that had been "photographed, labeled, then packaged, cataloged" in small evidence packages that were marked either "bullet evidence" or "firearms evidence" and placed on the steam table. Regardless of which version is correct, there is no official report of any such evidence being recovered from the crime scene.

Toward the end of our first interview and without informing him of the significance of what he had told me, I asked Butler to rate Wolfer's handling of the Robert Kennedy murder case?

"Ten," Butler replied. "At least to the technical aspects. He did everything that was necessary, everything that was required. He went a few extra steps, like taking the gun [Iver Johnson H18602] out of the gun collection, using that for certain testing and not the evidence gun."

Detective Mike Rothmiller worked in the LAPD's Organized Crime Intelligence Division (OCID) from 1978 to 1983. In his book, *L.A. Secret Police: Inside the LAPD Elite Spy Network,* Rothmiller stated that he had "read the detailed file on Bobby Kennedy. Investigators accounted for ten spent .22-caliber slugs in the kitchen of the Ambassador Hotel where RFK was shot dead. Sirhan Sirhan's revolver held eight bullets. Nowhere did the file draw any conclusion about the discrepancy."[162]

In a subsequent affidavit, Rothmiller attested that soon after his transfer to the OCID, he found the secret "60–100" page file, prepared by the OCID, about the Kennedy murder. "I recall that it stated that two (2) bullets had been recovered from a wall, and other bullets had been recovered from victims. . . .

"The Report contained the names of a number of individuals involved in the case or in the investigation, but I do not remember most of them. I do recall that one of the names in the report was William Bailey. The name stuck in my mind because of the song, 'Why don't you come home, Bill Bailey?' "[163]

" 'FELT HIM FIRE GUN,' HOTEL WORKER SAYS," was the headline of the page-one story which appeared in the *Chicago Tribune* on June 6, the day Senator Kennedy died and the day after the initial crime scene search. Written by Robert Wiedrich, a respected veteran police reporter, the article recounted his observations of the crime scene and his interview with Karl Uecker.

Wiedrich told me that he had flown from Chicago to Los Angeles hours after the shooting and received clearance from the LAPD to enter the pantry area after the SID had completed its work. The police detective who accompanied Wiedrich, according to the story, was Sergeant James MacArthur, who told me that he "vaguely" remembered the reporter.

Buried in Wiedrich's article was this observation:

"On a low table lay an 8 foot strip of molding, torn by police from the center post of the double doors leading from the ballroom.

---

[162] Mike Rothmiller, *L.A. Secret Police: Inside the LAPD Elite Spy Network* (New York: Pocket Books, 1992), p. 106.

[163] Rothmiller, whom I interviewed in October 1993, added in his August 26, 1992, affidavit, "During the years I was an officer of the LAPD, I saw officers destroy evidence, alter or falsify reports, or try to intimidate witnesses into changing their stories."

These were the doors thru which Sen. Kennedy had walked, smiling in his moment of victory.

"Now the molding bore the scars of a crime laboratory technician's probe as it had removed two .22 caliber bullets that had gone wild" (emphasis added).

Clearly, Wiedrich did not realize the significance of what he had written. Sirhan's eight bullets would soon be accounted for by the LAPD, and here was crime reporter Wiedrich unwittingly noting the discovery of two additional bullets that Sirhan's eight-shot gun could not possibly have held.

When I finally interviewed Wiedrich—who had not actually seen the bullets removed—and explained the significance of what he had written for the first time, he paused momentarily and then stood by his story. "That's exactly what happened," Wiedrich insisted. "That's exactly what I saw, and that's exactly what I was told."

26. *The FBI*
and the Extra Bullets

S imultaneously with the LAPD's probe of the murder of Senator Robert Kennedy—from the night of the shooting to Sirhan's conviction—the FBI was conducting its own parallel investigation. At first, relations between the two respected law enforcement agencies were minimal, even adversarial. However, within a short time, the LAPD and the FBI began to work together.

In May 1976, Greg Stone, the former aide to Congressman Allard Lowenstein, began reviewing FBI files about the Kennedy murder case, which had been made available in the wake of a Freedom of Information Act release. Having assisted in Paul Schrade's legal battles the previous year, Stone was well aware of the issues concerning the crime scene bullets and the alleged unaccounted-for bullet holes.[164]

The initial FBI catalog of documents on the assassination, dated June 9, 1968, contained a section titled "Charts and Photographs Showing Layout of Ambassador Hotel Area Where Shooting Occurred."[165] Stone was dumbfounded by the contents of this report: what appeared to be unequivocal FBI documentation that a minimum of twelve bullets had been fired in the assassination of Robert F. Kennedy!

And unlike LAPD photographs available on the Kennedy murder case, the FBI photos were presented in an orderly format, keyed to individual locator maps, and furnished with captions.[166]

Among the photographs was one labeled E-1, a picture of the wall to the immediate left of the double swinging doors at the west end of the pantry that Kennedy had walked through moments before being shot. At the top of the wall was a strip of paneling that had been cut out. In his identification of E-1, an FBI special agent wrote, "In lower right corner the photo shows two bullet holes [in the left door

---

[164] Greg Stone committed suicide on January 29, 1991. A lengthy February 17 article in the *Los Angeles Times* by reporter Gary Abrams blamed Stone's death on his own "obsession" with the investigation of Robert Kennedy's murder.

A few days after Stone died, I received a handwritten note from him in the mail that simply said, "Sorry about this, Dan. Stay a survivor."

True to form in death as in life, Stone attached a list of "Things To Do" on the Kennedy case.

Like Allard Lowenstein, Greg Stone mattered.

[165] The contents of the FBI reports were formally released in Los Angeles in June 1976 by former American Academy of Forensic Sciences president Robert Joling. Incredibly, there was virtually no reaction from the media.

[166] Washington, D.C., attorney Jim Lesar, on behalf of plaintiffs Greg Stone and Philip Melanson, filed a suit under the Freedom of Information Act against the FBI in 1987, demanding the names of those FBI employees who worked on the Robert Kennedy murder case. In an affidavit filed on behalf of Stone and Melanson, I stated, "This official case record of the FBI is fundamentally self-contradictory: It assumes that Sirhan was the lone shooter, but it reports unequivocal findings which, if correct, show that he was not. The failure of the official reports to resolve this paradox illustrates the limited probative value of documentary records standing alone."

The case has been dismissed. The court has, thus, upheld the FBI's refusal to release the names.

frame] which are circled. The portion of the panel missing also reportedly contained a bullet."

Photograph E-2 was labeled by the FBI "A close-up view of the two bullets holes of area described above."

Photograph E-3 was labeled "Close-up view of two bullet holes which [are] located in center door frame inside kitchen serving area and looking towards direction of back stage area [the center divider]."

And Photograph E-4 was labeled "Close-up view of upper hinge on door leading into kitchen area from back of stage area. View shows reported location of another bullet mark which struck [door] hinge."

These additional sightings by the FBI left open the possibility of six extra bullets—four of which were flat-out labeled "bullet holes," a "reported" bullet hole, and a "reported" bullet mark—according to its own report of the crime scene search.

These identifications were buried in the FBI's initial catalog of documents, which was completed within four days of the murder and based, in part, upon a June 7, 1968, search of the kitchen by FBI special agent Alfred Greiner, who wrote the report, and civilian photographer Richard Fernandez, an FBI employee, who took the accompanying pictures.[167]

Thus, the FBI, the nation's most respected law enforcement agency, had essentially made a case for critics of the LAPD's investigation of the Kennedy murder that at least two guns had been fired the night of the murder.

On November 2, 1977, Harry L. Hufford, the chief administrative officer for the Los Angeles County Board of Supervisors, wrote a letter to Special Agent Hal Marshall of the FBI's Los Angeles office.

---

[167] I attempted to interview Fernandez, who was then still active in the FBI's photo lab in Los Angeles. Understandably, Fernandez said that he did not want to talk to me—unless he received clearance from the FBI. He told me to call Fred Reagan, the FBI's chief spokesman in Los Angeles, to request that clearance. Reagan refused to authorize the interview.

I asked nearly every FBI source I have on the West Coast to persuade Greiner to talk to me, but they were all unsuccessful. I located the now retired Greiner in West Covina, California. Because I could not find his telephone number, I tried to ambush him at his home twice. The first time, his wife refused to allow me to see him. The second time, I caught Greiner in his driveway. But he said that he was not interested in talking about the Robert Kennedy case and ordered me off his property.

Hufford stated, "[Q]uestions have arisen concerning certain FBI photographs. These photographs . . . are captioned 'bullet holes.'

"If these were, in fact, bullet holes, it could be inferred that more than one gun was fired in the pantry during the assassination. . . . If the captions had said possible, probable, or apparent bullet holes, one could assume that no precise examination had taken place at the time the photographs were taken. However, the captions would lead one to believe that a determination had been made by someone with the requisite knowledge and skills. . . .

"If more bullets were fired within the pantry than Sirhan Sirhan's gun was capable of holding, we should certainly find out who else was firing. If, in fact, the FBI has no evidence that the questioned holes were bullet holes, we should know that so that the air may be cleared."

There was no known response from the FBI to Hufford's letter.

When confronted with this apparent new evidence, the LAPD and the Los Angeles District Attorney's Office either trivialized or simply misrepresented the FBI's initial catalog of documents. Addressing it, the Kranz Report stated, "FBI photographer [*sic*], Grinner [*sic*], stated in his signed report that there were 'four reported bullet holes' [*sic*] in the area of the two swinging doors. Photographs of the swinging doors taken by Grinner [*sic*] to substantiate his one page [*sic*] report were included in the file.

"However, no other reference is made to these 'reported four bullet holes' [*sic*] in the other 802 pages of the FBI files. Special Counsel Kranz . . . interviewed FBI investigators who had conducted the 1968 assassination investigation, including Deputy Chief [Roger] LaJeunesse in June and July 1976. No ballistics evidence or other references to Greiner's one page [*sic*] report were found to substantiate the report of photographer [*sic*] Greiner."

In his error-ridden and high-handed report, Kranz didn't bother to name the "FBI investigators" he interviewed. However, he did *not* speak to at least one FBI special agent who was part of the crime scene search and personally inspected the suspected bullet holes: FBI special agent William A. Bailey.

In November 1976, attorney Vincent Bugliosi delivered a speech at Glassboro State College, in New Jersey. Asked about the Robert

Kennedy murder case during the question-and-answer period, Bugliosi discussed the investigation, noting the extra-bullets issue. After he finished, a member of the audience asked to have a word with him in private.

The man was William Bailey, an assistant professor of police science at nearby Gloucester County College. He told Bugliosi that he had been an FBI special agent in Los Angeles at the time of the Kennedy shooting and had been dispatched to the Ambassador Hotel later that night.

Bailey's execution of a sworn affidavit at Bugliosi's behest in November 1976 has become one of the key pieces of evidence in demonstrating that more than eight shots may have been fired on the night of the Kennedy shooting.

Bailey stated in his affidavit, "I was assigned to interview witnesses present at the time of the shooting. I was also charged with the responsibility of recreating the circumstances under which same took place. This necessitated a careful examination of the entire room and its contents.

"At one point during these observations I (and several other agents) noted at least two (2) small caliber bullet holes in the center post of the two doors leading from the preparation room [the pantry]. There was no question in any of our minds as to the fact that they were bullet holes and were not caused by food carts or other equipment in the preparation room."

Bailey later reaffirmed what he saw in the center divider, in response to an inquiry from Los Angeles county supervisor Baxter Ward. Bailey said that the matter was "not even subject to speculation. I definitely recall closely examining those two holes, and they definitely [contained] bullets."

In follow-up inquiries, Bailey has confirmed and amplified this basic recollection of his observations on the morning of the assassination. Remembering the night of the shooting, Bailey told me, "I was at home in bed. My wife was watching television, and she came in and woke me up and said, 'Kennedy has been shot.' About two hours after that, I was called by the office, which told me to go to the Ambassador Hotel right away. My first assignment was to interview witnesses who were at the scene, who saw the shooting.

"Prior to conducting interviews of witnesses, I took the opportunity to walk around the crime scene. It's just good, basic investigative procedure to familiarize yourself with the crime scene before you interview witnesses. It helps you clarify points, understand what they're saying. If there are discrepancies between what one witness says and another has said, you can straighten those things out. Sometimes witnesses have a tendency to forget things or dismiss things. They consider them unimportant. They're not aware of all the facts.

"So I took a look at the entire pantry area. In the process of doing this, there were a number of Los Angeles Police Department officials there, marking and noting evidence. And there were a number of other FBI people there also.

"I took particular note at the time of two bullet holes which, according to the LAPD later on, did not exist: two bullet holes in the center divider between two swinging doors, the doors that Senator Kennedy came through on his way through the pantry en route to a press conference.

"I looked at them. I will go to my grave, knowing that they were two bullet holes. There were clearly two bullet holes lodged in that center divider. I looked at them. I didn't have a thing to do with the actual notation or collection of them. I just noted, 'Yes, two bullet holes.' I noted that police officers were making similar notations, taking photographs, etc. I did it, as I said, so that I could conduct an intelligent interview of witnesses. I then went on about the business of interviewing witnesses to the shooting."

When I asked Bailey how the Kennedy investigation could have gone awry, he replied, "Here's what happens in an investigation like this. Early on in this case—from the moment it happened—the investigation became focused. They had numerous witnesses who saw the suspect pull out a gun, point it toward Senator Kennedy, and begin shooting.

"What is coupled with this case is a very severe deadline in which we are under pressure to get an initial report to Washington. There is a lot of pressure to resolve something. Get questions answered, get issues resolved, get the evidence. 'Get going; the press is pushing us.' What happens to an investigator is that he becomes ripe for going from focus into tunnel vision, especially when you have a lot of evidence that initially points you in a specific direction.

"The tendency moving from focus to tunnel vision is to start ignoring, dismissing not so obvious evidence—evidence, in another set of circumstances—you really ought to look at. If you were looking at a case that had no clear focus, you would take all of these bits and pieces of evidence, and you would literally work the hell out them. If there were a lot of 'loose ends,' you would take every bit and piece of evidence, and you would just push and push and work and work on them. That wasn't true in this case. It's a two-edged sword, because you're crazy if you don't follow the obvious, but you're just as crazy if that's all you do.

"I think that's probably where the breakdown occurred in the Kennedy investigation. And that was very early on."

The FBI's deputy chief in Los Angeles, Roger "Frenchy" LaJeunesse, who coordinated the FBI's work on the Kennedy case with the LAPD and whom Kranz referred to in his report, described Bailey to me as "a good agent and a decent guy."

27. *Frenchy on the FBI Reports*

F renchy LaJeunesse did not hear about the Kennedy shooting until he arrived at his office at 7:45 on the morning of June 5.

"The night of the shooting," LaJeunesse told me, "I got some information from a snitch that a load of color televisions were going to be taken off a truck. And rather than come home for the evening, I stayed with a single friend of mine, an agent, because I figured that I would be getting a call and have to go out and dance. And nothing happened.

"I got up the next morning and walked over to the office, which was maybe two blocks away from where I was staying. We saw flares on the road in front of the hospital at Central Receiving, and [the other agent] made a comment that there must have been an accident or something. So I walked in the office, and all hell had broken loose.

"When I got into the office about a quarter to eight, Bill Nolan [a supervisor in the Los Angeles FBI office] wanted to know where the hell I was. I jokingly said, 'This morning started at 12:01. What part of the morning to you want?' He said, 'Don't be a smart ass. Where the hell were you?' And he tells me what happened. And that was my first knowledge of it."

Immediately, LaJeunesse received the assignment to go to Parker Center to coordinate the FBI's investigation with the LAPD. "I went down to the ECC, Emergency Control Center. They were using it for major events, when they had a problem. So they immediately activated it.

"I'm trying think which one of the police detectives, one of the brass, told me that they had identified the guy, and his name was Sirhan Sirhan. And I said, 'You're stuttering; you're repeating yourself,' or some smart-ass crack like that. And he said, 'No, that's his goddamn name; he's Sirhan Sirhan.'

"At that point in time, nobody was certain there wasn't—they were ready to believe that there weren't other people involved, but they weren't taking any chances. So my purpose in being down there was to monitor, as the FBI representative, what was going on with the ECC, so we coordinate our efforts. You don't send twenty agents; you send one or two agents down there. I had been there before on some other different things the police had. I knew most of their personnel."[168]

LaJeunesse told me that all FBI personnel in southern California were activated as part of the law enforcement agency's special emergency plan. "It's a major-case concept, drawn up by the bureau and revised and refined and honed that they followed at that time. Kidnapping would come under a major-case concept. The minute they

---

[168] LaJeunesse added, "I was told that President Johnson had instructed J. Edgar Hoover that he, Johnson, desired the FBI to remain active in the investigation and maintain contact with local authorities. So I got anointed."

LaJeunesse remained on the Kennedy case, nearly full-time, until Sirhan's conviction, in May 1969.

have a major case problem, they activate people, the personnel for it. They have stenos to do the clerical work and clerks. And they had agents who were assigned to the major cases concept unit. I think at that time we had a little over five hundred agents in the Los Angeles Division, which goes from San Luis Obispo to San Clemente over to the Nevada line. Everyone was pressed into service."

I then asked LaJeunesse, "Was there any doubt in your mind that Sirhan did it?"

"Never," he replied.

"And did it alone?"

"Alone. There was never any doubt in my mind. When a shooting takes place, and you have a man of his [Kennedy's] stature, you have to assume that the possibility exists that there was more than one person. To that extent, everyone was preparing for it. And we all made up our minds that this was not going to be another Jack Ruby thing, John Kennedy thing."

"Another Dallas?" I asked.

"Right," he replied.

"Were you working with the LAPD guys individually?"

"No, I was on the eighth floor [SUS headquarters in Parker Center], and I went there every day."

"So the [FBI] and the LAPD worked well together?"

"Oh, yeah."

"I hear everybody telling me about the early problems between the FBI and the LAPD. I mean, without exception, they tell me that."[169]

---

[169] Generally, there is a one-way street when one deals with the FBI. Investigators from other agencies are expected to share all of their information with the FBI, which simultaneously holds its cards close to its chest.

One top official who discussed the early problems between the FBI and the LAPD in the Kennedy murder case with me was William Jordan, the officer who interrogated Sirhan and then later became a principal in Special Unit Senator. Jordan told me, "We said [to the FBI], 'This is going to be run as a LAPD investigation. We have primary jurisdiction. We welcome your help and assistance. We will share with you. But you get on the white phone or the red phone or whatever it is, and make sure that your boss understands that if there is any holding back or any of this one-way street business, you guys are out. . . .'

"Oh, they had problems. They're cops just like anybody else. I believe that we should get along with people. Get the job done. Get the bad guys off the street. That's the name of the game. And I worked with those guys very closely. Manny [Pena] and I worked robbery together; I knew Manny when he was assigned to all this. So we were close together. And Manny didn't particularly trust the FBI as an organization. But he trusted certain guys. I was one of them."

LaJeunesse added, "The decision to prosecute Sirhan by Los Angeles County authorities was made by the prosecutorial authorities [i.e. Los Angeles County District Attorney's Office and the U.S. Justice Department]. The FBI, as an investigative agency, would have no decision-making responsibility with respect to prosecution matters. However, I preferred that Sirhan be prosecuted by local authorities since California had, at that time, the death penalty available to prosecutors, whereas the federal government would have had to rely on the recently enacted Civil Rights Act of 1968. The federal statute did not provide for the death penalty."

I then asked LaJeunesse about the FBI special agent who identified the four extra bullets at the crime scene, saying, "Tell me about Al Greiner. I ambushed him out at his house a couple of times."

"Oh, you're the guy he told me about at a lunch. Al's easygoing. He's not an aggressive guy. He doesn't want to talk about it."

"Why not? Why doesn't he want to talk about it?"

"Whatever picture taking Al did, or supervised, was strictly not forensic in nature. They were not taking pictures to show blood spots. Joe Smith was coordinating that aspect of it—I think Joe's dead now, too. They sent Richard Fernandez, nice kid, I like him. And the pictures they were taking were for agents to be used in interviewing witnesses to fix their physical presence. For example, you take a picture of a stove in the kitchen—or picture of this booth [at the restaurant where my interview with LaJeunesse was being con-

---

"Everybody liked Frenchy, because his instructions were 100 percent cooperation.

"Let me tell you something, I used to work with Frenchy and his partner, and if we wanted to get together to talk about bad people, exchange information, put people in jail, they'd have to sneak it, make sure that they weren't tailed.

"I always thought we were doing the same job."

ducted]. And three days from now, you're going to interview these
people standing here. And you say, 'Here's what we're concerned
about: Frenchy and Dan were sitting in a booth. And here's a picture
of the booth. Where was Dan sitting in relation to Frenchy in that
picture?' That was the purpose of the picture taking."

"There was a series of pictures."

"Crime scene forensic picture taking, which the police department did from the get-go. The picture taking the FBI did was not for
that purpose. It was for orientation for subsequent witness interviews."

In an effort to get an official quotation from LaJeunesse about the
FBI photographs that identified four bullet holes not accounted for
by the LAPD, I gave LaJeunesse my thoughts about the investigation
and the controversies revolving around the case, particularly the extra
bullets reported by the FBI.

I said, "So, let me get this straight: the picture taking the FBI did
was for orientation purposes to establish locations . . ."

LaJeunesse continued, "To assist in interviewing witnesses or
potential witnesses. You could show them a picture. There was no
attempt to characterize what was in the photographs. I suppose they
could be used for anything, but, basically, that's what the pictures
were taken for. Al was up there—what, two or three days after?"

"Yeah, two days after, and then his report came out on June 9."

"Because by that time, the police department had been crawling
all over the place—the fingerprint men, the forensic men, the hair
fiber men, everyone had been there."

"Okay, so the picture taking the FBI did was for orientation
purposes to assist in interviewing witnesses?"

"Yeah."

"There was no attempt to characterize what was in the photographs?" I asked.

"That's right," LaJeunesse replied.

"But he did characterize them."

"Who did?"

"Greiner. In this report."

"What did Al say? I've heard so much about that 302 [an FBI
official report]."

"Have you ever seen these photographs?"

"I might have seen them at the time, but I don't remember."

I then pulled out the four controversial FBI photographs, and I asked about each of them. During this line of questioning, I told LaJeunesse that numerous LAPD officers and officials, along with FBI special agent William Bailey, had appeared to corroborate Greiner's FBI report with their own sightings of bullets and bullets holes at the crime scene.

While reviewing the pictures, I asked LaJeunesse, "Where did these bullets come from? I'm no ballistics expert. I'm no firearms identification expert. I don't know land from a groove. But I do know this: an eight-shot revolver cannot fire more than eight bullets. And all eight bullets have been accounted for. You've got four bullets extra in that room. And this is not some crazy person saying this: this is the FBI saying this; this is the LAPD saying this!"

LaJeunesse argued, "Well, if a police officer or a detective is on the scene, and he's not with SID, he wouldn't know a bullet hole from a nail hole! The average working detective, he just wouldn't! He's not trained! His job is to isolate the scene! Don't touch it! Don't move anything! . . . I know that SID conducted the forensic crime scene search, because that was entrusted to them. I'm saying this for you, Dan: Dave Fitts was, in my opinion, the lead prosecutor. . . . Dave was sharp enough and independent minded enough that if he saw something that was kinky or questionable, he would not have danced with it. He would have checked into it. And I was with Dave after they started putting the case together. I was with Dave and John Howard and those guys, daily—and the investigators in the DA's office, I went over almost daily. And knowing Dave like I did—he later became a judge—and he could cut through all the bullshit that's going on in a trial, and get to the meat of it. But he was the kind of guy who would say, 'Hey, what about these bullet holes.' He would question it! He would bring them [Wolfer and the SID] in and question them!"

"Yeah, but it was never an issue," I replied. "Wolfer said that 'all these bullets were accounted for,' and that's it. All the bullets were accounted for."

When I returned to Greiner's FBI report, LaJeunesse said, "Well, only Al can explain that. I don't know. I just don't know. Dan, I tried to prevail upon him to talk with you. I talked to him. He said, 'French, I told you before, I don't want to get involved in this.' Now, I don't think Al is hiding anything."

I replied, "I think he [Greiner] is just a guy who did his job. And he feels that he did his job, and he did a good job. And he just doesn't want to relive it."

"Well, I'm being unfair to Al, but I'm going to say it: I think that he probably feels regret for the fact that he should not have said 'bullet holes.' He should have said 'reported bullet holes' or 'alleged bullets.' "

"Did he say that?"

"I don't know. What does the report say?"

I started laughing and repeated, "The report says 'bullet holes'!"

"No, he didn't say that to me. I'm speculating that he probably wishes now in retrospect that he would have said, 'Somebody told me they were bullet holes, so I called them bullet holes.' . . . Honestly, Al wouldn't know bullet holes from nail holes. Why did he characterize them as bullet holes? Somebody had to plant that in his head. I know Al well enough to know that he couldn't determine bullet holes from holes."

"Right," I replied. "That's what I think, too. I think he was with some cops, and somebody says, 'These are bullet holes; these are bullet holes.' He says, 'A bullet is reportedly removed from this panel.' I mean, somebody obviously told him that."

"He didn't make that up," LaJeunesse said, seemingly thinking out loud.

"That's what I'm saying. I think Greiner was there with somebody, somebody was giving him a tour through the pantry: 'These are bullet holes; these are bullet holes—we just removed a bullet from up there.' I don't think Greiner did anything but his job. Without the forensic experience, how's he going to have Fernandez take a picture of a . . ."

"Yeah," LaJeunesse agreed, "he's telling Richard what to do."

Then, trying to continue to obtain an acceptable quote from LaJeunesse, I said, "Okay let's say this: 'If . . .'"

He interrupted, "And we don't know that there were other

weapons or bullet holes. You're telling me that there were. But people have told you—or at least you've told me that people have told you that."

"Okay, I'm just trying to word this so that you're not making a leap of faith with me," I said.

"Let me say this to you: A weapon with an eight-round capacity, and eight rounds are accounted for—let's assume that happened. We don't know that happened in connection with that evening. Has anyone told you that there was a possibility that these goddamn things could have happened [before]?"

"There have never been any reports [of prior shootings in the pantry]. We checked it out."

"Speaking, not from a scientific [point of view]—because I'm not a forensic person—that was not my bag when I was in the bureau—if you have eight and you have four, you have twelve. So you have four extra to be explained away."

Finally, after several minutes of discussion, LaJeunesse authorized his quoted statement: "I undoubtedly saw the pictures when the initial FBI report came out. I didn't pay any particular attention to the text, because I knew that the pictures Fernandez took and Greiner supervised were for the purpose of witness orientation. The SID had the responsibility of preserving crime scene evidence. If these are, in fact, bullet holes, then the origin should be pursued."

Clearly, LaJeunesse still had some questions about the investigation of the Kennedy case—but he was in good company. The late William C. Sullivan—the assistant director of the FBI's Intelligence Division in 1968, who became the number three man in the FBI two years later—had his doubts, too. In his 1979 autobiography, Sullivan wrote, "[W]e did finally decide that Sirhan acted alone, but we never found out why. Although he was fanatic about the Arab cause, we could never link Sirhan to any organization or to any other country. He never received a dime from anyone for what he did. We sometimes wondered whether someone representing the Soviets had suggested to Sirhan that Kennedy would take action against the Arab countries if he became president. But that was only a guess.

"There were so many holes in the case. We never could account for Sirhan's presence in the kitchen of the Ambassador Hotel. Did he know Kennedy would be walking through? Intelligence work is exasperating. You can work on a case for years and still not know the real answers. There are so many unknowns. Investigating Sirhan was a frustrating job, for in the end we were never sure."[170]

[170] William C. Sullivan, with Bill Brown, *The Bureau: My Thirty Years in Hoover's FBI* (New York: W. W. Norton, 1979), pp. 56–57.

Sullivan was accidently shot and killed during a hunting trip on November 9, 1977. The series of interviews between Sullivan and his co-author, Bill Brown, a NBC news reporter, were completed the previous July.

28. *The Cesar*
Polygraph Test

On the basis of what FBI reports had stated and LAPD officers and officials had told me, I believed in the possibility that two guns had been fired in the kitchen pantry at the Ambassador Hotel on the night Robert Kennedy was fatally wounded. Thus, I targeted Gene Cesar as my principal suspect as the second gunman—just as many other investigators had before I came into this case.

The difference was that I had exclusive and unlimited access to him, even though Cesar was well aware that I had become fixed on him like a cruise missile.

After my numerous interviews with Cesar, over the telephone and in person, I finally concluded that I had asked him every question I could think of. At the end of one of our lengthy taped interviews, Garland Weber, his attorney, saw a puzzled look on my face and asked me what I thought. I replied that I still didn't know *what* to think. However, I did express my belief that Cesar was not a sinister force at the crime scene; he did not intentionally shoot Robert Kennedy. Yet, questions remained for me as to whether he had fired his gun accidently or in retaliation to Sirhan's barrage of gunfire. I still suspected that, somehow, Cesar might have shot Senator Kennedy during all the confusion at the crime scene.

Without any foolproof way to extract the truth, I simply decided to start treating Cesar just like any other witness to the murder. I called him on occasion from my home in Washington to see how he was; I visited him during my frequent trips to Los Angeles. I found the time I spent with him and his wife to be pleasant.

During one of those trips to the West Coast, Cesar and I had lunch at a restaurant near his place of employment. I brought no tape recorder; I took no notes during our conversation.

In the midst of lunch, Cesar casually told me about some unusual diamond purchases he had made with his own money. He added that he had bought the diamonds from a local businessman who was an associate of the Mafia in Chicago.

Needless to say, the story intrigued me, and I questioned him about it at subsequent meetings, which were tape-recorded. There were several discrepancies in the date of the initial purchase, which Cesar had ranged from 1968 to 1974.

Because of such discrepancies—and because of the enormous amount of time and money I was spending trying to prove or disprove Cesar's innocence—I asked Cesar if he would be willing to be either hypnotized or polygraphed. Surprisingly, he immediately agreed to such a test—with no particular preference.

I contacted a federal prosecutor whom I had known and trusted for several years and asked his advice about which test to arrange. He warned against hypnosis, because it could be tantamount to tampering with a potential witness. Thus, he suggested that I have Cesar polygraphed. He also proposed that I hire Edward Gelb, a Los Angeles polygraph expert, to administer the test.

I decided that if Cesar clearly passed this long-awaited test, I would back off and accept his innocence. However, if he failed the test or it proved inconclusive, I would spend every waking hour trying to bring him down. And I told him that.

The former president and executive director of the American Polygraph Association, Gelb, who served with the LAPD, had become publicly known for his 1983 syndicated television show, "Lie Detector," co-hosted with well-known attorney F. Lee Bailey. On June 19, 1994, the *New York Times* wrote, "With more than 30 years' experience in the field, [Gelb] approaches his job with scientific precision, following the same ritual that would be required by any American court."

Like anyone in such a situation, Cesar was understandably nervous. He and his attorney arrived at Gelb's office a few minutes early while I was briefing Gelb about Cesar and the Kennedy murder case.

"How do you feel?" I asked Cesar.

"Let's do it," he replied with some irritation. "Let's get it over with."

Gelb invited us into his private office and had Cesar sign several pro forma documents and releases. After a quick explanation of what would be happening over the next few hours, Gelb politely asked Weber and me to leave. As Weber and I went off to breakfast, Gelb and Cesar got down to business.

A tape recorder memorialized every moment of their exchange, as well as the test itself.

Because few people understand how a lie detector works, the following is a detailed description of Gelb's polygraph test with Cesar.

While they were getting started for the pretest interview, Cesar asked, "Is it possible to tell the truth and not show up for being the truth?"

"No," Gelb responded curtly.

"I've heard people say, 'Well, polygraphs had shown a person lying, and actually it wasn't a lie.' "

"Generally, Gene, they're talking about the competency of the examiner. It is not perfect. There is no perfect way of discerning perfect truth from deception."

During Gelb's extensive pretest interview, Cesar recounted his movements before the Kennedy assassination.

Yes, on the night of the shooting, Cesar's .38-caliber Rohm revolver, which he had purchased from a gun shop in Simi Valley, was on his hip. Yes, he also owned a .22-caliber H & R, which he had purchased from Bud Sutherland for his wife for home protection. No, he was not carrying the .22 with him at the Ambassador Hotel.

Gelb asked Cesar, "Tell me, did you ever go to the range and practice with these guns?"

"No," Cesar replied.

"Did you ever fire the .22 at the range or anything?"

"No."

"After you bought it, did you ever try it out?"

"I fired it one time after the assassination, the Kennedy assassination. I had that .22. And one of the guys at work said, 'How in the hell could Sirhan fire [eight] rounds' or whatever he fired 'that quick.' And I said, 'Well, I got a .22 at home like it. Next time we go rabbit hunting, I'll take it out there, and we'll try it.' So we did. We saw how fast we could fire that .22. And we timed it. It was unbelievable how quick you could rap off [eight] shots."

"This was a revolver?"

"The little H & R revolver I had."

Asking about the sale of the .22, Gelb said, "Let's [talk about] the gun. So some time after this, how long after did you sell this .22?"

Cesar replied, "Probably less than six months, because I sort of knew Yoder from Lockheed, and he was due for retirement. So it was in that six-month period I sold it to him. He wanted a gun to keep in the house, a little .22 for his wife. And that was exactly what I had it for. The reason why I went ahead and sold it was I had this .38 in the house. I didn't need a .22. I told my wife that I didn't need it anyway, because I quit working for Ace a little bit after that. Not because of that [the murder]. It was getting too much of a hassle doing two jobs."

Clearly, Gelb had become intrigued by Cesar's story, asking, "To the best of your knowledge, did the .38 go off at any time during that evening?"

"No. I never fired it."

"Did you have any other gun on your person other than the .38?"

"I never carried a backup gun. I wasn't smart enough to carry a backup gun. Somebody asked me that one time, and I said, I wouldn't do that, because that would never enter my mind, to carry a backup gun. I wasn't that good at my job to carry a backup gun. If I did that as a full-time career, I would probably know to carry a backup gun. I would at least know what the hell was going on. That's the fact of being naive and stupid."

Asked by Gelb about his support for George Wallace's 1968 presidential campaign, Cesar replied, "I contributed a little bit of money [for Wallace] and passed out some pamphlets at work. I wasn't a real staunch supporter of him, but I liked his ideas."

"He was the governor at the time?" Gelb asked.

"Yeah. I liked his ideas. I maybe liked him because he didn't take any crap from nobody. He told it like it was."

As Gelb later reported from his notes of the pre-interview, "Cesar was working crowd control in the kitchen area at the Ambassador. After Kennedy's speech he was helping clear the way through the pantry for the Kennedy party to get back to the press conference. At the steam table, Kennedy reached over to shake hands with a busboy and Cesar heard, what he thought was, a firecracker. Cesar said he has made conflicting statements about when he drew his gun but he thinks it was after he fell forward as Kennedy fell back bleeding. Cesar said he had never seen things like that before. He put his gun away after he saw they had Sirhan in custody. Cesar said he did not fire his weapon."

When Gelb completed his lengthy pre-interview, he remarked to Cesar, "Well, I think certainly your recollections of the incident are sufficient to make me believe that if you had any involvement, you certainly haven't buried it away in some niche in your mind where it won't come out during this examination. And I certainly think that you're a fit subject for a polygraph test. If you had nothing to do with this, maybe this will put it to bed for some of these people."

"That's why I agreed to it," Cesar insisted.

"And, I think, because you're not making money out the thing, you might as well put it to bed. I say, hey, if you were getting stardom out of this, then keep it alive. But if it's just a pain in the ass, so to speak, then put it to bed."

Cesar explained to Gelb, "See, Moldea said, 'Would you agree to hypnosis?' I said, 'I'll agree to anything.' I said, 'People who don't agree to it have something to hide. I got nothing to hide.' Only the guilty are afraid to do something like this. You know? That's the way I look at it. If I was guilty, first of all, I wouldn't have interviewed with him. If I was guilty, I wouldn't be down here. If I was guilty, I wouldn't be around here. You never would've found me."

Gelb laughed, "That's a good approach."

"You don't kill somebody, and then be open about it."

"Yeah. That's a good approach. Probably it doesn't bear out in every instance . . . because a lot of people who take polygraph tests fail them and admit that they were involved in such and such. Why did they take that test in the first place? And then probably we get into the whole psychology of why they committed the crime in the first place. They possibly had a need to be punished, to be caught, etc. There's a percentage of people who opt for polygraph tests, who opt for everything else, because down deep, they either want to be punished or they think they can beat the system. And that's why so many people are, in fact, punished. Because they come forward one way or another. They leave clues at the scene of the crime that they never should have left."

"Subconsciously, yeah."

"But I'm not sure that I see that in this case. Okay, another trip to the bathroom or just go on to the exam?"

"No, I'm fine."

"Let me check and see that everything's rolling here. And then you and I will review the questions, the specific questions, that will be on the test. And then we will run charts, and you'll be all through."

Before the actual examination began, Gelb challenged Cesar to a little game—just to see if Cesar could beat the polygraph.

Gelb explained, "Okay, Gene, with your right hand, I want you to give me a big seven in the middle of the page. A big one. What number did you write?"

"Seven," Cesar responded.

"Okay, I'll write, 8-9-5-6; you wrote the seven. I want you to intentionally lie to me, and see if you can get away with it. I'm going to ask you if you wrote any of those numbers. And I want you to say no to everything, including the seven. Now, what's going to happen is your blood pressure is going to rise, anticipating the seven. But I want you not to let that happen. . . . In other words, I want you to try to beat the test. I want you to play any mental game you want to play."

After configuring his equipment, Gelb said, "The test is about to begin.

"Gene, did you write the five?"
"No."
"Gene, did you write the nine?"
"No."
"Gene, did you write the seven?"
"No."
"Gene, did you write the six?"
"No."
"Gene, did you write the eight?"
"No."

Looking at the results of this practice test, Gelb told Cesar, "Relax. Gene, you're probably as good a responder to the polygraph as I've ever seen in my life."

Gelb then showed Cesar how the machine's needles jumped quite noticeably on the graph when he answered no to whether he had written the number seven.

Preparing for the actual test, Gelb explained the control questions that would be interspersed among the home run questions. He also told Cesar that the same questions would be asked three times in a different order each time. The polygraph would chart his responses to all three tests.

Just before the last of the three graphs, Gelb said, "Here we go. Look straight ahead. Try not to move. Answer the questions simply yes or no. This is the last chart we're going to run. You are a very good subject for a polygraph, excellent, a very good responder to the test. You'll feel the blood pressure cup for the last time, Gene. The test is about to begin.

"Are you in California?"
"Yes," Cesar replied.
"Do you intend to lie to me on the test about whether or not you

fired a gun the night Bobby Kennedy was killed?"

"No."

"Between the ages of twenty-eight and forty-five did you ever start an argument?"

"No."

"Did you fire a weapon the night Robert Kennedy was shot?"

"No."

"Between the ages of twenty-eight and forty-five, other than your kids, did you ever hurt anyone?"

"No."

"Regarding Robert Kennedy, did you fire any of the shots that hit him in June of '68?"

"No."

"Is today Wednesday?"

"Yes."

"Could you have fired at Kennedy if you wanted to?"

"No."

"Were you involved in a plan to shoot Robert Kennedy?"

"No."

After the final question was asked and answered, Gelb said, "The test is over. Remain still for ten seconds, please. Gene, I'm going to have you—as soon as I get you undone here—sign these charts, so that nobody can say that these are any charts other than yours. How'd you do?"

"I told the truth," Cesar told him. "I don't know what the machine says. The only thing is if it picks up your subconscious in a fifteen-, twenty-year period, I might have started an argument and couldn't remember consciously—or I might have hurt my wife maliciously, because of our marriage, unconsciously. Consciously, I don't remember doing those things. Now, whether that picks that up or not, I don't know. When I told you no to a few things, in my mind, I don't remember doing either one of them."

Gelb told Cesar not to worry about the control questions.

Then Gelb gave him his spot-check opinion of the results. "I'll numerically score these charts, Gene. That will take me somewhere around thirty minutes to do carefully. But I've been doing this a long time. And these charts are so clear and so blatant that I can tell you right now that you had absolutely nothing to do with the Kennedy assassination. I can see the way the scores are adding up right now, indicating that you didn't fire a weapon, you didn't shoot at Kennedy, and that you weren't part of any plan to assassinate Robert Kennedy."

Gelb then invited Weber and me into his private office, where Cesar relaxed.

"Are you okay?" I asked Cesar.

Laughing, Cesar replied, "I didn't shoot Bobby, but I've been thinking about shooting you for making me go through all of this."

As I started laughing with him, I said, "You're going to be happy. You passed, right?"

"That's what he told me."

"Okay, now you're set," I said. "You don't have to do this any more."

Laughing along with us, Gelb began to explain the results, "As far as I'm concerned, it's a single-issue test.[171] When I say I don't

---

[171] Here's how Gelb described the results of the test: "Now, we used on this test three what we call relevant questions. And I'll read them to you. The [first] relevant question [was] 'Did you fire a weapon the night Robert Kennedy was shot?' The reason why we formulated the question in that fashion was to cover the fact that somebody might try to second-guess us and say, 'Yeah, but what if he accidently discharged his weapon and what if he was falling, and that's where the extra bullet holes came from.' So this question includes not only a shot that might have hit Bobby Kennedy, but it also includes discharge from his weapon at all that evening. And, because it says, 'a weapon,' it could have been the .38 Rohm that he was carrying. It could have been the .22, which was an H & R, which he ultimately sold to someone. So this question determines for us whether or not he fired any weapon on the night Robert Kennedy was shot. And we all agree that date was June of '68.

"In the next question, you'll see I don't even stay with June 5, because I don't want somebody saying, 'Well, he might have thought it was [before] midnight.' You ask June 5 and it could have been June 4. So listen to the next question, 'Regarding Robert Kennedy, did you fire any of the shots that hit him in June of '68.' Now, this would cover any shots that actually hit Kennedy. So in the first question, we have any shots at all, whether they hit him or not. This is: Did you fire any of the shots that hit Kennedy. Whether they are from a .22 or a .38 is of no interest. This covers any shots that hit Kennedy in June of '68 as opposed to June 4 or 5, so nobody starts arguing that it was close to midnight. His watch was off. He was on Central Time or some other nonsense. This covers any shots that hit Kennedy. He said no to that.

even have to numerically score this, it's because you gentlemen sitting here right now can very simply look at these charts and come to your own conclusions."[172]

If a polygraph test is only as good as the person who conducts it, then I have full confidence in Gelb's work. He is arguably the best in a very

---

" 'Were you involved in a plan to shoot Robert Kennedy?' Whoever did, in fact, shoot Kennedy was involved in a plan with himself, let alone with others, if there were any others. So this covers the conspiracy theory. It also directly relates to the other two questions, because if he had his own plan to shoot Kennedy, he would have responded deceptively to that question. What I mean by that is that you can now take the numerical scores of each one of those questions and add them together to get a composite total for the examination, because it is, in fact, a single-issue test. So nobody can say, 'Well, yeah, but wait a minute, if he did this, he couldn't have had to do that.'

"Anybody who did one of these three things did all of those things. Whoever shot Kennedy planned to shoot Kennedy. Whoever shot Kennedy did in fact fire a shot that night. And one of those shots hit Kennedy."

[172] Gelb wrote in his formal report, "Cesar was examined with a Stoelting Ultrascribe polygraph calibrated to factory specifications prior to the examination. He was tested in accord with the Zone Comparison Technique validated in a study for the United States Department of Justice under contract number 75-N1-99-0001. . . .

"The four resultant polygraphs were numerically scored in accord with the aforementioned technique. In a single issue examination a cumulative numerical score of + 6 or above indicates truth telling to the relevant issue. A score of − 6 or below indicates deception or withholding information. Scores in between are deemed inconclusive with no determination possible. This examination was designed so that each question was necessarily included in the other question making it a single issue examination.

"Question 1 ['Did you fire a weapon the night Robert Kennedy was shot?'] scored + 12. Question 2 ['Regarding Robert Kennedy, did you fire any of the shots that hit him in June '68?'] scored + 9. Question 3 ['Were you involved in a plan to shoot Robert Kennedy?'] scored + 7, for a total score of + 28 for the examination.

"Based upon the polygraph examination and its numerical scoring, Thane Eugene Cesar was telling the truth when he answered as above to the relevant questions regarding the Kennedy assassination. In other words, Cesar did not fire a weapon the night Robert Kennedy was killed nor was he involved in a conspiracy to kill Kennedy.

"The polygrams were 'blind scored' by a second expert polygraphist [Richard J. Sachelli] who independently corroborated the findings of the primary examiner. The 'blind scorer' did his evaluation of the polygrams without seeing the questions or interacting with the examinee."

cluttered market. Thus, there could be no doubt about it: Cesar had passed the polygraph test with flying colors.

As Cesar sighed with considerable relief, he sensed that his long ordeal was now over. Pleased that I was helping to clear an innocent man, I slapped him on the back and asked, "Gene, what are you going to do now?"

"I'm going to Disneyland!" Cesar laughed, acting as if he were spiking a football.

To sum up, Gene Cesar proved to be an innocent man who since 1969 has been wrongly accused of being involved in the murder of Senator Kennedy.[173]

Caught up in the euphoria of Cesar's vindication, I suddenly wondered out loud, "Then, who really did kill Senator Kennedy?"

[173] Actually, I had two truth tests conducted, the more recent in June 1994. The second test, a voice stress analysis, corroborated Gelb's polygraph results.

29. Confronting Sirhan

S irhan Bishara Sirhan became my last hope for any glimmer of evidence of a second gunman or other co-conspirators. I guess I had known all along, whether I fully realized it or not, that this entire case would begin and end with him.

As I faced a Coke machine and fumbled for change in my pocket in the visitation room at California's Corcoran State Prison—a maximum-security facility, tucked between Bakersfield and Fresno—I was anxiously awaiting my first meeting with the key figure in the 1968 murder of Robert Kennedy. It was September 26, 1993, and I had made the three-hour-plus drive from Los Angeles to see Sirhan Sirhan.

Adel Sirhan, Sirhan's loyal older brother, had arranged the interview and come along with me.[174]

After I placed two quarters in the slot and heard a can of soda drop, Adel, in a quiet voice behind me, introduced me to his younger brother. "Dan Moldea," he said, "Sirhan Sirhan. Sirhan, this is Dan Moldea."

We smiled at each other. Sirhan then bowed modestly, gently clasping his hands together as if in prayer. He took my extended hand and pumped it heartily like a politician on election day, placing his left hand over my right hand for emphasis. I couldn't help being struck by how kind and polite he appeared.

Dressed in blue denim prison fatigues and a pair of simple black canvas shoes, Sirhan was much shorter than I expected. He was slightly built but in good shape and well groomed. He had a full head of black but slightly graying hair, cut conservatively. His deep brown eyes were bright and clear. His natural bronze coloring made him appear like he had spent the summer on the beach. He looked pretty good for a guy who had spent the past twenty-five years in prison.[175]

Our six-hour interview in September 1993 went well, as did our second, four-hour interview two weeks later, on October 10. I recounted my work in the Kennedy murder case—which he was already well aware of—that indicated that two guns had been fired at the crime scene. For the most part, I had been lobbing softball questions, allowing him to smack them over the fence.

As I drove north from Los Angeles for my third interview with Sirhan, on June 5, 1994—the twenty-sixth anniversary of the shooting of Senator Kennedy—I assumed that this would be my last formal interview with him. Thus, I decided to go over some of the ground we had

---

[174] Lynn Mangan, a close friend of the Sirhan family, and Bill Klaber, who had recently produced a controversial program on the Kennedy murder for National Public Radio, were also present during the first of my three interviews with Sirhan.

[175] From the time of his conviction, in 1969, to 1975, Sirhan lived at San Quentin; the first two of those years, he spent on death row. From 1975 to 1992, he did his time at Soledad Penitentiary. On June 1, 1992, he moved to Corcoran. At the time of my first interview with him, he lived with thirty-four other "high-profile" inmates in the prison's protective unit.

covered during the previous two interviews and then to go for his throat to see how he would react.[176]

Early during our conversation—even though Sirhan and I are both members of the Eastern Orthodox faith—I offered him a little gift: a Roman Catholic scapular, which I wear around my neck. One side read, "Whosoever dies wearing this Scapular shall not suffer eternal fire." Sirhan seemed to be moved by my gesture and turned to a prison guard, who came over to our table and examined the cloth object. After several telephone conversations, the guard returned, telling us politely that Sirhan could not accept the scapular. Obviously disappointed, Sirhan gave it back to me.

After a few minutes of small talk with Adel and Sirhan, I marveled out loud that Sirhan, who spoke English and Arabic quite well, had also studied German and Russian. I lamented that had this crime not occurred, he probably would have done well with his life. Without missing a beat and still clearly agitated over the scapular, Sirhan shot back, "I had as many All-American values as the next guy. I have never viewed myself as a sociopath or a person on the margin."

Sensing that Sirhan wanted to get down to business, I asked, "Tell me again about the purchase of the gun, the Iver Johnson."

Allowing me to go over some old ground from our previous interviews, Sirhan replied, "My brother Munir was there when I bought it. He knew the guy we bought it from. Munir wasn't the gun enthusiast; I was. I don't remember the money changes, but the gun was for me and not my brother. Munir had no interest in guns at all. I paid him back all the money he loaned me."

"When was this?"

---

[176] At the insistence of Sirhan, I had to visit him on the weekend, when family and friends met with inmates. Although the prison had cleared me to visit Sirhan as a journalist during the week, Sirhan refused to allow me to do so when I would be toting recording equipment. I sensed that he didn't want to go literally "on the record," perhaps because of a previous bad experience. He never explained why.

So I had to meet with him at times when no recording equipment, pens, pencils, or notepads were permitted through prison security. In lieu of these, I scrounged up some paper and a small pencil from the prison guards who were standing watch nearby. When the pencil went dull, I sharpened it with the edge of a Coke can. During all three interviews with Sirhan, I frequently read his quoted comments back to him, allowing him to amend or expand on what he had said.

The following is a composite made from the notes of my three interviews with Sirhan, who, along with Adel Sirhan, has read and confirmed its accuracy.

"This was in early 1968. This was my first gun purchase. I've seen cheap .22s, Saturday night specials. But this gun was of good quality. There was no wear, no sign of usage."

"How did you become acquainted with guns?"

"I was familiar with guns because of my Cadet Corps training in high school, which was a state-sponsored program. I've fired M-16s, M-14s, .45s, .22s. I could tear a gun apart and put it back together. We used to have competitions."

"Were you a good shot?"

"I could shoot."

"Tell me about your job at the farm in Corona."

"At Corona, they bred horses. I had seen a note on the bulletin board at Santa Anita, offering a position as an exercise boy. I responded and met Frank Donnarumma, who was the trainer. I was into life not death. I watched horses being born. It was a life-affirming experience."

"Tell me about Donnarumma. His real name was Henry Ramistella. What did you know about him?"

"First of all, I didn't know that 'Frank Donnarumma' was an alias. I didn't know that. Frank always seemed to be having financial problems, which probably stemmed from his gambling. He was a heavy gambler."

"Did you know that he had a criminal record?"

"No, I knew nothing about that."

"When you fell off your horse in September 1966, what happened?"

"I was unconscious after falling off the horse. It was on a Sunday. We were working a filly. Frank was there. It was a foggy day. She was flying, and I couldn't make the turn. The saddle was loose or something. But I never felt the fall. There was no pain, because I was unconscious. The next thing I knew, I was in a hospital bed. I had a concussion, and I was bruised up. I had stitches under my chin and next to my eye. I was in the hospital for two or three days. Frank also drove me to get the stitches removed. It was mostly my face that was messed up."

Adel Sirhan interrupted, "After the fall, Sirhan started to change. I couldn't believe how badly he was hurt."

"How do you mean 'changed'?" I asked. "How did he change?"

"He just became a different person," Adel continued. "He changed through the experiences he encountered with the people who were trying to treat him and make him well. The changes probably manifested themselves as a result of the physical scars he received after the fall. We knew he was in pain, but he didn't want to show it."

"Is that true, Sirhan? Were you morose after your fall? Did you change?"

"I just felt different. I wasn't the same person."

"At Corona, did you ever know of anyone who was associated with organized crime, the mob?"

"I didn't know anything about crime and criminals."

"What kind of a gambler were you? The LAPD claims that you were betting sixty to eighty dollars on a single race."

"I made bets of ten dollars or fifteen dollars. Anything more was too much, and I couldn't afford it. I was broke most of the time. Also, I never knew of a fixed race or a doped horse. And I never had any fights with my mother over my gambling. That's another thing the police said."

"The LAPD claimed that you once worked at Del Mar racetrack. Did you work there, at Hollywood Park, or at Caliente, in Tijuana?"

"I never worked at Del Mar or Caliente. I once went to Caliente to watch a horse run. I don't remember ever working at Hollywood Park. I never even visited Del Mar. But in 1966 or 1967, I went to Tijuana once to watch a horse I exercised race at Caliente."

"Did you know John Alessio, the king of horse racing in Tijuana?"[177]

"No, I never heard of him."

[177] Longtime reputed bookmaker and associate of numerous organized crime figures and southern California political figures, John S. Alessio was born in West Virginia and made his fortune in San Diego. He owned, among other enterprises, the Caliente racetrack, near Tijuana, and almost succeeded in taking over Del Mar in 1966 before being denied by state racing officials.

Speaking of Alessio, Bert Altfillisch, Sirhan's former boss at the Corona horse farm, told me, "We certainly could have had a horse or two of his here, but I never met the man. I know him by his notoriety."

Several writers have tried, unsuccessfully, to link Alessio to Sirhan and Gene Cesar. There is no evidence of any such connection.

After a few minutes of conversation about his interest in horse racing, I abruptly changed the subject, asking, "What impact did the murder of Martin Luther King, Jr., have on you in April 1968?"

"I was at the racetrack that day. Pink Pigeon, a horse that broke the track record, was racing at Santa Anita in the afternoon. A black fellow with a portable radio walked up to me, and he was crying. I thought he had lost a race. He cried, 'They shot him! They shot him!' Someone said, 'They shot who?' And he said, 'Brother Martin Luther King.' Everyone was excited, concentrating on the next race. It put a damper on everything. It was a very sad time."

"What did you think of Senator Kennedy?"

"I had a lot of admiration for Kennedy as a humane, caring, and gentle person. I would've campaigned for him. But I couldn't see him reconciling his caring for blacks and the downtrodden but not the Palestinians. I remember him talking about sending the fifty jets to Israel. That's when I started to change my feelings about him. I had viewed him as a role model."

"Were you stalking Robert Kennedy?"

"No, I wasn't."

"Did you attend a Kennedy rally on May 20 in Pomona?"

"I didn't know anything about that."

"Did you attend a Kennedy rally on May 24 at the Los Angeles Sports Arena, where other witnesses claimed to have seen you?"

"No, I didn't."

"Were you present at a Kennedy rally on June 2 at the Ambassador Hotel? You were supposedly seen there, too."

"I never followed Kennedy, period. I still don't remember ever seeing him in person."

"Did you know anyone who worked at the Ambassador Hotel back then?"

"I never knew anyone who worked at that hotel. I had never been to the Ambassador before. I had heard about the Coconut Grove, but I had never been there."

"Did you drive to Corona during the weekend before the murder? Supposedly, you had put over three hundred miles on your car."

"My car was in such bad shape, I didn't trust it to drive for such a distance. And Corona is only about forty or fifty miles away. That's how bad my car was."

"Do you remember writing in your notebooks—the ones found in your bedroom at your home in Pasadena? Among the writings in these notebooks were very specific statements that 'RFK must die!' "

"I can't visualize this."

"You can't visualize this? Does this mean you didn't write in the notebooks?"

"No, it means that I can't remember writing in the notebooks."

"You can't remember?"

"No, I can't remember anything about them."

"Why did you say in your notebooks that Frank Donnarumma owed you some [money]? What was that all about?"

"I just don't remember any of that. All Frank and I ever talked about was horses. Sometimes, when my friends and I would go to the track, we saw Frank there. But Frank and I never hung out together. I never went to the track with him."

"I understand that you practiced self-hypnosis. What was that all about?"

"It was a kind of meditation, silence and quiet. It's like the New Age movement toward tranquillity and peace of mind."

"Nothing more than that?"

"No. Well, I was trying to improve myself. I started to learn about the metaphysical occult after the death of my sister. I was hit hard when she died. But no one knew that I was into self-hypnosis or interested in The Beyond."

"Tell me about your encounter with the occult."

"I had a lot of talks with people about occult literature. A guy I knew when I was down in Corona pushed me along the way to reading more.[178] It was more intellectual and abstract. It was more about Theosophy, which is about the spiritual afterlife. It expanded

---

[178] The man who encouraged Sirhan to read about Theosophy was Thomas Rathke, a groom on the Corona horse farm, who was investigated and cleared by the LAPD of any nefarious involvement with Sirhan. Rathke, who often went to the racetrack with Sirhan, was frequently mentioned in Sirhan's notebooks. As with Peggy Osterkamp and Gwendolyn Gum, Sirhan refused to allow his defense attorneys to call Rathke as a witness at his 1969 trial.

my knowledge and horizons of life, as well as my own nature and spiritual being."

I then took Sirhan through his day on June 4, 1968.

Chapter 1 of this book chronicles his recollection: leaving the gun range, restlessly wandering through Pasadena, searching for a party in downtown Los Angeles, arriving at the Ambassador and drinking Tom Collinses; then, after going back to his car, returning to the Ambassador for coffee.

"At that point," Sirhan told me, "I blacked out."

Sirhan insisted that he doesn't remember getting his gun and putting it in his pocket. "I guess I was afraid the gun would be stolen. It must have been out in the open."

He doesn't remember returning to the Ambassador. "I have no idea how I got back in there. I only know that my goal was to get some coffee."

Other than his memory of the room where the teletype was clicking away, Sirhan said that he doesn't remember talking to anyone at the hotel who claimed to have talked to him. "I just remember the bright lights in the big room. Then somebody referred me to the kitchen for coffee."

He remembered that, as he had stood by the coffee urn, a woman in a plain white dress was also there. He added, "I don't remember any woman in a polka-dot dress."[179]

When I asked about the moment of the shooting, he replied, "I don't remember being in the kitchen pantry. I don't remember seeing Robert Kennedy. And I don't remember shooting him. All I remember is being choked and getting my ass kicked."

"You don't remember anything about the shooting?"

[179] Rightly or wrongly, I have never placed much stock in the polka-dot-dress-girl controversy. If Sandy Serrano and the couple who talked to Sergeant Paul Sharaga did not err in what they reportedly had heard, then, I believe, the girl and her companion, who were gleefully boasting of killing Senator Kennedy, were apart from Sirhan, simply among those in the anti-Kennedy group at the Ambassador Hotel—described in Chapter 21, n. 141.

To me, it has always seemed to defy all belief and logic that people involved in a complicated murder conspiracy would boast of their involvement immediately after the murder had been committed.

"No, nothing. It just isn't in my mind. I just remember being choked."

"You have no recollection about the shooting at all?"

"I don't remember aiming the gun and saying to myself that I'm going to kill Robert Kennedy. I don't remember any adrenalin rush."

"Do you remember being handcuffed and arrested by the police?"

"All I remember is having some words with a police officer with the badge number 3909. I just remember his badge number and the fact that he was shining a flashlight in my eyes."

"That was Art Placencia. He was one of the arresting officers. He was sitting in the back seat of the car with you on the way to Rampart. Do you remember him checking your eyes to see if you were on something?"

"No. I don't remember that."

"That's what he was doing with the flashlight. Do you remember having your eyes checked at Rampart?"

"No, I don't. I do recall being in a little room and somebody counting the money that had come from my pocket."

"Do you remember being interrogated by Sergeant Bill Jordan at Rampart and then, later, at Parker Center?"

"I don't remember Bill Jordan or anything about the interrogation. I only remember a female judge."

"Joan Dempsey Klein. She presided at the arraignment. Let me ask you, What *do* you remember about that night?"

"Nothing. I have no recollection of anything else that happened that night."

"You don't remember being interrogated? You don't remember being transferred downtown? You don't remember being examined by a doctor?"

"I just don't remember anything about it."

"Let me ask you this, What do you think about the theories that you were programmed to kill and programmed to forget? Do you think that you were the victim of mind control by a person or persons unknown, as has been suggested by Dr. Eduard Simson [the prison psychologist who examined Sirhan] at San Quentin, among others? What did you think of him?"

"He might have been right. I was on death row at the time. But he gave a good analysis of the work of the Jewish psychological team—which was supposedly part of my defense. They dismissed me as a paranoid schizophrenic."

"Why do you think Dr. Simson was dismissed from his job at San Quentin?"

"He might have been getting too close to what really happened."

"Do you really think it's possible that you were under mind control, that you had been programmed?"

Sirhan smiled politely and replied, "It's probably too diabolical to suggest that I was controlled by someone else—but I don't know. I only know that I don't remember anything about the shooting. And I only remember being choked."

"Do you think the contributing factor to your memory loss was the fact that you had drunk too much that night?"

"I didn't know anything about beers or liquors. I was a square. The Tom Collins tasted just like lemonade. I was tired. It was late. I was an early-to-rise, early-to-bed person. I was out of my element. Whether I was drunk, programmed, or outmaneuvered, what has happened has happened. They never gave me a Breathalyzer, and they only drew my blood the next day."

"Do you know of anything that could help you remember?"

"Baxter Ward [of the Los Angeles County Board of Supervisors] wanted to do something after the Kranz Report. He wanted to get permission to take me back to the Ambassador, hoping to jog my memory. But the judge wouldn't allow it."

"Were you a participant in a conspiracy?"

"Do you think I would conceal anything about someone else's involvement and face the gas chamber in the most literal sense? I have no knowledge of a conspiracy."

"But, yes or no, were you part of a conspiracy, Sirhan?"

"I wish there had been a conspiracy. It would have unraveled before now."

"Then, why do you even talk about the possibility of being mind controlled?"

"My defense attorneys developed the idea of *The Manchurian Candidate* theory."

"Then, once again, why don't you just accept responsibility for this crime?"

"If I was to accept responsibility for this crime, it would be a hell of a burden to live with—having taken a human life without knowing it."

"Then you are saying that you are willing to take responsibility, but you have no memory of committing the crime?"

"It's not in my mind, but I'm not denying it. I must have been there, but I can't reconstruct it mentally. I mean no disrespect here, but I empathize with Senator Ted Kennedy in the Chappaquiddick incident. He was supposedly under the influence of alcohol and couldn't remember what he had done. When he finally did realize what had happened, someone was dead."

"Why did you take credit for the murder at your trial?"

"Grant Cooper conned me to say that I killed Robert Kennedy. I went along with him because he had my life in his hands. I was duped into believing that he had my best interests in mind. It was a futile defense. Cooper sold me out. Charles Manson [with whom Sirhan has done time] once told me that defense attorneys treat their clients like kings before their trials. After the trials begin, they treat their clients like shit. This was true of the manner in which Grant Cooper treated me. I remember Cooper once told me, 'You're getting the best, and you're not paying anything. Just shut up. I'm the lawyer, and you're just the client.' "

"You were willing to go to the gas chamber for a crime you didn't remember committing?"

"I did a lot of self-exploration while I was on death row. It changed my whole vision of the world. I was trying to justify that I was going to the gas chamber. I wanted to search myself to find the truth, but I could never figure it out. I had nothing to lose."

"Did you ever examine whether you had acted with premeditation?"

"When I got to death row, I started reading the law about diminished capacity and the requirements for premeditation. There was no way that I could have summoned the prerequisite for first-degree murder. That was no part of me. They said that I didn't understand the magnitude of what I had done. They're right. I don't truly appreciate it, because I have no awareness of having aimed the gun at Bobby Kennedy."

"Why did you admit to the murder before the parole board?"

"They want the prisoner to admit his guilt and take responsibility for the crime. They want us to confess and to express remorse, which is what I have done. In fact, I have been told that I won't be paroled because of the Kennedys."[180]

"So, once again, you were willing to take credit for the crime without remembering that you had committed it?"

Sirhan then seemingly became overwrought, exclaiming, "It's so damn painful! I want to expunge all of this from my mind!"

As if I had been punched with a straight right hand, I suddenly thought to myself, "This fucking guy has been lying to me all along."

In response to Sirhan, I stated firmly, "I am not a court of law; I am not a parole board. I'm a reporter who doesn't want to be wrong. I want to know, Sirhan: Did you commit this crime?"

Sirhan fired right back, "I would not want to take the blame for this crime as long as there is exculpatory evidence that I didn't do the crime. The jury was never given the opportunity to pass judgment on the evidence discovered since the trial, as well as the inconsistencies of the firearms evidence [the bullet evidence] at the trial. In view of this, no, I didn't get a fair trial."[181]

---

[180] Sirhan had been slated for release in 1984. However, Los Angeles district attorney John Van de Kamp persuaded the California Board of Prison Terms to rescind its decision in 1982. Since then, Sirhan has appeared before the parole board on numerous occasions, pleading for release. In doing so, he has apologized for killing Senator Kennedy, saying, "I wish it had never occurred, for the Kennedy's sake, and for my own." However, he has always maintained that he does not remember the key events of June 5, 1968. Sirhan lost his most recent parole hearing on December 1, 1994. His parole can be reconsidered in 1996.

In 1985, Rudolph Castro, the chairman of the board of prison terms, stated that Sirhan's act was "an attack on the democratic system of government [which] with three shots disenfranchised millions of people. . . . Sirhan still does not accept the enormity of his crime."

[181] When I asked Sirhan on June 5, 1994, what his thoughts were, he replied, "Give me another chance. Let me go home and mind my own business. Justice has been more than served in this case. I am not deportable by law, but I am willing to return to the Middle East, if necessary. I hold no grudges against anybody; I am no threat to anybody."

With that reply, I finally began to understand Sirhan's entire strategy: As long as people like me continued to put forth supposed new evidence, he still had a chance to experience freedom. And I also understood why he was talking to me in the first place. More than any other person in recent years, since the heyday of Paul Schrade, Allard Lowenstein, and Vincent Bugliosi—all respected and honorable men who had only sought out the truth about the case, without absolving Sirhan of any guilt—I had been helping to keep this case alive with all of my supposed new revelations about alleged extra bullets and the possibility that at least two guns that had been fired at the crime scene.

As I sat there, I became furious with myself for having nearly been hoodwinked by Sirhan and the bizarre circumstances of this entire case. I didn't even attempt to conceal my feelings.

At that moment of my stark realization in that prison visitation room—and with Adel present—I barked angrily at Sirhan, "You don't remember writing in your notebooks in which you articulated your determination to kill Robert Kennedy and why—That's motive! You don't remember getting your gun when you returned to your car from the Rafferty party—That's means! You don't remember having been in the pantry, getting close to Kennedy, and firing your gun— That's opportunity!

"Every time you have a memory lapse, it goes to motive, means, or opportunity!"[182]

In response, Sirhan sat quietly, saying nothing but looking puzzled, probably wondering where the hell I was going with all of this. But I could tell that he wasn't very concerned. He knew, probably more than anyone else, that I had already bought into the second-gun theory and made a damn good case of it. "What's Moldea going to do now that he's in so deep," Sirhan must have been thinking, "turn around now and say that I acted alone?"

Knowing how close Sirhan was to his ailing mother, who, besides Adel, had been his most ardent defender—and understanding how much pain Sirhan knew he had inflicted on her—I asked, "Sirhan,

---

[182] I offered to arrange a polygraph examination for Sirhan in order to determine what he did and did not do, as well as what he did and did not remember. He refused.

when your mother dies, God forbid, are you going to remember everything and come clean?"

Now furious with me for having brought his mother into this, Sirhan exclaimed, raising his voice with each syllable, "Change my story? *Mr. Moldea,* you're a motherfucker! *Mr. Moldea,* you're a fucking asshole!"

I smiled at Sirhan and started jabbing my finger in his face. "Sirhan, it's '*Dan,* you're a motherfucker. *Dan,* you're a fucking asshole.' " As I started to laugh out loud, Sirhan paused for a moment and started laughing, too, breaking a very tense moment.

But he wasn't laughing for the same reason I was.

I had just wanted Sirhan to remember the first name of his last hope.

And then I wanted nothing further to do with this assassin.

30. *What Really Happened?*

> "Wisdom too often never comes, and so one ought
> not to reject it merely because it comes late."
>
> —Justice FELIX FRANKFURTER

Complicated investigations sometimes have very simple solutions. However, in order to recognize and appreciate the simple solution in the Robert Kennedy murder case, one must pass through a gauntlet of intricate and often contradictory evidence.

The LAPD's probe appears to provide extremely persuasive evidence of Sirhan's guilt. But, simultaneously, a close study of the controversies in this case—such as challenges to the ballistics and firearms evidence—seems to provide equally persuasive evidence that a second gun may have been fired at the crime scene.

When I entered this case in 1987, I published an article in *Regardie's* in an effort to help force open the official case file. In that first

...stigation, I had concentrated my research on eyewitness testimony and on Gene Cesar. Without the LAPD's sealed investigative files, though, numerous questions remained unanswered. In effect, this case became more complicated than necessary because of the LAPD's stubborn insistence to keep its files secret.

In the wake of the *Regardie's* article, the city of Los Angeles finally transferred the files to the California State Archives for public release. However, many documents and photographs were missing or had been mysteriously destroyed; thus, suspicions about the LAPD's investigation and ultimate conclusions persisted. Yet, despite problems with the condition of the existing files, the LAPD and the district attorney's office continued to be cavalier and high-handed with those who asked reasonable questions about obvious discrepancies. So instead of providing a good-faith effort to resolve these matters, the LAPD gave its critics, like me, more ammunition for accusations that a cover-up was still in progress.

After being criticized by LAPD homicide detectives for relying on the statements of eyewitnesses who were "not trained or experienced or qualified to make judgments" about what they saw at the crime scene, I began locating and interviewing numerous law enforcement personnel directly involved in the original LAPD investigation.

To my surprise, nearly all of my best evidence of a possible second gunman came from many of these officials, who identified what appeared to have been extra bullets at the crime scene.

Because of overwhelming quasi-official corroboration that two guns had been fired, this new evidence of a second gunman nearly constituted conclusive proof. And I was not alone in this opinion. To me and others who examined my work, a simple solution to this case did not seem likely, since a second gun appeared to have been fired.

But personal and professional restrictions forced me to fade in and out of this case, depending on how much time and money I could afford to spend satisfying a basic curiosity: Do we really know the truth about Robert Kennedy's murder?

It was not until I received the backing of a major publisher, W. W. Norton & Company, that I could do what was necessary to resolve my own questions about this case.

Had I settled for the mere appearance of proof—muzzle distance discrepancies, alleged extra bullets at the crime scene, and the inability of independent firearms experts to match victim bullets with Sirhan's gun—this book would have had a very different ending. In my own defense, I decided not to settle for the sensational without examining more mundane considerations: the simple explanations for why the evidence appears as it does in this murder case, which has been characterized by an astonishingly complex and contradictory array of data.

In order to do this, I had to interview numerous law enforcement personnel while acquiring an understanding of the official version of the case, as well as the legitimate challenges to the LAPD's investigation leveled by reasonable people with honorable intentions.

These numerous interviews and record searches, as well as the Cesar polygraph and my talks with Sirhan, brought me to the point in which I could recognize and appreciate the simple solution to this complex case.

And based upon my research, I have concluded that Gene Cesar is an innocent man, who has for years been wrongly accused of being a murderer, and that Sirhan Sirhan knowingly shot and killed Robert Kennedy.

Some readers may be disappointed with this sudden twist in the plot of this book, but I, for one, am relieved.

Placing into a new context what I had known all along about this case, I now realize that even law enforcement officials—who possess the training, qualifications, and experience to determine the significance of crime scene evidence—*do* make mistakes if their abilities are not put to the test under the proper circumstances and conditions.

In other words, if one does not account for occasional official mistakes and incompetence, then nearly every such political murder could appear to be a conspiracy, particularly if a civilian investigator—with limited access and resources—is looking for one.[183]

---

[183] Even though I do not believe that Sirhan participated in a conspiracy to murder Senator Kennedy, I think that the LAPD and the FBI were negligent in not thoroughly investigating organized crime in a *possible* conspiracy amid its more massive investigations of such red herrings as the polka-dot-dress girl, horse-selling ministers, Arab hit squads, Sirhan's passing interest in the occult, and speculation that Sirhan may have been mind controlled. Clearly, of all the groups studied by the law enforcement community for their possible involvement in this murder, the underworld had the strongest motive, means, and opportunity to eliminate Senator Kennedy.

And, like author Robert Blair Kaiser before me, I still have questions about

This is not to say that I am now embracing the entire official version of the Kennedy case. I am not. However, I am saying that the Los Angeles Police Department came to the right conclusion for some of the wrong reasons.[184]

Clearly, the law enforcement community should have been much more vigilant in its handling of such crime scene evidence as photographs, door frames, and ceiling tiles.[185] It should have minimized its bullying tactics against people like Sandy Serrano and Donald Schulman, which really wound up causing more speculation than their stories deserved. It should have expedited the release of its ten-volume report on the case, as well as the central records supporting

---

Sirhan's racetrack connections—all of which should have been resolved by the LAPD and the FBI years ago.

[184] The mainstream media, particularly the *Los Angeles Times,* have also been right. However, the establishment press demonstrated a remarkable lack of curiosity about the state of the evidence in this case, tolerating and even supporting the complete suppression of the LAPD's investigative files for nearly twenty years.

In the end, the critics and independent journalists were responsible for prompting full disclosure.

[185] On April 2, 1992, a large group of celebrities, law enforcement officials, journalists, and politicians, as well as the American Civil Liberties Union of southern California, filed a request that the Los Angeles County Grand Jury investigate alleged "willful and corrupt misconduct" by the LAPD in its handling of the Robert Kennedy murder probe. At a press conference, Paul Schrade, a member of the group, told reporters, "We are not charging any grand interlocking conspiracy." Instead, the group asked for an investigation of the LAPD's procedures and practices during the Kennedy case.

Los Angeles attorney Marilyn Barrett represented the fifty-member group, which included Cesar Chavez, Robert Joling, Frank Mankiewicz, Arthur M. Schlesinger, Jr., and former counsel to the U.S. Senate Watergate committee Sam Dash. I participated on the working group that prepared the submission, and I continue to support its efforts.

To date, the grand jury has not accepted the proposed investigation.

California state archivist John Burns told me, "Based on the records on file at the California State Archives, LAPD appeared to conduct exhaustive inquiries into every alleged conspiracy connection, no matter how seemingly remote or tangential. Predictably, most of these resulted in quick dead ends. . . . The archives has a large array of documentary and audio materials. The files that we have do not support a presumption of conspiracy, nor do they prompt one to think that further study of the subjects investigated would be productive, since these files appear relatively complete. This is in contrast to those records relating to the crime scene, for which the LAPD admits to destroying a substantial amount of material that may have possessed evidential value."

---

it—instead of suppressing this information for twenty years and allowing so many important questions to remain unanswered. And it should have been more complete and definitive in its probe of Gene Cesar, who became a lightning rod for people, like me, who believed that a second gun might have been fired.[186]

Finally, the dismal manner in which records were handled implies disorganization within the LAPD, which might explain its reluctance to be candid in later years. LAPD officials knew they had made serious errors but didn't understand why they had been made.

In the end, the most serious mistakes made by the LAPD were errors of omission rather than commission.

Although I still have problems with certain aspects of this case—which will probably never be resolved—I believe that most of the principal questions can now be satisfactorily answered. Thus, I must painfully disassemble the evidence of a second gunman that I have both collected and uncovered over the years. The irony here is that a civilian investigator will do what the LAPD and the FBI have been capable of doing but have refused to do.

On the basis of what I have learned during the research of this book, here are my conclusions about what I consider to be the six remaining controversies in the Kennedy murder case: Whom did Sirhan hit with the first shot? What was the sequence of the shots hitting Kennedy? How did Sirhan manage to hit Kennedy at point-blank range? Were there bullet holes in the door frames? Why didn't the 1975 firearms panel conclude that the victim bullets came from Sirhan's gun? What was Sirhan's motive for killing Senator Kennedy?

---

[186] During the spring of 1993, television producer Beaux Carson found Gene Cesar's Harrington & Richardson .22 revolver in a swamp near Jim Yoder's home in Arkansas. One of the young men who had stolen the gun in 1969, now fully grown, had tipped Carson off as to its whereabouts.

Firearms identification testing arranged by Carson between this gun and the Kennedy neck bullet, now on file at the California State Archives, has reportedly been inconclusive—because of the deteriorating condition of the bullet and the gun.

California state archivist John Burns told me, "There have been, and continue to be, repeated efforts to reexamine the bullets. Conclusive results are even less likely, though, due to the deterioration of the bullets and weapon over time, caused by twenty years of storage outside of archival custody and being subject to repeated handling."

1. Whom did Sirhan hit with the first shot?

In his official July 8, 1968, bullet-accounting report, DeWayne Wolfer stated that the first shot fatally struck Kennedy in the head; the second passed harmlessly through Kennedy's shoulder pad and hit Schrade; the third struck Kennedy under the right armpit and lodged in his neck; and the fourth entered Kennedy's back near the entry site of the third shot and exited through his chest and into the ceiling, where it became lost. Wolfer then stated that the remainder of the eight shots hit the other victims.

I believe that this scenario, which has contributed heavily to the second-gun theories, is wrong.

Describing the initial shot from Sirhan's gun, all of the eyewitnesses identified by the LAPD as "reliable" said that the distance between the muzzle of Sirhan's gun and Senator Kennedy was between one and a half and three feet. If this is true, the first bullet could *not* have hit Kennedy—who both Wolfer and Coroner Thomas Noguchi verified had been shot at contact or near-contact range.

Eyewitness Lisa Urso—who was falsely thought to have been the LAPD's key "point-blank" shot witness and had an unobstructed view of both Kennedy and Sirhan when the shooting started—stated, "At the same time I saw the fire and I heard the first pop, I saw the Senator grab his head, behind his right ear."

Did she really see Kennedy get shot, or did she simply see him react defensively to the sound of the first shot?

Although Urso heard the other shots, she saw the flame coming from the gun only with the first shot, to which, she said, Kennedy reacted by raising his right arm. And what did she say the muzzle distance was for this first shot? "Three to five feet."

If her account is true, this bullet did *not* hit Kennedy or his clothing.

I believe that the first shot missed Kennedy, and hit Paul Schrade in the forehead—which contradicts a major conclusion by Wolfer but also helps to provide a better explanation for how Sirhan shot Senator Kennedy at point-blank range.

Schrade was looking directly at Kennedy when the first shot was fired; in fact, Schrade didn't even see or hear it. The last image in Schrade's mind before he lost consciousness was seeing Kennedy smiling and turning toward the steam table.

Also, in his sworn testimony, hotel waiter captain Edward Minasian, a key eyewitness, testified, "I saw the fellow [Schrade] behind the Senator fall, then the Senator fell."

And then, while dying on the kitchen floor, Senator Kennedy asked, "Is Paul all right?" Kennedy probably saw Schrade get hit with the first shot.

2. What was the sequence of the shots hitting Kennedy?

During my October 1993 interview with former Los Angeles county coroner Thomas Noguchi, I asked him what, on the basis of his years of experience, he believed to be the correct sequence of the shots that hit Kennedy or his clothing. Noguchi replied, "If one person is the shooter, one person can still do it, but the senator had to be facing away from the assailant. Then, three shots must have been very close—although no one actually saw them. Two of the shots in the right armpit had a very tight blackening. With the infrared photography, it was clear that there was a tight powder deposit. I would think that it was a matter of a few inches if not actually contacting. Someone had to be close.

"If there was just one gun, of course, the arm had to be extended further. So the assailant didn't have to be next to the senator—but he had to be within arm's reach.

"So the question is, How can one receive such an injury if one person is shooting? Of course, I was reasonably trying to place the senator in certain positions so that he could receive the injuries."

Noguchi continued, "The injury to the back of the right ear, specifically, the right mastoid area, would be fatal and also would render him helpless. Kennedy could not be standing if he had such an injury. He would collapse to the floor. This was a severe injury. The bullet from this .22 had a great deal of power. Striking the hard bone and the bone shattering would have taken him off his feet. The fragmenting bullets caused the swelling of the brain which took away his consciousness after he was able to speak only a few words.

"That means that the other shots must have been *prior* to the senator collapsing. Based on the examination of the clothing, there had to be three other shots. One went through the right shoulder pad of Kennedy's jacket. One stopped in back of his neck in the soft tissue, and [that bullet was recovered].

"One of the shots that has prompted the second-gun theorists went through his right armpit [and exited out of his chest]. Again, it was a very tight, contact shot. That means that the senator's arm had to have been raised enough so that the location of the wound was accessible to the gunman.

"Of course, Kennedy could have been waving his arm to guard off from an oncoming assailant or action. Or he could have just heard the gunfire and then raised his right arm whereby his shoulder pad was raised and the bullet went through, not striking his body. The shoulder pad shot could not have struck the right mastoid, because the pattern of the powder didn't match."

Noguchi concluded, "So I believe that there were four shots fired at him, at least. The sequence? The shoulder pad shot as he was raising his arm, the two shots to his right armpit, in which one of the bullets lodged in the back of his neck, and, lastly, the shot to the mastoid. This was the shot that was fatal.

"In other words, the nonfatal wounds first and then the fatal wound."

3. How did Sirhan manage to hit Kennedy at point-blank range?

Like many others, including the LAPD, I have been guilty of trying to re-create the murder by characterizing the people at the crime scene, including Senator Kennedy and the other five victims, as being stick figures, standing tall and upright throughout the incident. Many of us have failed to consider realistically the kinetic movement of the crowd, that everyone in that room must have been in motion after the first or second shot.

The most common description of the first shot by those inside the pantry was that it sounded like a firecracker. With the firing of the second shot, most in the crowd realized that they were in the midst of a shooting and responded predictably: they recoiled, contorted their bodies, raised their arms, turned their eyes and heads away, lost their individual and collective balances, and crashed into each other and onto the floor.

Before the dense crowd reacted in a wave of panic, I believe, it is more than likely that Kennedy was innocently propelled toward the steam table and into Sirhan's gun by the people in back of the senator, who had not reacted as quickly to the first shot and were still moving forward into the senator, who was trying to get out of the way. With falling bodies literally obstructing Kennedy's body motion, Sirhan— who had been rapid-firing his weapon all day at the gun range— managed to fire four point-blank shots into the senator's body and clothing.

Although no eyewitness saw Kennedy get bumped into Sirhan, *none* of the twelve LAPD-identified eyewitnesses saw Kennedy get shot either, and their estimates of muzzle distance are based on the position of the gun when—*and only when*—the first shot was fired.

However, busboy Juan Romero did remember seeing Kennedy appear to lose his balance at about the same time that Karl Uecker, who never saw the senator after the shooting started, lost his grip on Kennedy's hand. Also, Lisa Urso's last image of Kennedy during the shooting spree was seeing him "jerk a little bit, like backwards and then forwards."

I now believe that the backwards then forwards jerking motion came as Kennedy had recoiled after the first shot; he was then accidently bumped forward, toward the steam table and into Sirhan's gun where he was hit at point-blank range.

4. Were there bullet holes in the door frames?

I no longer believe that the holes in the door frames, particularly in the center divider, were bullet holes. And I now think I understand how this controversy began.

After the arrest of Sirhan and the removal of Kennedy and the other five victims from the pantry, a handful of LAPD officers, along with a contingent of LASO deputies, attempted to preserve an already messy crime scene.

As part of the LASO's human wedge to clear out the pantry, LASO deputy Tom Beringer told me that he had witnessed a man in a tuxedo trying to recover a souvenir by prying out what he believed to be a bullet from the wooden center divider between the two swinging doors at the west end of the pantry. Deputy Beringer stopped the man and reported the incident.

Whether acting on his own or ordered to mark this evidence, LASO deputy Walter Tew saw what he believed to be bullet holes in the door frames at the same location. Without any experience in criminalistics or firearms identification, Tew, I discovered, marked what he erroneously believed to be bullet holes, *circling* the holes and placing "LASO," his badge number, "723," and his name, "W Tew," inside each hole.

Significantly, despite all of the holes in the woodwork all over the kitchen, the only known ones that law enforcement personnel later positively identified as bullet holes were the ones circled by Tew. And those who worked at the hotel and claimed that they had never noticed the holes before, particularly in the center divider, more likely had never even noticed the holes before they were circled. These employees included maître d' Angelo DiPierro, waiter Martin Patrusky, and carpenters Wesley Harrington and Dale Poore. (DiPierro, who had accompanied non-SID personnel through a cursory crime scene search, does believe he saw the bases of bullets in the holes. However, his experience with bullet holes is limited to his service in the infantry and does not include criminalistics.)

LAPD sergeant James Jones, who directed the LASO's crime scene sweep, immediately noticed Tew's markings and told me that he believed that a bullet hole had been identified—a natural assumption after a shooting.

Then, at 2:00 A.M., after the crime scene had been secured, Officer DeWayne Wolfer and Sergeant Bob Lee of the Scientific Investigation Division arrived at the kitchen pantry, along with their staff. LAPD photograph Charles Collier, who was so sure during his interview with me that bullet holes were present in the door frames, might have been confused by the circled holes—which he repeatedly photographed—as were other SID staffers who told me that they thought they had seen bullet holes in the door frames.

Significantly, LAPD officer Pete Despard—who appears in numerous official photographs, aiding the crime scene search—told me, "I saw suspected bullet holes, but I never confirmed that they were bullet holes."[187]

Sergeant James MacArthur, the experienced Rampart detective who had been responsible for the overnight security of the crime scene, told me that he had nothing to do with the crime scene search—yet he also told me about bullet holes at the crime scene. He, too, probably read too much into the circled holes, as did those officers who guarded the crime scene—who also told me that they had seen or knew about bullet holes: LAPD officers James Wilson, Edward Crosthwaite, and Albert Lamoreaux; as well as Rampart watch commander Ray Rolon, Sergeant William Unland, Lieutenant Albin Hegge, and Inspector Robert Rock.

None of these honest police officers were criminalists; none of them had actually seen bullets in the wood; and none of them had witnessed the physical recovery of any bullets.

Later on the morning of the shooting, *Chicago Tribune* crime reporter Robert Wiedrich appeared at the crime scene to do a story for his newspaper. According to Wiedrich, Sergeant MacArthur told him that two bullets "gone wild" had been removed from the center divider. MacArthur, again not being a part of the crime scene search, had unwittingly misled Wiedrich.

Coroner Noguchi also executed a 1976 affidavit for Vincent Bugliosi, claiming that he had suspicions that the holes in the door frames had been caused by bullets. However, during my 1993 interview with Noguchi, I asked him whether he had *specifically* asked Wolfer if bullets had gone into the door frames during the crime scene search several days after the murder. Seemingly contradicting

---

[187] Although LAPD officers Robert Rozzi and Charles Wright both believe they were photographed by the Associated Press examining a bullet hole in a door jamb, independent firearms experts—even those critical of the LAPD's investigation—who have studied the LAPD's photographs of the "object," have insisted that the object is simply too small to be the base of a .22-caliber bullet.

his earlier affidavit, Noguchi replied, "Yes, and it was for more than just curiosity. I felt that in order to understand what had happened and the specific sequence of events, I needed to know the direction of the gunshots. I wanted to know how the trajectories would be determined.

"I remember that I asked for photographs to be taken at each [reconstructed shooting] sequence so we could analyze the scene. One of the pictures was of a center door divider.

"I asked Mr. Wolfer, 'Is this a bullet hole?' And he said, 'No.' He said that they had done X rays or something to that effect, and that no bullets were there. Of course, I have no reason to doubt that."

On June 6, the day after the shooting, John Shirley and John Clemente walked through the crime scene, and Clemente took a photograph of the circled holes on the center divider—which had been pointed out to them not by a criminalist but by a hotel employee; these same circled holes were viewed by CBS radio reporter Bob Ferris two days later.

These accounts of bullet holes were featured in Lillian Castellano and Floyd Nelson's 1969 article in the *Los Angeles Free Press*, initiating suspicions that extra bullets were present. Consequently, the can of worms had been publicly opened, and the LAPD did nothing definitive to close it.

The 1975 discovery during the Schrade litigations that SUS had destroyed the door frames, along with the supposed X rays of these items, only enhanced suspicions that the door frames contained extra bullets, which would prove the existence of a second gunman.

Further complicating the controversy over the alleged bullet holes was Greg Stone's discovery in 1976 that FBI special agent Alfred Greiner had identified and FBI photographer Richard Fernandez had photographed four "bullet holes" in Sirhan's line of fire.

As FBI special agent Frenchy LaJeunesse told me, both Greiner and Fernandez had been sent to the crime scene to provide "orientation" information to the FBI. Neither Greiner nor Fernandez was a criminalist or a firearms identification expert.

Further, according to a recently discovered June 8, 1968, FBI memorandum prepared by Greiner, the person who gave Greiner and Fernandez their tour through the crime scene the day before was not a criminalist, a firearms identification expert, or even a police officer. Instead, according to the report, he was Frans Stalpers, assistant manager of the Ambassador Hotel.

Greiner's report clearly states, "Stalpers directed [Special Agent] Greiner and Photographer Fernandez over the entire area where Senator Kennedy had been immediately prior to the shooting and the route taken by him to the point where he was hit."

There is no mention of anyone else accompanying Greiner and Fernandez on this tour. Clearly, the FBI men learned what they had learned about the crime scene from Stalpers, a civilian.

For years, many of us have wondered why Greiner has been so averse to settle the controversy over how and why he had identified the four circled bullet holes in the door frames. In light of his own memorandum, showing that he had received his information from a hotel clerk, Greiner might well be a little reluctant to recount the circumstances under which he drew his conclusions and wrote his report.

Then, in January 1990, SID staffer David Butler, a LAPD Medal of Honor recipient, told me that he had witnessed DeWayne Wolfer remove two .22-caliber bullets from the center divider. Butler equivocated on this version, telling me during our second interview—after he realized that he had given me evidence of more bullets in the room than Sirhan's gun could hold—that he had seen only evidence packages of bullet slugs on the steam table.

On this matter, Butler has self-destructed.[188]

However, what etched in stone such sightings as Butler's, as well as Greiner's FBI report, was attorney Vincent Bugliosi's accidental discovery in November 1976 of FBI special agent William Bailey, who said that he had actually inspected the two bullet holes in the center divider and found the base of a .22 slug in each hole during his fifteen- to twenty-minute pass through the crime scene on the night of the shooting.

---

[188] When I called Butler to give him an opportunity to amend and expand upon his quotes, I asked him to pick a position and stand by it. However, he refused to say anything further—other than to stand by what he had already stated during my tape recorded interviews with him, in which he had claimed to have, and then recanted having, witnessed Wolfer remove two bullets from the center divider.

Bailey's story is harder, if not impossible, to discredit, even though Bailey has become an ardent and vocal supporter of the two-gun theory. Like many others, I had used him for years to bulk up my own evidence of at least two shooters at the crime scene.

Thus, if Bailey—for whom I have great respect—is correct, then there is no doubt that at least two guns were fired that night. But I now believe that Bailey simply made a mistaken identification during his quick examination of the crime scene. I believe that he, too, had been misled by the holes in the center divider circled by Walter Tew.

If Bailey is right, it would mean that DeWayne Wolfer had literally perjured himself on numerous occasions during his sworn statements about whether bullets had been recovered at the crime scene. And Wolfer has hung tough all of these years and even filed a defamation suit, insisting that he found no bullets in the walls and the door frames of the kitchen pantry. Was he capable of committing this monumental act of obstruction?

To continue to suggest that Wolfer lied is also to suggest that Wolfer, the officers in the SID, and the LAPD wittingly engaged in a conspiracy to permit the escape of Sirhan's co-conspirators. And that defies the evidence, as well as all logic.

Indeed, Wolfer has a well-established record in this case, alternating between flawless work, such as his muzzle distance tests, and obvious errors, such as the mislabeled test bullets.

Although it is clear that the bullet fragments found on the floor of the crime scene and identified by the SID's Dave Butler, crime lab photographer Charles Collier, and LAPD officer Kenneth Vogl were never booked as evidence, I contend that there is *no* evidence to suggest that Wolfer either committed perjury or intentionally destroyed evidence that would have proven two guns had been fired at the crime scene.

In short, Wolfer's detailed crime scene search on the morning of the shooting—during which he was specifically searching for bullet holes—must outweigh Bailey's cursory examination of two circled holes, especially when Bailey did not appreciate the significance of his alleged discovery until eight years later, when he met Bugliosi.

5. Why didn't the 1975 firearms panel conclude that the victim bullets came from Sirhan's gun?

The 1975 firearms panel matched three victim bullets with each other but could not determine which gun had fired those three bullets. This has fueled the speculation about a second gun ever since.

The 1975 panel claimed that Sirhan's gun had been damaged because of a "heavy leading" of the barrel, which could have altered the characteristics of subsequently fired bullets.

The Los Angeles District Attorney's Office in 1971 and 1974, as well as the Kranz Report in 1977, charged that Sirhan's gun had been tampered with and suggested that the tampering had occurred while the weapon was in the possession of the Los Angeles County Clerk's Office.

Allowing the clerk's office to take the fall, but without answering the key question raised by the firearms panel, the Kranz Report stated, "The experts [in 1975] conceded that the dirty and leaded barrel could possibly change striations and characteristics on fired bullets. None of the experts could give any explanation for the leaded barrel."

Thus, the answer to this "leaded barrel" question could hold the key to proving that Sirhan's gun—and no other gun in the world—fired the three victim bullets analyzed by Wolfer in 1968 and the firearms panel in 1975.

When I talked to Lowell Bradford, a prominent member of the 1975 firearms panel, in April 1990, I asked him about the leaded-barrel problem raised by the panel and later in the Kranz Report. Bradford explained that the "lead buildup" in the barrel of Sirhan's gun could have "simply resulted from an unknown firing" between the time of Wolfer's test firing of Sirhan's gun in June 1968, and the refiring by the firearms panel in September 1975.

Had there been an unknown firing between this period of time?

During my tape-recorded interview with LAPD/SID criminalist David Butler, we were discussing Sirhan's gun when Butler stated, almost matter-of-factly, "I've still got test bullets from that gun."

"Really?" I replied with some surprise.

"Yeah. We fired some extra tests, and I saved them. I don't know what the hell I did with them. They're somewhere at home rattling around."

When I conducted my second tape-recorded interview with Butler, I brought up the additional, unauthorized test firings of Sirhan's gun again. This time, Butler said, "Much to Lee and Wolfer's credit, we shot extra test shots out of the gun. We saved those test shots."

I asked, "Was that out of Sirhan's own gun?"

"That's out of Sirhan's gun."

"How many test shots were fired?"

"I don't know. We fired a bootful of test shots."

"What's that mean? More than ten?"

"Yeah, more than ten."

"More than twenty?"

"Yeah. What we do is submit *x* amount [of bullets] to the court as evidence that comparisons were done on. But extra rounds are saved, and they are maintained in our files. Well, when the [Schrade suit] came up, the gun barrel was grossly changed internally. This would, if it was the first examination, indicate that it was not the same gun. To Wolfer and Lee's credit, they had the original test shots. The [seven firearms] examiners basically found out that the gun barrel had been tampered with. . . . They found that the gun barrel had been changed. And they couldn't come back with a positive comparison. Now, there is no doubt that that was the gun."

I later asked Butler, "Now, the test bullets: where are the test bullets now?"

He replied, "The Lord only knows where the test bullets are. Some were entered into evidence. We may have kept some back. I know I've got a set.

"You keep them at the office or something?"

"I took them home."

"You took them home?"

"Yeah. . . . A set."

"And these are from Sirhan's gun?"

"Yeah."

"Not from the test gun [Iver Johnson H18602] but from Sirhan's gun?"

"Yes."

"Did anyone else get a set?"

"I don't know. I just took out two bullets and two casings."

"And this is from the test firings?"

"Yeah, this is before the gun's released [to the grand jury]. This is after the main test-firing."

In other words, Butler's forthright admission finally explains that the leading of, and consequent damage to, the barrel of Sirhan's gun had come from the extra test-firing by souvenir hunters from the SID—*after* Wolfer had completed his initial test-firing.

Thus, Wolfer and only Wolfer could have positively matched the three victim bullets before the leading of and permanent damage to the barrel of Sirhan's gun. Wolfer legitimately made these matches and testified honestly. His analysis could not be confirmed by the firearms panel or anyone else, because the barrel became damaged immediately after he conducted his tests.

I now believe that Sirhan's gun fired all three of the victim bullets analyzed by Wolfer and the firearms panel. Thus, DeWayne Wolfer should be finally vindicated on this matter. For years, Wolfer has been wrongly accused of sloppiness and incompetence in his identification of the victim bullets.

6. What was Sirhan's motive for killing Senator Kennedy?

To me, the evidence is clear that Sirhan stalked Senator Kennedy for days prior to the murder and went to the Ambassador Hotel for the sole purpose of killing him. Apparently, it wasn't until June 5, 1968, at 12:15 A.M., that Sirhan had his opportunity to catch his prey at close range. Unfortunately, he finally had guessed right when he decided that Kennedy would take the shortest route from the stage of the Embassy Room to the Colonial Room, via the kitchen pantry.

Because of lax, almost nonexistent security at the victory celebration for Senator Kennedy, Sirhan had no problems getting into the Kennedy party. For the same reason, he encountered no difficulty getting into the kitchen pantry.

Did Sirhan kill Robert Kennedy because of the senator's support for Israel? I don't believe that for a second, and Sirhan certainly never mentioned anything about Kennedy's position on the Middle East in his notebooks.

A lifelong Christian who demonstrated only a minimal interest in joining groups and causes, Sirhan preferred to spend his free time at the racetrack. And I received a sense from him that he would never allow any person or any group to represent his views on anything. Sirhan liked to see himself as his own man: bold, daring, and misunderstood.

Thus, I believe that Sirhan's motive had less to do with politics and more to do with his own personal problems.

In June 1968, as his personal notebooks show, Sirhan's confused life revolved around personal introspection and a stated hope for self-improvement; flirtations with fringes of the occult and an individualized but unsophisticated form of left-wing politics; and, of course, horses and the racetrack.

However, his problems had begun to get the better of him. He was still unemployed, a college dropout, living at home with his mother, whom he loved dearly but had begun to rebel against. He was also down to his last $400, which was found in his pocket at the time of his arrest. Also, his car, which provided his only real means of escape and freedom, was falling apart. He did not have money to buy the Ford Mustang he fantasized about in his notebooks. He had become a desperate young man, somehow losing all hope.

At the racetrack, where he had lost much of his insurance settlement, Sirhan was developing a reputation as a loser. As a rider, he had already received the reputation as having "lost his nerve." His worst fear realized, he was being humiliated; and he was becoming a local clown.

So why would a good son with no criminal record or history of overt violence commit such a heinous crime?

I believe that Sirhan's unilateral motive consisted of nothing more than his desire to prove to himself and those who knew him that he still had his nerve. He wanted everyone to know his name and be forced to recognize him.

As a man who had unfairly prejudged himself as a failure at age twenty-four, Sirhan decided to make his mark, even if it was by committing a terrible and violent act.

As Sirhan claimed during my interviews with him, he felt no particular malice toward Senator Kennedy—in fact, for many years, he admired him. But, to Sirhan, Kennedy had become a symbol of everything he wanted and didn't think he would ever have a chance to get. Thus, the angry and trite rhetoric in his notebooks about power and the powerless and the haves and have-nots referred to nothing more than his own life.

For instance, one passage in his notebook reads, "I advocate the overthrow of the current president of the fucken [*sic*] United States of America. I have no absolute plans yet—but soon will compose some. I am poor—This country's propaganda says that she is the best country in the world—I have not experienced this yet."[189]

If Sirhan could not achieve the American Dream, as well as a level of public appreciation and respect, murdering this popular symbol provided the means by which he could achieve, at the very least, a level of notoriety.[190]

Vilified in the wake of the crime, Sirhan needed a scapegoat. After being captured, he said nothing about getting drunk or being drunk. The arresting officers concluded that he was not under the influence

---

[189] Before his testimony during his trial, Sirhan put up a defiant clenched fist in lieu of simply raising his hand to take the oath.

Moreover, Sirhan, who had come to view himself as a great defender of minorities and the downtrodden, told author Bob Kaiser in May 1969, "It's just like wanting to have some sex and, instead of going out with the most beautiful broad, you go into nigger territory and pick the ugliest whore they've got. [How] have you satisfied yourself? Sure, you got a piece of tail. But, you know, where's the satisfaction of it?" See Kaiser, *"R.F.K. Must Die!"*, p. 518.

[190] Sirhan also told Kaiser in May 1969, "They can gas me. But I am famous. I achieved in a day what it took Kennedy all his life to do."

of anything. Sergeant Bill Jordan, his principal interrogator, deemed him to be coherent and sober during his interrogation immediately after his arrest.[191]

However, seeing that his act had only brought him and his family more devastation, he concocted, I believe, the tale that he was drunk. Thus, he created the opportunity to plead amnesia when questioned about the key events of the evening: getting his gun, maneuvering his way into the kitchen pantry, and then firing his gun—with no memory of his interrogation.

And, as a backup to that, he did not really try very hard to dissuade others from suspecting that he had been the subject of hypno-programming.

With these devices—drunkenness and the possibility of mind control—he thought he could, at least publicly, escape direct responsibility for his crime and have some cause to look his long-suffering mother in the eye. "Mom," he told her as the wrath of the world came down on him and his family, "I'm sorry. I don't remember anything." Of course, Mary Sirhan stood by her son, and the Sirhan family continued to be innocent victims in this tragedy.

Without the ability to evade responsibility, Sirhan—a nice, quiet kid with no criminal record who regularly drove his mother to church—could not, I think, have handled the magnitude of his crime and the impact it had on his family.

However, when his story of being drunk or hypnotized met considerable skepticism, Sirhan created another cover story—that he had done this for his Arab brethren, who had also immediately denounced his actions. Somehow, he presumed that he could achieve a degree of respect by portraying himself as a political assassin and later a political

---

[191] Dr. Edward H. Davis, on behalf of the defense, performed an electroencephalographic examination to gauge Sirhan's reaction to alcohol. On October 12, 1968, Sirhan received "6 ounces of Gordon's Gin made up as several Tom Collins drinks. This was consumed in 8 minutes."

At the end of the test, Dr. Davis concluded, "The patient did become agitated and tended to hyperventilate for a period of time after the administration of the gin but the [EEG] tracing only showed various movement artifacts during this period. The record failed to reveal any abnormalities either at rest or with hyperventilation before and after the administration of gin."

prisoner rather than allowing others to cast him as just another cold-blooded and cowardly murderer.

Even his own attorney, Emile Zola Berman, said of Sirhan in open court, "In his fantasies, he was often a hero and savior of his people. In the realities of life, however, he was small, helpless, isolated, confused and bewildered by emotions over which he had no control."[192]

Clearly, Sirhan's plan to portray his murderous act as "politically motivated" also backfired on him. It is unlikely that he ever thought that such a plan would continue to bring on him the scorn of the world, even that of the Arab community.

Perhaps, over the years, Sirhan has somehow managed to convince himself that he does not remember the events of that terrible night. But I doubt it. I believe he relives that moment every day, but, I'm sure after speaking with him at length, he has now twisted reality, justifying his deed and believing that he has become the victim—while expressing a willingness to say and do whatever it will take to get out of prison.

Amateur psychology aside, does Sirhan really not remember his threats against Kennedy, as well as firing a gun at him?

After Robert Blair Kaiser released his 1970 book, *"R.F.K. Must Die!"*, he went on a book promotion tour, appearing on radio and television programs. In an undated, handwritten letter to Sirhan's defense counsel, Grant Cooper, Sirhan referred to Kaiser, who had earlier studied for the priesthood.

Addressing Cooper, Sirhan wrote:

Hey Punk,
        Tell your friend Robert Kaiser to keep mouthing off about me like he has been doing on radio and television. If he gets his brains splattered he will have asked for it like Bobby Kennedy

[192] Dr. Bernard L. Diamond, the psychiatrist for the defense, seemed to agree in his testimony at Sirhan's trial: "Sirhan would rather believe that he is the fanatical martyr who by his noble act of self-sacrifice has saved his people and become a great hero. He claims to be ready to die in the gas chamber for the glory of the Arab people. However, I see Sirhan as small and helpless, pitifully ill. . . ."

did. Kennedy didn't scare me; don't think that you or Kaiser will: neither of you is beyond my reach. [A]nd if you don't believe me—just tell your ex-monk to show up on the news media again—I dare him.

R.B.K. must shut his trap, or die.

Michael McCowan—who, like Kaiser, had been an investigator for Sirhan's defense team—told me a similar story, indicating Sirhan's clear knowledge of his crime. During a prison visitation, McCowan tried to reconstruct the murder with Sirhan.

Suddenly, in the midst of their conversation, Sirhan started to explain the moment when his eyes met Kennedy's just before he shot him.

Shocked by what Sirhan had just admitted, McCowan asked, "Then why, Sirhan, didn't you shoot him between the eyes?"

With no hesitation and no apparent remorse, Sirhan replied, "Because that son of a bitch turned his head at the last second."

Sirhan Bishara Sirhan consciously and knowingly murdered Senator Robert Kennedy, and he acted alone.

Index

Index

Index

Index

San Gabriel Valley Gun Club, 26, 90*n*, 108*n*, 109*n*, 202
San Quentin Penitentiary, 129, 130*n*, 154–56, 292*n*, 299–300
Santa Anita racetrack, 26, 103–4
Sartuche, Phil, 183
Sayegh, Anwar John, 27
Schabarum, Peter F., 156
Schiller, Howard L., 39
schizophrenia, 122, 123, 155, 300
Schlei, Barbara L., 195
Schlesinger, Arthur M., Jr., 195, 308*n*
Schmidt, D. G., 156*n*
Schorr, Martin, 123, 154–55
Schrade, Paul, 33–35, 54–55, 120*n*, 178, 181, 187, 189, 193–94, 195, 220, 222*n*, 240, 264, 303, 308*n*
  background of, 167
  in kitchen pantry, 34–35
  personal injury suit filed against Sirhan by, 170
  reopening of investigation demanded by Lowenstein and, 165–73
  RFK campaign work of, 33
  wounding of, 35, 43, 85, 86, 87*n*, 95, 167, 310–11
Schulman, Don, 146–47, 308
Schulte, Valerie, 97, 116
Scientific Investigation Division (SID), LAPD, 67, 86, 90, 132, 172, 173, 178, 237, 238, 239
  author's interviews with, 243–53
  crime scene responsibilities of, 244–45, 278
  at interagency meeting, 100
  Iver Johnson .22-caliber revolver tested by, 88–89, 91, 93, 159
  see also Wolfer, DeWayne A.
Scotland Yard, 178
Second Gun, The, 151*n*, 170*n*, 198
second gunman, 168, 224, 227*n*, 303, 306
  Bugliosi on, 185*n*
  Cesar suspected as, 145–53, 179, 198, 201*n*, 203, 204, 216, 219, 280–90, 309
  Cooper's disbelief in, 124, 144*n*
  FBI's disbelief in, 278–79
  firearms evidence reexamination and, 176, 178–79
  Harper's belief in, 142, 156, 157, 161–64, 176
  Kaiser's disbelief in, 134
  LaJeunesse's disbelief in, 273

muzzle distance conflict and, 89, 139, 191
pantry door bullet holes and possibility of, 130–32, 181, 266–67
Ward hearing on, 156–59
Secret Doctrine, The (Blavatsky), 107
Secret Service, U.S., 24, 78*n*–79*n*
Senate, U.S., 18, 24
  Rackets Committee of, 17, 191
Serrano, Sandra, 72*n*, 115, 116*n*, 141*n*, 308
  girl-in-the-polka-dot-dress reported by, 70–71, 112–14, 298*n*
Seventh Day Adventist Church, 106
Sharaga, Paul:
  girl-in-the-polka-dot-dress reported by, 39–40, 60, 71–72, 115, 298*n*
  as head of command center, 59–60, 62, 65, 71
Sharp, William G., 142–43
Sheehan, Joseph and Margaret, 109
Sheen, Martin, 195
Sheridan, Walter, 117*n*
Sherman, Tony, 79*n*
Shirley, John, 131, 132, 233, 316
SID, *see* Scientific Investigation Division, LAPD
Sillings, Robert K., 39, 62–63, 65*n*
Simi Valley, Calif., 30, 199, 201, 202, 283
Simson, Eduard, 154–56, 299–300
Sirhan, Adel, 27, 80–81, 101, 119, 292, 293, 294, 303
Sirhan, Aida, 101, 103, 297
Sirhan, Bishara Salameh Ghattas, 101, 102, 123
Sirhan, Mary Bishara Salameh, 27, 80, 101, 102, 106, 119, 125, 129*n*, 130*n*, 303–4, 322, 324
Sirhan, Munir (Sirhan's first-born), 101
Sirhan, Munir (Sirhan's second-born), 27, 80, 102, 293
Sirhan, Saidallah, 101, 102
Sirhan, Sharif, 101, 102
Sirhan, Sirhan Bishara, 26–30, 70, 74–82, 171*n*, 188*n*
  alcohol test not given to, 52*n*
  analysis of handwriting of, 108*n*, 121*n*, 155
  apprehension and arrest of, 43–44, 45–52, 58
  arraignment of, 79–80
  author's belief in sole gunman as, 302–4, 307, 326

Index